AF624353

# STUDIES IN QURAN

ENCYCLOPAEDIC SURVEY OF ISLAMIC CULTURE SERIES—2

# Studies in Quran

*Edited by*
**MOHAMED TAHER**

**ANMOL PUBLICATIONS PVT. LTD.**
**New Delhi-110 002**

**ANMOL PUBLICATIONS PVT. LTD.**
4374/4B, Ansari Road, Daryaganj
New Delhi-110 002

*Studies in Qvran*
© Reserved
First Edition 1997
ISBN 81-7488-536-6

All rights are reserved. No part of this publication may be reproduced, stored in a retrieval system or transmitted, in any form or by any means, mechanical, photocopying, recording or otherwise, without prior written permission of the publisher.

**PRINTED IN INDIA**

Published by J.L. Kumar for Anmol Publications Pvt. Ltd., New Delhi-110 002 and Printed at Mehra Offset Press, Delhi.

# Preface

The Encyclopaedic Survey of Islamic Culture is a unique reference source. This series seeks to anthologise the most important primary and secondary materials on a wide variety of topics and writers of Islamic culture and civilisation. The scholar, the student and the layman will find in various volumes not only a generous selection of reprinted articles, but original essays, bibliographies, and other materials brought for the first time in a comprehensive and exhaustive fashion.

The need for this collation grew out of our awareness that there is no comprehensive source of information for the study and research of the field. Other published works are too specialised in the topics discussed or neglect the institutional as well the individual role which the Islamic system plays. Few encyclopaedic works do exist, and few anthologies also have appeared. Fewer books, again, have systematically covered such topics as Islam in Africa, Islamic sociology, Islamic polity, Islamic thought, etc. Although these topics have been addressed separately, no attempt has been made to discuss them as part of a united treatment of the literature of the field.

Islam brought a total change in all spheres of life. It revolutionised many societies, both in the east and the west. But this is not always accepted and acknowledged. To quote Major Arthur Leonard from his work: Islam; her moral and spiritual value:

"Never to this day has Europe acknowledged in an honest and whole hearted manner the great and everlasting debt she owes to Islamic culture and civilisation. Only in a lukewarm and perfunctory way has she recognised that when, during the dark ages, her people were sunk in feudalism and ignorance, Muslim civilisation under the Arabs reached a high standard of social and scientific splendour that kept the flickering members of European society from utter decadence."

"Do not we, who now consider ourselves on the top most pinnacle ever reached by culture and civilisation, recognise that, had it not been for the high culture, the civilisation and intellectual, as well as the social splendours of the Arabs and soundness of their school system, Europe would to this day have remained sunk in the darkness of ignorance. Have we forgotten that the Muslim maxim was that, the real learning of a man is of more public importance than any particular religious opinions he may entertain, that Muslim liberality was in striking contrast with the then intolerant state of Europe? Does the magnificent valour of the Arabs, inspired as it was by a theism as lofty as it was pure, not appeal to us? Does not the moderation and comparative toleration shown by them to the conquered, notwithstanding the fierce and burning ardour to regenerate mankind that impelled them onward to conquest, also appeal to us? Does it not all the more appeal to us when we contrast this with the bitterness of the attitude of the Christian sects towards one another? Especially when we consider that in Christendom, as it was then constituted, extortion, tyranny and imperial centralisation, combining with ecclesiastical despotism and persecution, had practically extinguished patriotism, by substitution in its place schismatic and degenerate Church?"

Further the same writer continues to say:

> "Is it possible that Europe is unmindful of, and has the ingratitude to ignore the splendid services of the scientists and philosophers of Arabic? Are the names of Assamh, Abu Othman, Alberuni, Albeithar, Abu Ali Ibn Sina (Avicenna) the great physician and philosopher, Ibn Rushd (Anempace) besides a host of others but dead letters? Is the great work that they have done and the fame they have left behind them in their books to be consigned to the limbo of oblivion, by an ungrateful but antipathetic Europe?

"It cannot be that already we have lost sight of the amazing intellectual activity of the Muslim world during the earlier part of the `Abbaside' period more especially. It cannot be that we have quite forgotten the irrecoverable loss that was inflicted on Arabian literature, and on the world at large, by the wanton destruction of thousands of books that was promoted by Christian bigotry and fanaticism? It cannot be surely said of Christian Europe that for centuries now she has done her best to hide obligations to the Arabs; yet most assuredly, obligations such as these, are far too sacred to lie much linger hidden."

This is one side of the story. The other side is that the West has definitely absorbed much of the Islamic contributions and is "unaware." To quote Marcus Marby and William Underhill "Bold new visions from ancient landscapes" (Newsweek May 29, 1995): Christian and Islamic civilizations have been in conflict for most of their history. But as often as they have clashed, they have enriched each other. In this ninth century, Moors brought advanced architecture, astronomy and medicine to occupied Spain. While Europe lingered in the Dark Ages, courtly poetry from Persia inspired the troubadours, whose verse evolved into the literature of the early French Renaissance. Even whiling away hours over coffee and conversation—the basis for the cafe—came from Arab culture... France's most popular dish today is not escargots but couscous. French slang is peppered with Arab words like kif-kif (50-50) and Insha Allah (God willing). The hottest new music is Arab-inspired rai" (p. 28). The list of Arabic borrowed words in English and Western usages are many more, not mere algebra, alchemy, azimuth, albatross, timbal, zenith, etc.

There is, in short, a lot of misinformation and incorrect representation about Islam. And more so there is a need today to describe and interpret the issues and express in clear terms what this thought actually deals with. Due to social and cultural changes, the salient aspects of the field require examination. The post cold war era has left the world with a unipolar political system. Islam is a system which promises the world that if applied in toto it would solve the multi-dimensional problems of the modern era. But is there any one who wishes to test this module and try it in a space and time to see the truth of the statement?

The primary purpose of this encyclopaedic survey is to serve as a basic handbook on significant topics of Islamic culture. To facilitate an understanding of the field, the series presents a survey and an analysis of the various socio-cultural forces that shape both the structure and functions of the field as well as by the way this society has changed. We also analyse the larger forces outside the community, such as assimilation and acculturation, and forces inside the community, like, role of the leadership, role of the social and cultural groups and the so much alleged 'imbalance' in the theory and practice of the faith.

We are confident that this work will make a permanent and significant contribution to the study of Islam. Its style is simple, and it is presented in a style accessible to a wide audience. Its target audience is faculty, students, and all concerned with the understanding of the faith of the second largest following in the world. While it has scholarly materials, it is nevertheless also of use to those who have no knowledge of the field, as well as to those who are working in related and allied fields. Most important, we hope that this series will be useful in teaching and learning as an educational resource in the academic world.

The series is planned to be both, multi-volume and multi-facted set, which will run into hundreds of numbers. The compilation of such a huge set is a gigantic task and requires the support and encouragement of all concerned. It requires feed-back and also support from the literary market place and literary circles all over.

A collection of articles, or an anthology, has many benefits, like, it renews our acquaintance with literature which we have neglected, it reveals to us material of which we were ignorant, and it exposes relationships where we did not suppose them to exist. This is the ultimate purpose of our efforts and we wish and pray that this is fulfilled.

A word of acknowledgement is due to the inspiration of the idea of a comprehensive, commulative and compact set of literary works on the Islamic culture. These inspirers are from all walks of life and their efforts must be acknowledged which includes, contributors, authors and editors, as well as the publishers who have graciously contributed to this project and we duly acknowledge their cooperation. The well wishers are many more and listing all the concerned by names is impossible here. Each must be duly rewarded for this gesture, and this is our sincere prayer.

**Editor**

# Contents

# 1

# The Qur'an and Our Lives

**BADRUDDIN TAYABJI**

The Quran is a guide and a model for all the humanity and not merely for a sect. Even Muslims cannot progress if they donot go by the guidelines given in this Scripture. Quran calls for new interpretations and new effects with changing times.

I am attempting, in a modest way, to express my realisation of the impact on our lives of the Qur'an, first revealed to man fourteen hundred years ago. I use the term, "on our lives," instead of the more sectarian one "Muslim lives," deliberately. I do so because the impact of the Qur'an has been universal; it has certainly not been confined to those who may technically or otherwise call themselves Muslims.

The subject is "the Qur'an and the Modern World"— a vast ranging subject. Under its umbrella, matters as diverse as the perennially beguiling topic of whether the Qur'an enjoins an absolute prohibition on the use of liquor, or only temperance; whether a man who has bacon and eggs for breakfast is more culpable than one who has a whisky and soda at sundown, could be dealt with at length without getting oneself technically "wet"; almost to the same degree, as a discussion on what effect the progress made in Nuclear Physics has on our conceptions of the structure of the world.

This has, of course, been done before; but, perhaps, my readers will be relieved to learn at the outset, that I do not intend to follow suit. To those who are disappointed or feel cheated out of a disputation, that would certainly have the merit of being endless; and the capacity of leaving all parties to it absolutely convinced to their own rectitude, and of the fallaciousness of the arguments of those who differ from them, I can only say this. After fourteen centuries of experience of the working of the Qur'an on the minds of men, Muslims should at least realise that God wills that uniformity in its interpretation by, or uniformity in its effect on His creatures is ruled out. The diversity in the character and abilities of human beings has been stressed in the Qur'an.

If a person claims to be a Muslim and acts according to his own conscience and understanding of the Qur'anic precepts, no other human being has the religious right (I am not talking here of State or other man-made rights) to question his bonafides or deny his claims. The Qur'an does not recognize any priesthood set over Muslims, with rights or prerogatives to judge between them; to pass judgement on their respective observances, or interpretations of the junctions contained in it.

That is why, apart from other reasons, the Qur'an remains, and will remain eternally fresh, eternally inspiring and eternally speculative; for its meaning has to be sought by each seeker of the purpose of life, according to his own understanding, and the limits of the powers of mind and heart with which God has endowed him. A man can only help another in understanding it. He cannot force his own interpretation on others. Least of all can he make all the others see it exactly as he does himself. Anyone presuming to do this is attempting what the Prophet himself never presumed to do. In my opinion, it would be a gross presumption, and contrary to the spirit of the Qur'an.

One word about the term "modern" used in the title of my paper. "Modern" is defined as "of the present time" and as "not old fashioned." One is apt to use either definition rather loosely to suit one's own convenience or whim. The latter, in particular, plays a great part in what we choose to dub old-fashioned. To mutilate one of Oscar Wilde's casual and yet introspective witticisms

: "What we do is modern, what others do differently is old-fashioned."

Well, here the term "modern" means only "of or in present time," of in the contemporary setting. There is nothing modern or old-fashioned in the latter sense in the effect of the Qur'an on the contemporary world. It is the same old story in a different setting.

The danger in a Muslim dealing with Islamic subjects, particularly one like that of the Qur'an, which is the keystone of his beliefs, is that he is apt to assume that the justification of his beliefs is equally self-evident to others—Muslims as well as non-Muslims; and in any event, that if it is not, it should be. Too little effort is made to substantiate one's contentions or assumptions by reasoned arguments or by illustrative examples. It is true that belief frequently transcends reason. As Andre' Gide once remarked, and was subsequently quoted approvingly by Robert Bridges in his book "The Spirit of Man," it is not necessary to understand poetry to appreciate it. There is something intangible and undefinable about it that is beyond articulated understanding, or rather human expression in the accepted sense. This is even more apposite to religious beliefs and spiritual intimations. Something inside one responds to them, which it is impossible to explain or communicate to others.

Nevertheless, it is incumbent on all those who attempt to convert or to convince others, to support their contentions by reasoned arguments, leaving questions of "faith" to be decided by individuals, each according to his own inner promptings or response. Equally it is necessary for each believer to know for himself what he believes, and to judge the value of his beliefs by actual personal assessment. This has always been necessary, but in the present-day world it is perhaps more necessary than it has ever been before.

Human beings are so self-centred that they are always inclined to think that their world, their times in the world, are the most significant; the most fraught with consequence, the most revolutionary. Even allowing for this human frailty, the revolutionary changes of our times in thought, word and deed, seem startling enough to obtain for them a high place in the history of such periods. And whatever else they may or may not have accomplished, they have certainly succeeded in eroding faith and belief in traditional religion, dogma and precepts, in large numbers of people belonging to most of the principal religions of the world.

It is always difficult to judge the depth, or even the extent of religious belief at any stated period. This is difficult in regard to the followers of all religions, even those that have a regular priesthood, a religious hierarchy with powers to include or exclude followers from its fold. It is almost impossible to judge about the followers of Islam, as all those that say they are Muslim have to be accepted as such. None can gainsay their claim, though a Muslim in profession and a Muslim in deed, are not the same. I do not think it can be seriously disputed that the number of Muslims in name far exceeds the Muslims, indeed; and that this gap which has always been wide, has not become narrower in our times. If anything it has grown. Much of this has been caused by a conflict between the externals of tradition and religion, and the externals of contemporary living. Fundamentally, human beings have not changed. But because the bulk of humanity lives on the surface of things, their attachment to religions is also superficial; a concern with, and interest in forms, ritual, and companionship, or rather conformity with other human beings, instead of with God's will. Thus, they tend to take any change in the outward look of things as seriously as if it involved a fundamental alteration in the nature of our being, and in our beliefs. The result of such thinking is, that whenever there is a change in the outward symbols of life, in the ways of seeking human well-being on earth, in the relationship of man and his material environment, a hiatus develops. The conflict is between the letter of the moral and spiritual regulations, guidelines and stipulations that a particular set of people had formulated at a particular period of time, on the basis of their understanding of the board principles of human conduct, of Man's relationship with God as set down by the Prophet; and the actual needs of the situation as it exists in the living present. This dilemma can only be resolved in one of three ways—by obstinately shutting one's eyes to its existence; by adapting oneself in fact to the new envoirnment, and the compulsions of present-day facts of life, while outwardly continuing to conform to the letter of past practices, and by paying lip service to them; or by boldly reshaping one's life and conduct in conformity with the present needs, with the help of those eternal principles of morality and relationship with God as are set out in the Qur'an, and were illustrated by the Prophet in his own life.

In actual fact (I hope I am not maligning anybody) I think that most Muslims, consciously or unconsciously, tend to solve this problem of present-day existence, by steering a path of compromise between these positions in accordance with their own temperaments, and their own particular environment and upbringing. There cannot be the least doubt that such compromise between the actual performance of one's religious beliefs and one's profession of them, has the most deleterious effect, not only on one's own character, but on that of the community, and ultimately of the world as a whole. Double talk, double thinking and dubious or devious action is the bane of this century. It is, unfortunately, not the preserve only of politicians, but plagues even otherwise pious persons. The question therefore arises : why should this be so? Is there anything in the Qur'an that is incompatible with the essentials of the contemporary world and the way of life that it imposes upon me? The Qur'an is a comparatively short book. It can easily be read in translation, if not in the original. There is no excuse for not doing so, for anyone interested in Islam. It is not a code; in no portion of it does it profess to be a code complete in itself. Only a very short portion of it has any reference to law. It refers to itself thus:

"This is the Scripture whereof there is no doubt, a guidance unto those who ward off (evil), who believe in the unseen, and establish worship, and spend of that we have bestowed upon them; and who believe in that which was revealed unto thee (Muhammad) and that which was revealed before thee, and are certain of the hereafter." Qur'an ii 2-4.

Islam itself is not promulgated in the Qur'an as a new doctrine, but as a continuation of the old religious that were brought by the earlier Prophets. It says : "Say, (O Muslims) : We believe in Allah and that which was revealed unto Abraham, and Ishmael and Isaac and Jacob and the tribes, and that which Moses and Jesus received, and that which the Prophets received from their Lord. We make no distinction between any of them, and unto Him we have surrendered." Qur'an, ii 136.

The Qur'an taught man how to look at things, and from what point of view to regulate his conduct towards other men and his relationship with God. In a famous passage it says :

"It is not righteousness that you turn your face towards the East and to West; but righteous is he who believeth in God and the last day and the angels and the scripture and the Prophets; and giveth his wealth for love of Him to his kinsfolk and to orphans and the needy, and the wayfarer and to those who ask, and to set slaves free; and who is instant in prayer and payeth the poor-due (Zakat). And those who keep their agreement when they make one, and the patient in tribulation and adversity, and time of stress. Such are they who are sincere. Such are the God-fearing." Qur'an, ii-177.

Foreseeing the danger that might arise from the zeal of two devoted followers, the Prophet, when asked to advise on a point of horticulture, replied:

"I am no more than man, but when I enjoin anything respecting religion, receive it; and when I order anything about the affairs of the world, then I am nothing more than Man." As to the relative authority of the Qur'an and the Sunna, he said:

"My words are not contrary to the words of God, but the words of God can contradict mine." *Mishcat ul-Masabih.*

After a detailed examination, Syed Ameer 'Ali in his "Spirit of Islam" held that: "The Islam of Muhammad contains nothing which in itself bars progress or the intellectual development of humanity," He then went on to ask: "How is it then that, since the 12th century of the Christian era, philosophy has almost died out among the followers of Islam, and an anti-nationalistic patristicism has taken possession of the bulk of the people? How is it that predestinarianism, though only one phase of the Koranic teachers, has become the predominant creed of a large number of Moslems?" Ameer 'Ali pointed out that before the Abbaside Mutawakkil's accession Islam presented a spectacle similar to that of Christianity in the 17th and 18th centuries. It was divided into two camps, one of Authority, the other of Reason, the one advocated the guidance of humanity in matters natural as well as supernatural, by precedent, pure and simple; the other by human judgment, tempered as far as practical by precedent."

We need not pursue this matter further here. Ameer 'Ali wrote about it 45 years ago. Since then, much has happened in the world, including the world of Islam. The two camps—of Authority and Reason—still exist in Islam, as they do in most religions; but the latter has gained immeasurably in strength and influence, especially in the last twenty-five years. Writing of the effect of the Mongol conquest of Baghdad, Ameer 'Ali said in 1922; "The gleams of light which we have seen shining on Western Asia under the successors of Hulaku were the fitful rays of the setting sun. Policy worked with in born fanaticism in crushing any endeavour to introduce rationalism and philosophy in the Muslim world. The lawyers were not only strong, but also the main support of despotism. The result was, as we have already seen, Patristicism took possession of the hearts of large sections of Muslims, and has in course of time become a second nature with them. They can perceive nothing except through the medium of patristic glasses. The Prophet inculcated the use of reason; his followers have made its exercise a sin. He reached against anthropolatry and extravagant veneration of human beings; the Sunnis have canonised the Salaf and the Four Jurists, the Akhbari Shias, their Mujtahids,—and have called any deviation from the course laid down by them—however much the deviation may accord with the Master's own teaching and with reason—a crime. He had said: "Ghosts, apparitions and the like have nothing to do with Islam. "They now firmly believe in them. He impressed on them to go in quest of knowledge to the land of the heathens. They do not take it even when offered to them in their own homes."

Things have greatly changed since this was written, especially in Western Asia. In the last decade almost the entire world of Islam has come into political self-responsibility' and in one important particular, the new Muslim world is in marked discontinuity with the old. The Caliphate is no more. Suppressed in 1924 by the new Turkey, no serious Muslim opinion appears now to expect its revival. Whatever else this may have done, it has certainly given a greater impetus to rationalism in Islam, against the traditional and authoritarian. Muhammad Iqbal even went to the extent of comparing the changes implicit in the termination of the Caliphate to those brought about in Western thought and religion by the Reformation. There is much to support this; though like all comparisons of such sweeping nature, one has to be careful not to be too carried away by its seeming appositeness. Much more to the point, however, is the identical throwback to the original sources of inspiration in both the movements. Back to the Bible; back to the Qur'an, have been their dominating themes. It is right that this should be so.

I am convinced that Muslims can come to terms with the contemporary world, 'only, if they go straight back to the Qur'an, and renew their faith and belief by seeking direct inspiration and guidance from it.' The dogma of past centuries, labouriously and conscientiously elaborated, even by the most eminent divines and theologians of those days, can no longer serve their purpose. It was made for other times by other people. We have to forge our own code by our own study and understanding of the Qur'an in the light of our own needs.

---

[Revised and edited; originally appeared in *Islamic Culture,* April 1968].

# 2

# The Miracle of Quran
## ('Ijazu'l-Qur'an)

ABDUL ALEEM

How did this claim originate, because Quran does not use this word, 'Ijaz, or miracle of Quran. The article highlights the source material on this topic.

### 1. Origin of the Claim

The Qur'an says in unmistakable terms that its composition is beyond the powers not only of man but also of the Jinn who were thought to possess more capacities than Man. We will try here to find out how and why this extraordinary claim arose and how it grew to become a very important dogma in Islam. Before we proceed further it would be appropriate to examine the surroundings in which the Qur'an appeared, to find out the different literary forms that existed at the time, and to determine, as far as we can, the nature of the first reception accorded to the words spoken by the Prophet.

The first thing that strikes every student of the pre-Islamic literature of the Arabs is that the art of writing was almost non-existent amongst them. This had a very far-reaching effect on the form that their literary activities were to take. It is almost self-evident that the expression of the literary genius of a people depends very much on the method of expression available to the time. The Arabs did not know how to write, so all their ideas had to be expressed orally. This in its turn had a great effect on the development of the Arabic language itself, and that is why we find that the language before the appearance of Islam was a simple but forceful language, rich in synonyms and terms of exhortation, strong for the expression of one's passions, weak and, so to say, incapable of expressing a systematic train of thought, incoherent at times, but always picturesque and pure like the air of the desert in which it was born. It lies beyond our province to trace the whole development of the Arabic language, but we can trace here the different forms existing at the time when the Qur'an appeared.

The most important of all the forms, undoubtedly, was Shi'r or poetry. This was developed to such an extent that up to modern times the pre-Islamic period is thought to be the golden age of Arabic poetry. The poet was a man who was universally honoured and whose pleasure was as much sought as his wrath was avoided. It was the highest honour for a person or a tribe to be praised by a well-known poet; and on the other hand a satire by a famous poet was enough to tarnish the name for ever. Every tribe wished to have its own poet, and that day was a day of great rejoicing on which a poet appeared in a tribe. The chief form that poetry took at this time was the Qasidah, which varied very much in its length but remained almost constant in its nature. The ten most famous Qasa'id have reached us in more or less their original form.

The Arabs in this period had hardly any prose. This is not difficult to explain. Prose is the outcome of the art of writing. But what at this time took the place of prose were speeches that the Arabs used to deliver on the slightest provocation before their own tribe or a gathering of more tribes than one. The language of these used to be rhymed in a way which is called in Arabic Saj. The chief difference between Saj' and Shi'r is that the former has got no fixed metre and that the rhyming is not so strict as in the later. Not many of these have reached us but those that have are sufficient to give us an idea of their form and contents.

Another form in which Saj' played the leading part were the sayings of the Kahin. By his very nature he was bound to use ambiguous language and Saj' provided him with a handy material. Small compact sentences sounding very grandiose but devoid of any sense, or capable of being interpreted in innumerable ways, form the bulk of these sayings which are, to a very small extent, still preserved.

These in short, were the two forms to which the literary activities of the pre-Islamic Arabs were confined. The Arabs had no fixed life. Mostly they were nomads who were obliged to wander in search of pasture for their cattle and loot for their family. That is why most of this oral literature is lost to us. Only a few communities lived a stable life; the most important of them lived in and near Mecca, the holy city of Arabia, situated on the great highway for caravans coming from the south-east and going to the north-west and *vice versa.* Here came the Arabs from all parts of the country annually for pilgrimage and to buy and sell. Here at 'Ukaz used to be held an annual fair where thousands of people gathered, and the old tradition tells us that in this fair the famous poets used to recite their poems and the great orators used to deliver their Khutab. This was the place where literary standards were formed, and thither young aspirants after fame flocked together to compete. And it was in Mecca that the Qur'an appeared.

The Qur'an was something new, something unprecedented. It resembled in its outward form sometimes the Khutab and sometimes the sayings of the Kahin. It was Saj' more often than not. But in spite of all this it was in its very nature something diametrically opposed to all the literature existing at the time. It was the expression of the religious experience of the prophet Muhammad. The people of Mecca and the other Arabs who heard him were taken by surprise. Here was a man who opposed their deep-rooted traditions, who spoke strongly against their deities, who preached that their lives were lives of sin, who said that there was only one God and that he, the man who was in no way different from them, was His messenger. They examined his words. These were forceful and strong. Were they Shi'r? Yes, perhaps; but they were not sure. Was he a Kahin? Very likely; but a peculiar one who did not speak in ambiguous terms but in a language so clear. They were quite at a loss. How could they believe those words to be the words of God which they heard uttered by an ordinary man? In their perplexity they accused him of fabrication, they denounced him as a madman or a poet run amok, or a mere story-teller or at best a magician wanting to deprive them of their gods. Some thought they could also speak like him.

The Prophet heard all this. This was the reception that was accorded to the words of God which were revealed to him. Then came the verses:"They say he has forged it, the truth is they do not believe; then let them bring something like it if they are right" and again, "They say, he has fabricated it; tell them: bring ten surahs fabricated the like thereof and call to your help everyone you can except Allah, if you are right." Yet again : "They say, he has fabricated it; tell them: bring (even) one piece like unto it and call to your help any one you can except Allah, if you are right." Then the Voice addresses them directly through the Prophet "If you are in doubt about what We have sent down to Our servant, then bring a surah like it and call all your helpers, other than Allah, if you are right. But if ye bring it not, and ye cannot bring, then try to save yourself from the fire whose fuel is men and stones which is prepared for those who deny." This was the challenge to all those who doubted, or thought the Qur'an was the word of man. Either they tried to imitate the Qur'an and failed or they did not even try because they thought it beyond their power; and how could they bring anything like it unless they had had the same religious experience as the Prophet? and more, "Tell them, if human kind and the Jinn come together to produce the like of this Qur'an they cannot produce it, even if one help the other." The last word was said and this forms the basis of the dogma in Islam that the Qur'an is supernatural. The claim is clear and unmistakable.

In the Qur'an itself there is no direct evidence of the fact that anybody accepted the challenge and tried to bring forward anything like it. On the other hand we can deduce from the way in which the language of the challenge became more and more pointed that no serious attempt was made. At first there is a general challenge to bring something like it *(bi hadithin mithlih)* then it is limited to ten pieces only and lastly even to one, and with the last challenge there is also a strong conviction that they cannot bring anything like it *(wa lan taf'alu)*. Had any important attempt been made, it was bound to be mentioned in the Qur'an, just as all their doubts and criticisms are clearly mentioned. But it is also quite possible that some people tried to produce something like it and failed, and because they did not make a public claim, no notice of it was taken in the Qur'an. Tradition also does not enlighten us on this point. The consensus of opinion seems to be that the people did not trust themselves to take up the challenge and this forms one of the chief arguments in favour of the contention, as we are going to see later on. Many stories on the other hand have reached us about the magical effect of the Qur'an on the sceptics or the disbelievers when it was recited by the Prophet.

**2. Growth of the Dogma**

It takes a long time for an idea to become a dogma and it is very interesting to try to trace its growth and to find out the circumstances which have helped to give it a definite colour. But it is an extremely difficult task. Such growth is almost always invisible and, because the people living at the time are quite unconscious of it, no first-hand impressions are available. The only possible way is to follow the history of the time in the light of the particular question and to see whether one can distinguish some landmarks.

Just after the death of the Prophet the task of gathering together the different pieces of the Qur'an was taken in hand, and a collection was made. But it was only under the reign of the third Caliph 'Uthman, that the work could be properly completed. At the same time began the period of disturbance which lasted with a few short intervals of peace till the year 85 A.H., when Abdulmalik b. Marwan succeeded in suppressing every kind of opposition and made the path easy for his son Walid. But these disturbances had served one purpose. They gave to the people plenty of food for thought. The battles between Mu'awiya and 'Ali, the rise of the Khawarij, the battle of Karbala, the struggle between 'Abdullah b. Zubair and Abdulmalik b. Marwan, all these were not merely struggles for supremacy or power. They were more a conflict of principles, a conscientious struggle, at least on one side. The thoughtful people tuned again and again to the Qur'an to seek a light which could guide them in those dark days. This gave a fillip to the study of the Qur'an, which was naturally the chief occupation of religious-minded people.

But as yet the time for a systematic *Tafsir* (commentary) had not come, nor for seeking out the different problems in the Qur'an and dealing with them at length.

At the same time, Islam came in contact, on one side with the complicated dogmas of the oriental Christian churches in Syria, which was the seat of the Omayyad Khalifahs, on the other, with the Zoroastrain and Manichaean ideas in the newly founded Islamic towns of Kufah and Basrah. The Muslims were beginning to have free discussions with the non-Muslims, who questioned the very basis of Islam, the prophethood of Muhammad. They had to give proofs of the truth of their religion and their beliefs. Then by the middle of the second century A.H. began to be translated into Arabic works on natural sciences and philosophy from Greek, Syriac and middle Persian. The natural result was a current of free thought in Islam. People like Ibnu'l-Muqaffa,' Bashshar b. Burd, Salih b. 'Abdi'l-Quddus and 'Abdu'l-Hamid-al-Katib were bound to appear and to be called *Zindiq.* Orthodox Islam had to struggle not only with the non-Muslims but also with the agnostics. This was again a reason for turning towards the Qur'an, the fountain-head of religion, the sole determiner of beliefs, the guide of all the Muslims. In the meantime the Khilafat had changed hands. The Omayyads had passed out and the 'Abbasids had appeared on the stage which had been transferred from Syria to 'Iraq.

The time had come now for the systematic exposition of dogma and the foundation of different schools. The Mu'tazila appear and with them also appears the first notice that we have received about the question of I'jazu'l-Qur'an. It must have been discussed for the first time about the middle of the second century.

There must have been at least three ways which led to the discussion of this question. Firstly, the direct way of a systematic *Tafsir.* As we have already seen, the claim stands clearly in the Qur'an more than once, and those writing a commentary on it were bound to tackle this problem. Just at the beginning of the second Surah is the challenge thrown to the disbelievers in the divine origin of the Qur'an, and it is always at this point that the commentators discuss the question of I'jaz.

The other two ways branch off from the highway of *Kalam.* One of them which must have been a by-path, was trodden by those veterans, who traversed the ever-circling and never-ending road which had, as its milestone, the problem of Khalqu'l-Qur'an. Those discussing the question whether the Qur'an was eternal or created were bound to touch this problem, and there is plenty of evidence that they did so.

The third way, which seems to be a thoroughfare, and which led to this question most of those with whom we have to deal here, is the most important one. In the structure of *Kalam* there are two big wings which attract the eyes of every observer. One is Ilahiyat (Metaphysica) and the other is Nubuwat (prophetica). In the first, only a very small corner is dedicated to our question; but the whole of the second is not only occupied by, but without any exaggeration, also founded on this question.

After discussing the essence and attributes of God under Ilahiyat the Mutakallim turns towards the question of prophethood. He deals at first with the need of a prophet for mankind, with the possibility of a prophet being commissioned by God, with the tests of the truthfulness of a prophet, and then with individual prophets. Here he begins with Moses and Christ and ends with Muhammad. He has already decided that the test of the truthfulness of a person who claims to be the messenger of god is that he performs miracles. Now when he begins to prove that Muhammad was a true prophet, he goes out seeking for his miracles. He turns first to the Qur'an and finds himself amply rewarded for his search. The Qur'an itself claims that its composition is beyond the powers of all the creatures of God because it is the word of God himself. What other miracle can be greater? Then he finds a Hadith of the Prophet also : "There is no prophet but he was given a sign which made the people believe in him, and what I have been given is nothing other than the words revealed to me and I hope to have the greatest following on the Day of Resurrection." The matter is now settled. The Qur'an is the miracle of Muhammad and an everlasting miracle to boot.

We have seen how these different roads have led different people to this one question, but we ought not to lose sight of the fact that these paths are not parallel. They constantly cross one another as we shall see later on. Perhaps it is also true to say that in this case the straightest path seems to have proved the longest. Those who travelled by the way of *Tafsir* seem to have reached this point later than those who took the path of *Kalam.* As we have mentioned above, the first to reach there were the Mu'tazila. It is one of the saddest facts for those working in the field of the religious history of Islam that almost nothing is to be had today of the vast literature left by these wonderful people. Even the meagre and scanty notices that we have received about their ideas and beliefs have come through authors who are their admitted opponents in the realm of dogma like Ash'ari, Baghdadi, Ibn Hazm and Sahristani.

The notices of the views of the Mu'tazila on this question in particular are very short and we are quite in the dark about their arguments. The names mentioned in this connection are Nazzam, Hisham, 'Abbad and Muzdar, as taking a somewhat different view from the others who were in agreement with the general opinion. From among the Mu'tazila only Jahiz is reported to have written a book very likely on this subject, which was called Nazmu'l-Qur'an.

At this point we ought to take account of a very important work which has been rightly called a semi-official defence of Islam. 'Ali b. Rabban at-Tabari who was a client (Maula) of the 'Abbasid Khalifah Ja'far al-Mutawakkil (232-247 A.H.) is the author, and the name of the book is Kitabu'l-Din wa'd-Daulah fi ithbati'n-Nubuwah. The Khalifah himself helped in the compilation of this book, as the author has mentioned in his preface. The subject-matter of the book, as appears from the name, is the proofs of the prophethood of Muhammad. The sixth chapter is devoted to the argument that the Qur'an is a sign and a proof of the truthfulness of the Prophet. The style in which the author writes and the arguments that he brings show clearly that this problem did not, as yet, form a part of the big system of Kalam, nor had discussion of it, as yet, become a convention, as it later became. This was a time when problems which were destined to become a synthetic whole were being discussed individually, sometimes together but often apart. And our question was one of them.

Of the books on Tafsir written in the second or third century we have received, unfortunately, nothing but their names. The only representative of that time and perhaps the best of all times is Ibn Jarir at-Tabari (d. 310 A.H.) whose voluminous commentary, comprising thirty big volumes, has been to our exceeding good fortune completely preserved. It is all the more valuable because it is almost an encyclopaedia of the information about the Qur'an available at the time, and has been a prototype for all the later commentators. He discusses this question when writing the commentary on Surah II, 21, 22 in a very simple manner and does not seem to be encumbered with the technicalities of Kalam as later commentators obviously are. He does not bring arguments other than those mentioned in the Qur'an itself and contents himself with explaining and amplifying the verses.

The next among the early commentators whose work still exists is Hasan ibn Muhammad al-Qummi an Nisaburi (d. 378 A.H.). He also discusses this question at the same place but it is interesting to see what a difference the three-quarters of a century have made. Al-Qummi follows the way rather of the Mutakallimin than of the Mufassirin and uses all the technical terms of the former. He goes beyond his province and brings arguments from other fields of thought. The later commentators have more often followed the example of Qummi than that of Tabari. It seems like planting in one's own garden a tree grown in a foreign soil. But this is only the beginning of a long process. As time went by, the whole field of Tafsir was invaded by the Mutakallimin, and the simple art of explanation was superseded by complicated and puzzling discussions on matters of dogma. Every party tried to prove its thesis by the help of the Qur'an. They read into the simple unsophisticated language of the Qur'an all sorts of preconceived meanings. They tried even to reconcile the conceptions of Hellenistic philosophy with the verses of the Qur'an.

The above discussion shows the growth of dogma. Let's examine the literature on the subject and, then, survey the problem systematically. This literature can be divided into two parts. There are a number of special books but mostly this question has been discussed as part of one system or another. First in order comes the system of Ma'ani and Bayan. The books falling under this category can also be classified as special books on the subject, as their names invariably indicate. But it is better to deal with them separately for very important reasons, as we are going to see later on. The other two systems are those of Tafsir and Kalam, whose growth we have already followed.

**3. Special Books on the Subject.**

The following are the names of those authors who wrote a treatise with the title 'Ijazu'l-Qur'an. Ibn Nadim who completed his *Fihrist* in 377 A.H. mentions only the first two names. This may be safely taken as an evidence that no other book with this name was known at the time :

1. Muhammad b. Zaid (Yazid?) al Wasiti (d. 306 A.H.).
2. 'Ali b. 'Isa ar-Rummani (d. 384 A.K.).
3. Hamd b. Muhammad al Khattabi (d. 388 A.H.).
4. 'Abu Bakr Muhammad al-Baqillani (d. 403 A.H).
5. Muhammad b. Yahya ibn Suraqah (d. 410 A.H.).
6. As-Sayyid ash-Sharif al-Murtada (d. 436 A.H.).
7. Abdu'l-Wahid b. Isma'il ar Ruyani (d. 502 A.H.).
8. Ibn Babjuk al-Baqqali (d. 562 or 576 A.H.).
9. Qasim b. Firroh ash-Shatibi (d. 590 A.H.).
10. Nasir b. 'Abdu's-Sayyid al-Muttarazi (d. 610 A.H.).
11. Ibn Kamal Pasha (d. 940 A.H.).
12. Ibrahim b. Ahmad al Jazari (d. ?).
13. Muhsin b. Husan an-Nisaburi al-Khuzai (d.?).

Baqillani's book is reported to be the best ever written on this subject. The author, who is better known as Al-Qadi'l-Baqillani was a famous dogmatic theologian and a staunch follower of the Ash'ari school. He was a disciple of Abu'l-'Abbas ibn Mujahid at-Ta'i who in his turn was a disciple of the great Imam. Of his innumerable writings this is the only one which has reached us, but it is quite enough to give us an idea of his immense learning and his command of dialectics.

In the preface to his book Baqillani gives the reasons which impelled him to write on this subject in the following words; "One of the most important things, the examination of which is incumbent on the people who follow the religion of God, and the discussion of which is the most needed, is that which forms the basis of their religion and the groundwork of their theology, and which is a proof of the truthfulness of their Prophet and an evidence and an argument in favour of his miracles (He means the Qur'an) especially at the time when ignorance has pitched its tent and has a very brisk market, and has got mastery over all the world, and knowledge is on the way to obliteration and effacement and is in hiding and remote, and the learned are under the yoke of the black times, suffering from the roughness of time what one suffers when he encounters a ferocious lion, so much so that what they have to undergo has deprived them of the requirements of learning namely walking on its path and taking to its ways. So the people now are divided into two groups, one walking way from the truth and being diverted from righteousness, and the other prevented from helping and harassed in their own business. This has led the heterodox to engage themselves with the fundaments of religion and to make the weak doubt their every belief. The helpers of religion have become few, its allies have been distracted from it and its own people have given it up, so that it is now a target for everyone who wants to aim at it. The position is again the same as it was quite in the beginning when people used to talk about the Qur'an and some said it was magic, others that it was poetry, still others that it was the tales of the past, and all of them thought they could also produce something like it if they wanted, and there are so many other things which God the Almighty has quoted as being what they said about it. It has been related to me about one of the ignorant amongst them (he means his own contemporaries) that he has begun to compare it (the Qur'an) with some verses of poetry and to weight it with other categories of speech and it is not content with that alone but holds them to excel it in merit. This is not new to the heterodox of this age; their friends, the disbelievers the Quraish and others, had said most of all this before them. The only difference is that most of those who culminated it (the Qur'an) in the beginning saw clearly the right path, later repented and turned back, they recognised the truth, not because their tongues were tied but only through the guidance of their Lord and His succour. Ignorance in these days is more wide-spread and the heterodox are farther from the truth and quicker to abandon the needful. It would have been more proper for those of the linguists, who have written useful books on the meanings of the Qur'an, or for the dogmatists to have explained in detail the reasons why it is supernatural and to have assigned to its right place. This was more worthy of being done than most of what they have written on atoms and more important than their subtle discussions about the accidents and most of the fine points of grammatical analysis or syntax; because the need of it is more pressing and the tackling of it is more imperative. Some of them have neglected it so much that it has led a group of people to adopt the view of the Brahmins in this matter. These people thought that by the inability of their friends to defend this miracle it follows that it need not be defended at all and that it is without foundation. All the more when they observe, on the one hand, the excellence of these authors in what they have invented, and the limit they have reached in what they have innovated and they see, on the other hand, that what has been written on the subject is in complete in itself and unconvincing in argument, confused in its treatment and faulty in its arrangement.... In view of these facts somebody asked us to deal with this matter fully in a way which might do away with the doubts that occur to those who are ignorant and might strike a blow once for all at all the criticisms aimed at this miracle. We have complied with the demand, hoping in this way to gain the nearness of God and relying on His help and His succour."

By reading this preface it is possible to form an idea of the state in which this problem was at the end of the fourth century A.H. Even after allowing very much for the exaggerated style which is the hall-mark of the dogmatists of every age, at least this fact comes out clearly, that the question of Ijaz-ul Qur'an was being neglected at the time. The books that were written on the subject till then were not satisfactory and there was a demand that it should be dealt with in full. We may safely opine that this gap was admirably filled by Baqillani himself. This book has formed the basis for all those who wrote on the subject later. Before proceeding further, it will be proper to give a short sketch of the book.

Baqillani, like all other Mutakallimin, begins by putting forward the thesis that the miracle of the prophethood of Muhammad is the Qur'an. This forms the first chapter. Then in the second chapter he proceeds to prove that the Qur'an is really a miracle. He continues the discussion in the third chapter and enumerates in detail all the proofs in favour of this thesis. One of the arguments is that the style of the Qur'an is such that no human being could have composed it. Here he finds it necessary to show that the Qur'an is neither Shi'r nor Saj'. These form the next two chapters. Then he puts forward the question whether it is possible to find out the miracle of the Qur'an by examining its eloquence or rhetoric (Badi'). Here he mentions in detail the different forms existing and compares them with those passages of the Qur'an which have taken the same form. After doing this at length, he comes to the conclusion that this is not the right way, and one cannot be sure in this way of the fact that the Qur'an is supernatural.

Then, in the next chapter, he proceeds to describe how it is possible to come to the right conclusion. He says at the very outset that it is not possible for those whose language is not Arabic or even for those who only speak the language but have got no taste for its fine points to be certain of the fact. They must depend on the judgment of those whose business it is to distinguish between the ordinary and the extraordinary style. Then he quotes some of the speeches and letters delivered or dictated by the Prophet himself and asks us to compare them with the Qur'an and see what a difference there is in the style and composition of both. The idea is that the prophet himself could not compose in the same style and there is no way open but to believe that the Qur'an is revealed and is the composition of God Himself. After that he brings in the same way the *Khutab* or *Rasa'il* of the Companions of the Prophet and those of other earlier and later prominent men and comes to the same conclusion regarding them also. Here he gives an example of the words uttered by the two claimants of prophethood just after the death of Muhammad, viz., Museylimah, the man, and Sajah the woman, and ridicules them outright. Now he takes the poets. He prefaces his examination by enunciating a general principle that poetry cannot go the same length in the excellence of style as prose, because the former is handicapped by the requirements of rhyme and metre. So it is no use comparing poetry with the Qur'an for its very nature gives it a secondary position. But, as some people who had no understanding used to compare the two, he is bound to expose them. He selects as a representative poet the best of them Imrau'l-Qais and begins to examine at length the beauties and the faults in his verses. After finishing this, he describes some of the indescribable charms of the style of the Qur'an and asks all those who have got any taste to form their own judgment. He does not finish here but goes not to examine the poets of his own time, for there might be people who have doubts on this score, though it is very unlikely that any one could excel Imrau'l-Qais, and so, when his verses cannot be compared favourably with the Qur'an, it is quite out of the question for any one else to reach that level. This is by far the longest chapter and comprises almost half of the whole book.

In the following pages he discusses some of the small points, viz., (I) Is the supernaturalism of the Qur'an self-evident? (2). What is the amount of the supernatural in the Qur'an? (3). In what does it lie? (4). The question of the challenge (Tahaddi). (5). The real connotation of the world Mu'jiz, and lastly (6) Why it is not right to say that the Qur'an was composed by Muhammad, and some other matters related with I'jaz. There is also a separate chapter, which ought to have been rightly a part of the principal one described above, on the description of the different figures of speech and their examples from the Qur'an. Then he closes the book with a very eloquent discourse on the difficulties in the path of a person discussing such a vast subject. He is of the opinion that it is quite impossible for any one to fathom the depth of the Qur'an or to describe all its beauties.

Typical of his attitude is an anecdote that he relates. A Bedawi had lost his way one dark night. Suddenly the moon came out and he found his way again. Then he addressed the moon in the following words, "What should I say to thee? Should I say : god may rise thee high! but He has already raised thee; or, may He make thee bright, but He has already made thee bright; or may He give thee beauty, but He hath already given thee beauty."

It is a pity that many of these books are lost. The loss of the book of Ash-Sharifu'l-Murtada is all the more sad because he had taken a view very uncommon and, in early times, expressed only by Nazzam. It would have been of great value to us to see how he proved his contention. Some of his arguments have been quoted by other authors and, fortunately, a fragment of his own on this subject also exists. He used to answer theological and religious questions forwarded to him by different people in course of their correspondence with him, and a collection of such letters is still extant (MS. Berlin Pet. 40). Two of the letters discuss this problem and give us an inkling of his views.

### 4. As a Part of Others Systems

*(a) In Ma'ani and Bayan*

It is a well-recognised fact that Arabic Rhetoric is largely based on the Qur'an. But it has not been perhaps as yet realised that the origin of the whole science lies in this dogma of the supernaturalism of the Qur'an. There were naturally other causes also, but without any doubt this was the chief cause. In the discussions about the miracle of the Qur'an the chief problem was : in what does this miracle lie? We see that quite in the beginning there were two groups. One contended that it lay in the style and the composition of the Qur'an while the other saw nothing extraordinary in its style and put forward other arguments. But only a few people belonged to the second group. Most of the learned men belonged to the first. So it was quite natural for people to begin asking the question ; what, after all, was the standard of judgment? They began to collect specimens of literature existing at the time and to compare them with the Qur'an. This also explains clearly why Jahiz felt the necessity of writing a book which he called Nazmu'l-Qur'an. It is really very unfortunate that this book does not exist, but its very name is a picture of its contents.

This fact also remains to be appreciated in full that Jahiz was the person with whom Arabic Rhetoric came into existence. Anybody who peruses his work *Al-Bayan wa't-Tabyin* carefully, requires no other proof. It is a general belief that Abdu'l-Qahir al-Jurjani (d. 471 A.H.) was the originator of Arabic Rhetoric, but this should not be accepted without certain qualifications. There is no doubt that Jurjani was the first person who systematized all the ideas existing about the subject and made it a science. But he cannot in any way be called the originator. His two books *Asraru'l-Balaghah* and *Dala'ilu'l-I'jaz* are the first books in which the problems of Ma'ani and Beyan are discussed systematically. But most of the subject-matter existed before him in one form or other.

Now his book Dala'ilu'l-I'jaz is a living proof of our contention that this science originated because of the belief in the I'jaz of the Qur'an. The name suggests that he is going to enumerate in this book all the arguments in favour of the dogma of I'jaz. But what does he actually do? From beginning to the end he discusses problems of grammar and rhetoric. Why does he do such a thing which is obviously a paradox? The explanation which he gives is very simple. One cannot come to the conclusion that the Qur'an is supernatural unless he has the capacity to distinguish between the different forms of expression. He repeats the same argument in an appendix written later and called *All-Mudkhal fi Dala'ili'l-I'jaz.*

Jurjani is also said to have written two commentaries on the book of Khattabi already mentioned.

One of them was bigger and was called Al-Mu'tadad and the other was smaller. It is quite possible that while writing the two commentaries he felt the need of a system of literary criticism and later compiled his two famous books above-mentioned. This also shows the development of his ideas. He first wrote a small commentary on one of the earliest books on the subject, but later on was dissatisfied with it and wrote a bigger one. Then this also became insufficient and he found himself unable to remain within the bounds of a commentary. So he wrote a separate book *Dala'ilu'l-I'jaz.* But the basis remains the same. Had the original book of Khattabi and the two commentaries not been lost to us we might have been able to trace the development clearly and exactly.

These two books of Jurjani have been abridged and rearranged by Fakhruddin ar-Razi (d. 606 A.H.) in his book *Nihayatu'l-I'jaz fi Dirayati'l-I'jaz.* He says it himself clearly in the preface to his book. He moreover, puts the argument brought forward by Jurjani in favour of this way of treatment more clearly. Razi discusses this question in his other works also, namely his commentary on the Qur'an and the two books on Kalam, *Ma'alimu Usuli'd-Din* and *Muhassalu Afkari'l-Mutaq-addimin.* But in all this he brings almost nothing new himself.

The other authors who have followed the path pointed out by Jurjani are (1). Ibnu Abi Isba'-il-Qairawani (d. 654 A.H.) who wrote a book called *Beyanu'l-Burhan fi I'jazi'l-Qur'an* and (2). 'Abdul-Wahid az-Zamlakani (d. 651 A.H.) whose book is named *Kitabu't-tibyan fi 'Ilmi'l-Beyan al-Mutli 'ala I'jazi'l-Qur'an.*

The name of Hazim b. Muhammad al-Qartajani (d. 684 A.H.) is also mentioned in this connection. He is said to have dealt with the problem in his book *Minhaju'l-Bulagha.*

At this point it would be interesting to note how, as the time passed on, the very word I'jaz went on losing its particular colour till it came to mean simply eloquence and by *'Ilmu'l-I'jaz* nothing more was meant than the science of rhetoric. We come across a book written by Ghiath-ud-Din Lutfullah (d. 1035 A.H.) called *Al-I'jaz fi 'Ilmi'l-I'jaz* and the author does not find it necessary even to explain the relation between the name and the subject-matter which is nothing other than notes on Ma'ani and Beyan. What more proof is required for the connection between the dogma of I'jazu'l-Qur'an and Arabic

Rhetoric than this fact, that the word which was coined to signify the one came to mean the other.

*(b) I'Jazul-Qur'an*

We have already noticed two of the earliest commentaries, those of Tabari and Qummi. The outstanding amongst the later commentators who have also dealt with our problem are the following:

1. Ar-Raghibu'l-Isfahani (d. 502 A.H.) in the introduction to his commentary on the Qur'an (published at the end of *Tanzihu'l-Qur'an 'ani'l Mata'in* by 'Abdul Jabbar al-Asadabadi (d. 415 A.H., Cairo, 1329 A.H.).
2. 'Umar b. Muhammadi'n-Nasafi (d. 537 A.H.) in his commentary on the Qur'an (MS Berlin Mf. 41).
3. Mahmud b. 'Umar az-Zamakhshari (d. 538 A.H.) in his commentary on the Qur'an (published Calcutta, 1865 A.D.).
4. Ibn 'Ati'a al-Gharnati (d. 542 A.H.) in his commentary on the Qur'an (MS., Berlin Spr. 408).
5. Muhammad b. Ahmad al-Qurtubi (d. 671 A.H.) in his commentary on the Qur'an (MS. Berlin Spr. 436).
6. Muhammad b. Juzayy al-Kalbi (d. 741 A.H.) in *Kitabu't-Tashil li 'Ulumi'l Qur'an* (MS. Berlin Lbg. 85).
7. Ismail b. 'Umar ibn Kathir (d. 774 A.H.) in his commentary on the Qur'an (published Cairo, 1924 A.D.).
8. Muhammad b. 'Abdillahi'z Zarkashi (d. 794 A.H.) in *Al Burhan fi 'Ulumi'l-Qur'an* (The book exists in Medinah). See Ma'arif, Vol. 18 No. 6 Dec. 1926 p. 411; see also introduction to Suyuti's *Itqn.*
9. Majdu'd-din al-Firozabadi (d. 817 A.H.) in *Basairu dhawi't-Tamyiz fi Lata'ifi'l-Kitabi'l-'Aziz.* (There is no trace of the existence of this book). See Cat Berlin I, p. 286).
10. Jalalu'd-din as-Suyuti (d. 911 A.H.) in *Al-Itqan fi 'fi 'Ulumi'lQur'an* (published Cairo, 1344 A.H.).

*(c) In the System of Kalam*

We have already noticed the book of 'Ali b Rabban at-Tabari.

It is said that Ash'ari (d. 324 A.H.) also wrote on the subject in some of his innumerable books but unfortunately most of them are lost and there is no mention of this question in the existing ones. Some of his views on the matter have nevertheless reached us through other writers. Another famous Mutakallim, whose work has not reached us, was Abu Ishaq-al-Isfaraini who is better known by his surname of Al-Ustadh (The Master). d. 418 A.H. He dealt with this question in his book *Jami'u'l-Jali wa'l-Khafi fi Usuli'd Din wa'r-raddi 'ala'l-Mulhidin.* The other dogmatists who made this question a part of their systems and whose works still exist are:

1. 'Abdu'l-Qahir b. Tahiri'l-Baghdadi (d. 429 A.H.) in *Kitabu Usuli'd-Din* (published Istanbul 1928 A.D.).
2. 'Ali b. Muhammad al-Mawardi (d. 450 A.H.) in *A'lamu'n-Nubuwah* (published Cairo 1315 A.H.).
3. 'Ali b. Ahmad ibn Hazm (d. 456 A.H.) in *Kitabu'l fisal fi'l Milal wa'l Ahwa'i wa'n Nihal* (published Cairo 1899-1903).
4. 'Abdu'l-Malik b. 'Abdillahi'l-Juwaini (Abu'l Ma'-ali, Imamu'l-Harameyn, d. 478 A.H.) in *Kitabu'l Irshad fi Usuli'l-'tiqad* (Leid. 1983. Br. Mus. 1628/2).
5. Abu Hamid al-Ghazali (d. 505 A.H.) in *Kitabu'l Iqtisad fi'l-I'tiqad* (published Cairo 1916 A.D. MS. Berlin Lbg. 279).
6. All Qadi 'Iyad (d. 544 A.H.) in *Kitabu'sh-Shifa* (published Cairo 1911; MS. Berlin Spr. 460).
7. Muhammad b. 'Abdi'l-Karim ash-Shahristani (d. 548 A.H.) in *Nihayatu'l-Aqdam fi 'Ilmi'l-Kalam* (MS. Berlin Pm. 579) published Oxford 1931.
8. 'Ali b. Abi 'Ali-i'l-Amidi (d. 631 A.H.) in *Abkaru'l Afkar* (MS. Berlin Pet. 233).
9. Taqiu'd-Din ibn Taymiyah (d. 728 A.H.) in Al-Jawabu's-Sahih li man baddala Din al Masih (published Cairo 1323 A.H.).
10. Hibatu'llah-il-Barizi (d. 738 A.H.) in *Tauthiqu 'Ura'l-iman fi Tafdili Habibi'r Rahman.* (MS Berlin Spr. 127).
11. Badru'd-Din b. 'Umar b. Habib (d. 779 A.H.) in *An-*

*najmu'th-Thaqib fi Ashrai'l-Manaqib* (MS. Berlin Pet. 342).

12. Sa'du'd-Din at-Taftzani (d. 791 A.H.) is *Sharhu Maqasidi't-Talibin fi Usuli'd-Din* (published Istanbul 1277 A.H.).
13. Ash-Sharif ul-Jurjani (d. 816 A.H.) in *Sharhu'l-Mawaqif* (of Al iji d. 756 A.H.). Published Leipzig 1848, MS. Berlin Mf. 152.
14. Abu'l-Huseyn Sa'id b. Hibatillah ar-Rawandi (al-Qutb d?) in *Kitabu'l-Khara'ij wa'l-Jara'ih* (MS. Berlin Pm. 113).

    The whole book is incorporated by Muhammad Baqir al-Majlisi (d. 1011 A.H.) in his encyclopaedic work *Biharu'l-Anwar* (published Tehran, 1303-15 A.H.).
15. Yahya b. Hasan al-Qurashi az-Zaydi in *Minhaju't-Tahqiq wa Mahasinu't-Talfiq* (MS. Berlin Glas. 96).
16. Rahmatu'llahi'l-Hindi in *Izharu'l-Haqq* (published Cairo 1309 A.H.).

### 5. The Word I'jaz and the Idea Behind It

Before proceeding further it is necessary to discuss what the word *i'jaz* means. Literally it means incapacitating or rendering powerless. From this is derived the word *al-mu'jizah* which is a technical term of Kalam for a miracle performed by a prophet. The idea behind the word which is not difficult to discern, is that everybody else except the prophet is powerless to perform a miracle. In the Qur'an neither the word al-mu'jizah is used for "miracle" nor any other derivative from the same root. The words which are very common are al-ayah, the sign, or al-burhan, the proof. The idea behind these words is not the same. These words stop short after saying that a certain phenomenon is the sign or the proof of the prophethood of a person. Here begins the province of the word al-mu'jizah, which is an adjective and in it underlies the assertion that the phenomenon is special to the prophet and to him alone.

It is not easy to ascertain when this word was first used in its technical sense. The discussion of the question of prophethood had already begun in the first century A.H., but it is not at all certain that the word al-mu'jizah is as old as that. On the contrary, we find an author like 'Ali b. Rabban at-Tabari, who wrote his book somewhere between 232 and 247 A.H., still using the word al-ayah and not even once employing the word al-mu'jizah or any other derivative from the same root. We cannot, of course, assert on such slight evidence that till then the word had never been used in its technical sense, but we shall have no fear of being far from the truth if we say that up to the middle of the third century this word had not become dominant enough to exclude its predecessors al-ayah and al-burhan as it later did. As and evidence of this we find Ahmad b. Hanbal (d. 241 A.H.) using the word mu'jizah not only in relation to the prophets but other holy persons also. Later on the word *Karamah* began to be used for the second meaning. We know that the first book with the name *I'jazu'l-Qur'an* was written sometime in the latter half of the third century A.H. After that time, in discussions on the question of the prophethood, the words ayah and burhan are very seldom used. The words i'jaz and mu'jizah now take their place.

It is fascinating work to trace the process by which a certain word acquired a particular meaning, but at the same time it is an extremely difficult task; and especially in this case, on account of the scantiness of the available material, it is difficult to decide conclusively what the process has been. We can only say that the technical meaning of the word i'jaz has in some way or other been taken over from the ordinary use of the word. Now it is known that in the Islamic circle in Syria the particular question of the prophethood of Muhammad was being discussed long before the system of Kalam sprang up and the general problem of prophethood, as such, began to be discussed. It is also known that the chief argument in favour of Muhammad was that he was the recipient of a revelation. The Qur'an claims its own composition to be beyond the power of human beings or the Jinn.

In the books of Kalam we find pages devoted to the discussion of a comprehensive definition of al-mu'jizah. A representative one will suffice here. M.B.A. al-Qurtubi, in his book *Al-Jami' li Ahkami'l-*

*Qur'an* prescribes five conditions without which no act could be called a mu'jizah :

(1) The act must be such that only God could have performed it.
(2) It should break the law of Nature.
(3) The claimant should declare beforehand that such and such a thing is going to happen.
(4) The actual happening should conform exactly to his declaration, and
(5) Nobody else should be able to call the same phenomenon into action.

This in short is what the Mutakallim means when he use the words i'jaz or mu'jizah. We need not enter into details because here we are not chiefly concerned with miracles as such but with the miracle of the Qur'an. Our business ought to be to classify the arguments brought forward in favour of the thesis that the Qur'an is supernatural.

**Classification of the Arguments**

We have already seen that in the Qur'an the claim of supernaturalism is made in answer to those who did not believe in the prophethood of Muhammad. The Mutakallim also begins his arguments at the same point. First he proceeds to show that the miracle of the prophethood of Muhammad is no other than the Qur'an. So says Baqillani :

"The fact which requires complete attention in recognising the miracle of the Qur'an is that the prophethood of our Prophet is based on this miracle although he was supported, afterwards, by many other miracles. While these other miracles were performed at particular times, in particular cases and on particular persons...., the miracle of the Qur'an is such as prevails over human beings as well as the Jinn... and the force of its arguments is the same from the day of its appearance to that of the Resurrection." Baqillani quotes many verses from the Qur'an to prove his contention. One of them is : "They said, why then does he not receive a sign from his Lord? Tell them, the signs are with God and I am merely a plain warner. Is it then not enough for them that We have sent down the Book to thee, which is read to them?"

Then he proceeds : "So He states that the Book is one of his signs and distinguishing marks, and that it is sufficient as a proof and corresponds to the miracles and signs of other prophets." To the same category belongs the Hadith, already mentioned, in which the Prophet is said to have declared that the Qur'an is the only sign (Ayah) he has received.

The later Mutakallimin go still further back and formulate five premisses, namely : (a) that Muhammad did exist (b) that he did claim to be a prophet (c) that he performed a miracle, (i.e. produced the Qur'an) (d) that he challenged others to produce a similar thing and (e) that nobody could bring anything similar to it. They say that if these five premisses are established the conclusion necessarily follows that Muhammad was a true prophet.

The first two premisses, they say, are most obvious and do not require any proof; because nobody denies the existence of Muhammad or that he declared himself to be messenger of God.

Now the third premiss is the chief one, because here it is to be proved that the Qur'an is really a miracle. Most of the Mutakallimin have turned the last two premisses into arguments in favour of the third. The fact that Muhammad did challenge the people to bring something like the Qur'an is beyond dispute because more than one verse of the Qur'an itself bears witness to it. It is also certain that nobody did produce anything like the Qur'an because, if it were the case, we should have received the pieces so composed as we have received the pre-Islamic poetry or Khutab. There is no reason why they should have been concealed or lost. On the other hand, it should have been the greatest concern of the disbelievers to preserve them. The believers too could not have ignored them because, if any attempt to rival the Qur'an did succeed, the whole basis of their belief would have been lost. The very fact that all through the ages so many people have believed in the supernaturalism of the Qur'an is enough to prove that nobody succeeded in producing the like of it.

The pieces reported to have been composed by Museylimah are so ridiculously poor in style that nobody could seriously compare them with the Qur'an.

It is also quite evident that the easiest and the most convincing way of refuting the claim of Muhammad would have been to show that others too could compose something like the Qur'an and that there was nothing supernatural in it. But we see the Arabs doing everything in their power except this. They resorted to war and so underwent all the privations one could imagine. If it had been in their power to rival the Qur'an and so destroy the whole structure of Muhammad's claim, is it not reasonable to expect that they would have preferred that method? So the only conclusion one can draw is that, in spite of the fact that the Arabs were masters of style and composition, it was beyond their power to produce anything like the Qur'an.

This is the general argument. Now comes the question : What in the Qur'an is supernatural? Here we do not find a unanimous opinion. From the very beginning there has been a reference of opinion on this question. Together with the formulation of the dogma arose the problem whether the style of the Qur'an was supernatural or the subject-matter. The orthodox view is that both of them are supernatural, but there have been many exponents of only one of them. Very early did Nazzam assert that there was nothing extraordinary in the style of the Qur'an. If the Arabs were left alone they would have been able to compose pieces like those of the Qur'an. But they were deterred by God from attempting to rival the Qur'an and in this lies the miracle. This is, technically, called the argument of Sarfah. (Sarafa to deter). The other thing that he found supernatural in the Qur'an was prophecies about future events. After him came Jahiz who emphasized more the point of style and wrote a book to prove the thesis. From the time on the chief argument has always been the miraculous style of the Qur'an.

That the question of style was a controversial one in early times is clearly shown by the introductory words of 'Ali b. Rabban at-Tabari. "When I was still a Christian I used to say, as did an uncle of mine who was one of the learned and eloquent men, that eloquence is not one of the signs of prophethood because it is common to all the peoples; but when I discarded (blind) imitation and (old) customs and gave up adhering to (mere) habit and training and reflected upon the meanings of the Qur'an I came to know that what the followers of the Qur'an claimed for it was true. The fact is that I have not found any book, be it by an Arab or a Persian, an Indian or a Greek, right from the beginning of the world up to now, which contains at the same time praises of God, belief in the prophets and apostles, exhortations to good, everlasting deeds, command to do good and prohibition against doing evil, inspiration to the desire of Paradise and to the avoidance of hell-fire as this Qur'an does. So when a person brings to us a book of such qualities, which inspires such reverence and sweetness in the hearts and which has achieved such an overwhelming success and he is (at the same time) an illiterate person who did never learn the art of writing or rhetoric, that book is without any doubt one of the signs of his prophethood."

Here another element is added to the previous two. The fact that Muhammad did not know how to read and write becomes a third argument in addition to the style and the subject-matter of the Qur'an. Then comes Ar-Rumani who says :

"The miracle of the Qur'an lies in (1) the fact that nobody rivalled it in spite of the plenty of motives and the intense need and the general challenge, (2) the Sarfah, (3) the eloquence, (4) the prophesying of future events and (5) the breaking of the established rule, and (6) its analogy to all the other miracles. Now the breaking of the established rule is that (up till then) the well-known established forms of speech had been Shir, Saj`, Khutab, Rasa'il and the prose which was current in conversation. But the Qur'an opened a new path, unique and different from the established ones. It has a degree of beauty which surpasses that of all the other forms and excels even verse which is the best form of speech. Its analogy to other miracles lay in the fact that it was similar to the parting of the sea and the transformation of the rod into a snake, or other miracles of the same kind, in so far as it broke the established rule and so hindered the creatures from rivalling it."

Now, with the question of Style, arose the problem of a standard or criterion. How can one find out that the Style of the Qur'an is supernatural? The first answer to this was that it depended on personal taste. Only those who had got a right taste for Arabic style could be sure of it. Common people amongst the Arabs themselves or the foreigners could not be certain of the fact and had to depend on expert opinion. We find Al-Qummi asserting that the nature of the miracle of the Qur'an could only be realised, and it was impossible to describe it just like a good place of poetry or the beauty of a free. Anybody who asserted the contrary and tried to show that the miracle lay either in Sarfah or departure from the established forms of speech or freedom from contradictions or even the prophecies was absolutely wrong, in his opinion.

But Al-Khattabi opposed this view. He said: "Most of the speculative theologians are of the opinion that the reason why the Qur'an is supernatural lies in (its) eloquence, but it has proved difficult for them to explain it and they are inclined towards the judgment of taste only. But the fact is that the forms of speech differ and rank high or low when considered from the point of view of rhetoric.

Al-Khattabi adds another argument which, he says, had been neglected : namely, the effect that the Qur'an produces on people. He says : "No words, be they poetry or prose, when heard by the ear, produce on the heart sometimes the effect of sweetness and sometimes that of awe as the Qur'an does."

Now appeared Baqillani who collected all the arguments as yet put forward and added his own to them. We have already given a short sketch of his book. In the second chapter he argues at length why the Qur'an should be termed a miracle. The gist of it we have given under the general arguments. He is also against *Sarfah.* In the third chapter he puts forward three arguments at the start.

1. The Qur'an contains prophecies about future events and this is beyond the power of man.

2. It is well-known that Muhammad was an 'Ummi (one who could neither read nor write). It is also known that he was not conversant with the books of the ancients or their tales and biographies. Nevertheless he recapitulated all the important events that had happened from the creation of Adam down to his own call. So there is no other way but to conclude that he received all the information direct from God through revelation.

3. The Qur'an surpasses the limit man can reach in composition, style and eloquence.

These are the arguments which his predecessors had already put forward but his business is to enlarge upon them. So he proceeds to enlarge upon the third argument and draws the attention of the readers to ten points :

1. The first point, which is a general one, is that the style of the Qur'an, with all its different phases and aspects, goes beyond all the known styles and is special to the Qur'an alone.

2. That the Arabs have got no piece of composition which can rival the Qur'an in its eloquence and chastity of style and is at the same time so long as the Qur'an is.

3. That the style of the Qur'an retains its high levels in all the phases of expression. For example the Qur'an contains tales and sermons, arguments and exhortations, promises and threatenings, ethical teachings and so many other things. In spite of these different aspects the style never degenerates, as is the case even with the best of poets and orators. They excel only in one class of subjects while the Qur'an excels in all of them.

4. That in the composition of the best authors (even on one subject) one part does not compare with the other. It is particularly the case where the author shifts from one idea to another. But in the

Qur'an, on the other hand, we see that the most divergent topics are treated in such a way that they appear to be one whole.

5. That the style of the Qur'an is not only superior to that of men but also to that of the Jinn. It might be said that this is a claim about which we cannot be sure because it is beyond the range of our knowledge. We can be sure at least about this: that the style of the Qur'an is superior to the style of those compositions which the Arabs believed to be the compositions of the Jinn.

6. That all the different forms of expression, like dilation and elision, collection and distribution, metaphor and explicitness, etc., which are found in their compositions are to be found also in the Qur'an. Moreover these forms in the Qur'an excel their forms in every respect.

7. That it is more difficult to coin words for new ideas than to coin words for current ones. In the Qur'an we find such words which express the new Qur'anic ideas about Shari'ah in a way which is beyond the power of man.

8. That the excellence of a composition and the height of its eloquence is established when one takes out a word from it and puts it in another sentence or verse and if this word catches the attention of the reader or hearer. This is exactly the case with the words of the Qur'an. Its words when used in other compositions shine like jewels or pearls.

9. That the letters of the alphabet on which the Arabic language is based are 29, and the chapters of the Qur'an which begin with letters of the alphabet number 28, and the letters of the alphabet so used are 14 or exactly the half. This is to show that the composition of the Qur'an is based on the very alphabet which they use. Then again the letters of the alphabet have been classified in different categories by different people, as, for example, soft and hard, guttural and non-guttural, straining and non-straining, covering and open letters. The remarkable fact is that half the letters from all these classes are used at the beginning of chapters of the Qur'an. The

classification dates long after the appearance of the Qur'an and the fact that exactly half the number from every class are used is a proof of the knowledge of the future and this is possible only to God.

10. That the language of the Qur'an is simple and easy and its meaning is quickly understood. It does not contain uncouth words or expressions. Nevertheless it is impossible to rival its style.

These are the ten points of Baqillani. The rest of his book is devoted to the amplification of these points. The whole force of these points can only be realised by going through the book from one end to the other. It is impossible here to enter into details. The book of Baqillani is the central link in the whole chain of arguments brought forward to prove the dogma of I'jazu'l-Qur'an. All the arguments put forward by his predecessors converge in him and then flow again from him into different channels. By now we have reached the end of the 4th century, when most of the Islamic dogmas had acquired a sort of rigidity true of Kalam was completed at this time and the efforts of the later Mutakallimin are confined to the decoration of the building already erected.

The argument of Sarfah got another champion in As-Sayyid Ash-Sharif Al-Murtada, and he was perhaps the last man who saw the miracle of the Qur'an only in Sarfah. We are quite in the dark about all his arguments because his book is lost; but, as he himself mentions in one of his letters, the chief argument he brought forward was that the difference between the small pieces in the Qur'an and the best compositions of the Arabs is not evident to everyone although the difference between the good and bad compositions of the Arabs is quite evident. So the only sure way of proving the miracle of the Qur'an is to establish that the Arabs did not produce the like of it or in other words, that they were deterred by God from doing this.

Much does not remain to be said regarding the arguments. After this time the merit of a Mutakallim lies not in bringing new arguments but in putting the old ones in an original way. This can be judged only by reading the works of the authors themselves and cannot be put briefly in another language. We see, for example, Al-Mawardi counting twenty arguments in favour of the I'jaz but only one seems to be new viz., that the Qur'an can be committed to memory so very easily by everybody even by the Persians and the Copts. Then another thing which the later Mutakallimun have done is that they have example. Al-Qadi Iyad 'Ali al-Amidi and Shahristani writing pages after pages to make one argument clear. Al-Amidi has got a further peculiarity viz., that he puts questions which might arise in the mind of a reader and answers them, but strangely enough the questions are put in a finer way than the answers.

The name of Ar-Raghibu'l-Isfahani should also be mentioned here for the very fine style in which he writes and the original way in which he begins the arguments. The article of Ibn Hazm is more remarkable for the invectives he uses against those who differ from him than for the arguments he puts forward.

**7. Reports of Opposition and Refutation**

In the first section we have already noticed some of the comments of the Qur'an offered by the people of Mecca which are quoted in the Qur'an itself. In the life-time of the Prophet there appeared certain persons who either claimed prophethood for themselves or tried to produce something like the Qur'an. One of them who lived in or about Mecca was Nadr b. al-Harith. He did not claim to be a prophet, but he used to relate stories of the Kings of Persia with intent to rival the stories about the old prophets or peoples mentioned in the Qur'an. We can take him as a representative of those who said that Muhammad was merely a story-teller and the Qur'an nothing more than the tales of the past. Nothing either of the words or the contents of his stories has reached us.

Then came a number of persons who claimed to be prophets themselves. The most famous of them was Museylima b. Habib of the tribe of Bani Hanifah of Yamamah. He appeared in the last years of the life-time of the Prophet and is said even to have written a letter to him which ran : —"Verily, I have been made a partner of thine in this world. Half of the land belongs to us and half to the Qureysh. But the Qureysh are a rebellious people....." After the death of the Prophet he succeeded in getting quite a good following, and Abu Bekr had to send an army against him. He was killed in the battle which followed. Some of his sayings have reached us but they are mostly imitations of verses of the Qur'an and have no literary worth. It is very likely that they are later fabrications for the purpose of exposing Museylima to the ridicule of later generations. The others were : 1. 'Abhala b. Ka'b. (better known as Al-Aswad ul'Anasi) 2. Sajah, bintu'l-Harith of the tribe of Bani Tamim and 3. Tulaiha b. Khuweylid of Bani Asad. Of their utterances only a sentence or two have reached us and it is not possible to form any opinion.

About the middle of the second century there lived a number of people who were more or less freethinkers. The most prominent of them were Ibnu'l-Muqaffa, Bashshar b. Burd, Salih b. 'Abdi'l-Quddus and Abdu'l-Hamid al-Katib. All of them were well-known writers or poets. The report goes that they used to sit together and criticise the Qur'an or tried to excel it is composition and style. The report is particularly persistent in the case of Ibnu'l-Muqaffa. It is a most remarkable phenomenon in Arabic literary history that many of the best prose writers and also some poets of the early times are accused of trying at one time or other to rival the Qur'an. But the stories always end on the same note, namely, that they were obliged to abandon the attempt finding it beyond their power. In the same category fall also Abu't-Tayyib al-Mutanabbi (d. 354 A.H.), Qabus b. Washmgir (d. 403 A.H). and Abu'l 'Ala al-Ma'arri (d. 449 A.H.) In the case of Mutanabbi the surname itself shows that he was said to have claimed prophethood. The stories sound very circumstantial; firstly, because these people are known, without doubt, to have been not very orthodox in their beliefs, and secondly, and perhaps chiefly, because they were unquestionably masters of style. Popular imagination is at all times very fertile, and it is common knowledge that the passage of time turns vague rumour into established history and fiction into fact. Especially in case of those persons who oppose the popular beliefs it always happens that as time goes on additional sins are added to their charge-sheet. The evidence at our disposal does not warrant a summary judgment one way or the other. The age in which Ibnu'l-Muqaffa' and his companions lived was an age in which the process of the formation of dogmas had just begun. There were bound to be serious differences of opinion on every subject. We have already seen that approximately during the same period the question of I'jazu'l-Qur'an was being discussed for the first time. Actions and reactions were inevitable. These people, as forming a group of intellectuals, must have had opinions of their own, which were more likely than not to have differed from the common view. The popular mind always thinks in extremes. Either a person believes in everything or he believes in nothing. If he does not believe in one thing the chances are ten to one that he does not believe in the other also. That is popular logic, and that is how persons are judged by the tribunal of public opinion. Why should there have been any exception in the case of these persons?

Against Ibnu'l-Muqaffa' there is a more serious charge : that he wrote a book against Islam and criticised especially the Qur'an. There is only one evidence in favour of the charge. Among the writings of Al-Qasim b. Ibrahim Ar-Rasi (d. 246 A.H.), one of the Imams of the Zeydiya, there is a treatise which is named *Kitab'ur-raddi-'ala'z-Zindiqi'l-la'in ibni'l Muqaffa.* He quotes from the book of Ibnu'l-Muqaffa which was in his hards and then proceeds to refute the arguments. It has been fairly well discussed, and established almost beyond, doubt, that this treatise is the work of Al-Qasim, but what is very doubtful, and has not been yet discussed, is the question whether the book of which this is the refutation could have really been written by Ibnu'l-Muqaffa. The external evidence against this is that from no other source is Ibnu'l-Muqaffa'known to have written any such book. His works are well-known and, although not all of them have reached us, at least their names have been preserved. Also, from what we know about his life, manners and temperament, it seems very unlikely that he indulged in such controversies. There is also internal evidence against this. The passages quoted by Al-Qasim do not speak much for the ability of the author either in style or in argument. Al-Qasim himself remarks that the style of the book is un-Arabic (A'jami ul-Beyan). Ibnu'l-Muqaffa' on the other hand was one of the best writers of Arabic, and also a clever and learned man. We have no reason to doubt that a book criticising the Qur'an and Islam in general did reach the hands of Al-Qasim, and that it was written by one of the Thanawiya and also that Al-Qasim was made to believe that it was the work of Ibnu'l-Muqaffa. But Al-Qasim lived far away in Yaman and about a century after the time of Ibnu'l-Muqaffa. At that time the Thanawiya literature was spreading and was mostly anonymous. The authors had good reasons to keep back their names. Speculation must have been rife about the authorship of such books and it is not to be wondered at that one of them was attributed to Ibnu'l-Muqaffa' who was a well-known writer, had been accused of Zandaqah in his own time, and was also known to have translated some of the religious literature of his own people. Al-Qasim, who was every inch a zealous preacher, took this for granted and began to refute the book. To him it was naturally a secondary question as to who had written the book. The primary thing was that it was against orthodox Islam, and whosoever the author might be he was a *Zindiq* and *la'in.* He had no time and no need to examine the question of authorship.

In the reign of Ma'mun (198-218 A.H.), when liberalism was not only preached but also forced upon people, the one problem of the day was the question of Khalqu'l Qur'an. That is it dealt with the question, whether Quran is a created word not.

The question of I'jazu'l-Qur'an must have been either pushed aside or discussed only as subsidiary to the big problem. But a very remarkable thing happened at that time. A certain courtier of Ma'mun, who was also related to him and who is known as abdullah b. Isla'il al-Hashimi, wrote a letter to a friend of his, who had also been once a courtier of Ma'mun, but was a staunch Christian and is known as 'Abdul Masih b. Ishaq al-Kindi. In his letter he asked his friend to accept Islam, and gave his reasons for the superiority of Islam to Christianity. One of the arguments in favour of the prophethood of Muhammad was, naturally, the miracle of the Quran. The Christian, Al-Kindi, wrote back a long letter refuting all the arguments of Al-Hashimi and especially his argument concerning the Qur'an. In this he passes some very strong remarks on the way in which the Qur'an was collected, and on its subject-matter its language and its style. In short, he tries by every means at his disposal to disprove the Muslim belief in the supernaturalism of the Qur'an. This is very interesting reading, and is perhaps the best of the very few original documents written against the Qur'an in the early times which are still preserved.

Not long after this appeared a person whose name was Abu'l Huseyn Ahmad b. Yahya and who is better known as Ibnu'r-Rawandi (d. about 250 A.H.). His chief work seems to have been criticising the doctrines of orthodox Islam and especially the Qur'an. He is said to have written many books on this theme. The one in which he confined to criticism of the Qur'an was called Ad-Damigh. It is said that he wrote this book for some Jews while he was staying with them in hiding, having much to fear from the hands of justice. He resembled somewhat the so-called free-lance journalist of these days and could write for and against the same cause without any scruple. He changed his opinions as often as he thought fit, and wrote in favour of everyone of them with same amount of zeal and gust. Some partial quotations from his writings are all that we have received from the great mass of books and treatises that he is reported to have produced.

The criticism of the Quran offered during the ages by non-Muslims and freethinkers, and the response to this by Muslim writers is a subject of study by itself. It is a vast subject, concerning with a lot of material is to be found scattered in the books of Kalam. The Mutakallimin almost invariably devoted some pages of their books to answer such criticism after they had dealt with the issue of Ijazul Quran. Abul Hasan Abdul Jabbar al-Hamudani al-Asadabadi (d. 415 A.H) felt even the need of writing a seperate book on this issue which he titled Tanzilhul Quran ... It would be very instructive and of great value to students of the religious history of Islam and of literary history of the Arabic language if all these criticisms together with their responses were collectec and arranged systematically; but this is not the place for it. It must be dealt seperately and throughly.

# 3

# The Law of Crime in the Qur'an & Religion vs. Morality

SYED MAQBOOL AHMED & A KHALIQ KHAN

Islamic concept of morality and punishment are discussed. While the law of crime deals with theft, murder, rebellion, adultery etc., the question of morality is discussed under the different themes like, the laws of piety, fate of an apostate in Islam, etc.

The main heads of crimes (or sins against the rights of man), and punishment for the same, are laid down fundamentally in many verses of the Qur'an, particularly in those revealed at Medina. They form the basis of Islamic jurisprudence, which elaborately classifies crimes and the nature of their punishment; deriving the authority not available in the Qur'an, from the actions of the Prophet himself, and his four rightly-guided successors. I need not go into it, beyond what the Qur'an has laid down, for that is the purpose of my present remarks. The following passages relate to crimes and their punishment in the Qur'an :

**Theft**

And thieves, man or woman, cut their hands as a punishment of their deeds. This has been appointed by God, and God is all knowing and all powerful. And if he repents after his misdeeds and reforms himself, he shall be forgiven by God, for God is the Forgiver and merciful *(Almaida,* vi).

The Qur'anic injunction with respect to thieves is very much the same as was given through Moses to the Israelites; and Jesus has also recapitulated the same law, when he said : "If thy right hand commits a sin cut it off, it is better to remain armless than to be thrown into hell with a sinful arm, etc." This is an extreme punishment for thieves, *who cannot be reformed otherwise.* It has now been generally accepted that jail has failed to correct habitual thieves. It only confirms them in their habits, and makes them quite at home with jail life. The theory that such thieves, when put to work in jail, come out of it with the habit of following any trade taught them there, and become honest and useful members of society, has been shattered by repeated experience. Such have never been found to follow any trade taught in the jail, but only that for which they were sent to jail. England did well to hang thieves till very recently, for there is no other way of getting rid of these pests of society; and nothing short of putting such in perpetual irons, as an alternative, can deter them from their profession, and save others from their ravages. The perpetual manacling of their hands, or permanent deprivation of that sinful instrument, is what the Qur'an means. As I said, this punishment has been specially enjoined for habitual thieves, but it is quite inconsistent with the purpose of the Qur'an to go to such lengths with those who have not become confirmed in their habits. A handless man will also proclaim and warn others to beware of him. The modern Turks have adopted the Code Napoleon in place of the Qur'an, probably because the Turks, as a race, are reputedly an honest people, and this emergency has never arisen among them; but if they had been in India, and had come in contact with those professionals to whom it is their birthright and a caste obligation to follow the profession of thieving, they would have been wiser to adopt the measures given in the Qur'an. A false notion of soft-heartedness and civilization, is costing the British Government in India, many crores of rupees annually, for keeping watch over these gentlemen, and it has not succeeded in its attempt.

**General Retribution**

We have appointed in the law of Moses, A life for a life, an eye for an eye, a nose for a nose, an ear for an ear, a tooth for a tooth, injury for injury, and if the aggrieved one is compromised, then that will atone him of his sin (*Almaida,* vi).

This law given to Moses has been re-adopted by the Qur'an without any amendment; and it simply means that all mischiefs are to be punished in proportion to the injury done.

**Culpable Homicide (not amounting to murder)**

And it is not lawful for a Muslim to kill another Muslim, unless it be by mistake, and whoever kills a Muslim by mistake, he shall free a slave, and pay blood-money to his heirs, unless they excuse him from this payment. And if the murdered man be an alien, and the murderer a Muslim, then he shall free a slave, but if the murdered man be from those aliens, with whom you are at peace, then a slave shall be freed and blood money shall be paid to the relations of the murdered. If the man possess no slave, he shall fast continuously for two months. This has been appointed as a way of repentance, and God is all knowing.

Comment on this is not Necessary.

**Murder**

O believers, you are enjoined Qisas (capital punishment) for murder; free or slave, male or female (shall suffer equally), but if the family of the murdered forgiveth the murderer, then the blood money shall be paid according to rules, and if any one transgresses afterwards, for him shall be grievous chastisement. And, wise men, for you there is life in Qisas.

Life for life is of course the law of humanity, but the Qur'an allows the murderer opportunity to save his neck by compensating and reconciling the family of the murdered. The latest craze of civilization seeks to abolish capital punishment altogether. Has it taken its cue from the Qur'an allowing recompense by the murderer to the aggrieved, thus putting him entirely at the latter's mercy? Without this provision, punishment for murder would be merely vindictive, and vindictive punishment is not advocated now.

**Rebellion**

Those who cause disruption in the country, and thus make war against God and His Prophet, the punishment for such is that they should be killed outright, or (as an exemplary punishment) crucified, or their hands and feet cut opposite ways, or to be exiled from the country *(Almaida,* v).

Even the most civilized Governments of Europe have dealt with insurgents, chiefly coloured people, more barbarously than ever the Qur'an has conceived.

**Adultery**

And (to adulterer and adulteress, scourge each of them with hundred stripes, and show no favour to them in the ordinance of God, if you believe in God and the last day. And let a party of Muslims be present at the time of their punishment (so that they may be put to shame).

Adultery in Islam is punished not, as in Judaism, by stoning to death, but by stripes. The numbers are fixed, but it is left to the discretion of man to employ the punishment to such an extent of severity as may not cause the death of the victim, or in capacitate him for ever; or, in other words, a cruel lashing, which the writer of these lines has seen dealt out to the natives of Mesopotamia and South Kurdistan, by the new rulers of that country, and which would reduce any body (Kurd and Arab excepted) to pulp in fifty strokes; so, as the number fixed in the Qur'an will never be reached, the allotment will be quite superfluous. The fact that a number has been fixed, and that on the general principle that a man cannot be punished beyond his capacity of endurance, makes it necessary that the flogging should not be unduly severe. The "Cat-of-nine-tails" was never invented in Islam, where the "Durra" employed is a thick, flaț leather, or else a thick cane that does not cut the skin. Of course, nobody can be punished unless he is in a fit state of health, and in the story of Job, given in the Qur'an, in order that he might strictly conform with the ordinance of God, he was permitted a device that seems to set a precedent for the punishment of a very weak man. Job, it is said in the Qur'an, was allowed to bind a hundred sticks together, and give one single blow with it. On the question of the punishment of adultery, the stoning of an elderly man or woman, or rather married people, was, in the opinion of Khalif Omar, permitted in the Qur'an, and he is reported to have quoted the following verse : "Alshaikh wal shaikahto, eza zaina, farjumoohama albutta" (Elderly men or women, when they commit adultery, stone them to death certainly). As this verse is not found in the Qur'an, it has divided jurists in Islam into two schools. One, the Mutazzilite and Kharjittes, including Hanafis like Razi, Dr. Sir Syed Ahmed, and Maulvi Muhammad Ali (the translator of the Holy Qur'an) consider this report, in spite of its mention in such reliable tradition as Muslim and Almautta, to be absolutely spurious, and to have been interpolated by some busybody of a jurist, who thought Islam would otherwise only look tolerant towards adultery, as compared with Judaism. They base their argument on the fact that for Khalif Omar to say that this verse was in the Qur'an, would be absurd, seeing that the Qur'an in its present form was edited in the time of Khalif Osman, so there could have been no occasion for Omar to complain of the omission of this verse. Nor does it seem quite probable Khalif Osman, with all the care he bestowed in collecting the verses of the Qur'an, would have overlooked the inclusion of so important an ordinance, when special mention had been made of it by his immediate predecessor. The other school, of course, accepts this tradition as true. To them it is enough that this report is found mentioned in a reliable book, and it is, with them, no matter that the Qur'an should be reduced to the same level as the Bible, by this damaging report. Their logic (which I confess I am not able to follow perfectly) would seem to contend that this verse is *"mansukhuttalawa"* or "not readable," though it remains in effect as Qur'anic law. My own suggestion is that the report, as it is given, need not be contradicted, for the very words of the verse settle the matter, seeing that anybody who has studied the language of the Qur'an, would find this verse to be absolutely prosaic and un-Qur'anic Arabic; and that the misunderstanding was unfortunately due to the fact that the word "Kitab Allah," as given in the report, has been needlessly considered as referring to the Qur'an. Kitab Allah (revealed book or the book of God) is a term which extends to the Old Testament also, and the Jews are referred to in Islam as Ahlul Kitab. Before any law was revealed about adultery in the Qur'an, the Prophet was tested by the Jews at Medina, who brought an adulteress to him for punishment, according to the law of God. The Prophet called the Jews to bring their law, and asked them to read out the verse about adultery, whereupon, he who read, concealed it by placing his hand over that passage; and it is reported that a Jewish Rabbi, Abdulla ibne Salam, who had become the follower of the Prophet, exposed their villany. Nevertheless, the Jews persisted in denying that there was any verse about stoning in the Torah. The Prophet was, however, convinced by his supernatural power that there was indeed such a verse in the Bible, and he ordered the woman to be stoned according to that law. Then the Jews began to murmur, saying that the Prophet had acted against the law of God, and it was perhaps on this occasion that Omar had to emphasize the fact that the verse, in spite of its concealment by the Jews, was in the Kitab Allah, and the Prophet had not acted against the law in ordering the woman to be stoned. In any case, we need not be troubled about it, for the narrators of traditions have caused so remarkable a confusion in many reliable sayings recorded in Bukhari, that we can only opine that the unfortunate Malik and Muslim have gone astray in understanding the real purport of the Khalif.

In my translation of Al Mautta of Immam Malik into English (which is now ready for the press), I have dealt with this report the more thoroughly, because I advocate Al Mautta as the most reliable collection of tradition. I have taken pains accordingly in explaining it. Had it been a report only in Muslim and from Ibne Abbas, I should be disposed to follow Maulana Muhammad Ali and Dr. Syed Ahmed, for Nuwavi, himself the commentator of Al Muslim, who is seldom anything but liberal in his views, was forced to the conclusion that the verse being abrogated in the Qur'an, is not binding on us. The great absurdity involved in this, which apparently Nuwavi has forgotten, is that the punishment for adultery in the Qur'an for persons of very low status, like slaves, is half for an ordinary man; and for the most noble of us all, that is the Prophet's own women-folk, it is double; so if stoning to death be the order of the day, putting persons to death by halves or twice over would be ridiculous.

**Slandering Chaste Women**

And those who slander chaste women, and are unable to substantiate their charge by bringing four witnesses, scourge such persons (accusers) with eighty stripes, and never accept their evidence in future, for they are evil does, unless they recent from their accusation, for good is forgiving and merciful. And those who charge their own wives for adultery, and are unable to produce any evidence but of themselves, they may take oath four times that they are true, and a fifth time (add) that God's curse may be upon them if they speak lies. The woman will also take oath four times saying that her accuser lies, and a fifth time, add that God's curse may be on her if her accuser is true (if she wants to rebut the charge).

What a blessing would this verse be to those unfortunate women who, in the most civilized societies, are often subject to the tender attention of scandal-mongers, if the latter were called upon to produce four witnesses, or receive eighty stripes, by the law of society! And yet Islam is said to be not charitable towards the fair sex!

Other offences for which no scale of punishment is laid down, but a deterrent admonition is given, are as follows, the punishment for these offenders being apparently left to the discretion of the Khalifs.

**Defamation**

O believers, let not a party of you scorn another party, may be their party is better than yourself, nor females to other females, nor taunt ye each other, nor call each other bad names. It is not befitting to good faith to indulge in such misbehaviour, and those who will not repent, they shall be transgressors. O believers, keep yourself free from suspicions, for some suspicions are sins, and do not be inquisitive, nor blame each other behind the back. Would you devour the corpse of your dead brother? Wherefore save yourself from such evil, and God is forgiving and merciful. O people, we have created you from male and female, and made you in tribes and clans for recognition only (and not that one is superior from the other), verily the respectful among you before God is one who is pious.

**Cheating or Criminal Misappropriation**

O believers, do not misappropriate the property of each other, unless you gain it in fair trade... and if anybody misappropriates by force or dishonesty, it shall be easy for me to send such men to hell.

**Bribery**

And do not misappropriate each other's property, nor use the property to gain favour of judges, so that he may help you in your misappropriation.

**Breach of Trust in the Property of Orphans and Idiots**

And give the property of orphans to them, and do not mix their property with yours and eat it up, for it is a grievous sin, and if you are afraid that you cannot adequately discharge your trust to orphan girls, marry them in two, three or four, and if you cannot keep them on an equal footing then marry one alone, and give them their dowry without any grudge, unless they leave it out of their own free will to you. Do not let the property of idiots be wasted by them, spend it on their behalf in their food and dress and treat them kindly..... Those who devour the property of orphans entrusted to them, by force, they swallow hell fire in their stomach, and they shall go to hell.

**Gambling, Wagering and Drunkenness**

O believers, drink, gambling, wagering are Satan's work, meanly, so avoid them that you may be saved. Verily Satan desires to create enmity among yourselves by this means, and keep you from prayer and from the remembrance of God. So would you desist (or not).

**Unnatural Offences**

The story of the tribe of Lot in the Qur'an gives a stern admonition to this crime.

Some empty-headed persons have said that the Qur'an stands in the way of modern enlightened government, and that unless Islamic countries adapt themselves to "civilized" legislation, as for instance the codes of Justinian and of Napoleon, they will remain groping in the dark. The credulous Turk has listened to them, but with what result? It is the habit of these gentlemen from time immemorial to talk at random, when the bugbear of the "Qur'an of Mahomet" comes under their notice. For such men I have taken pains to give the above brief extract, as I know that they will be taking a great risk of losing faith in their own Church if they but once open the Qur'an and read it. Carlyle, I think it was, said that there is no such danger as far as the Englishman is concerned, as he knew full well that the English are a conservative people who do not take to any change, however good it may be, in an abrupt fashion. Has the present generation belied Carlyle? I wonder.

**Morality Vs. Religion**

The study of Anthropology would seem to disclose a strong connection between Morality and Religion, making them appear, as it were, to be strands in the same rope, or links of the same chain.

The customs prevalent in old-time society were directly controlled by imaginary gods, so that Morality and Religion were regarded as, in effect, synonymous. The laws of Piety, Morality and Religion were interlaced, as, for example, in the Ten Commandments, where the religious, the civil, and moral precepts are so beautifully linked together that, while we can trace each quite distinctly and separately, they nevertheless form one harmonious whole. Their partial transgression involved the gravest crimes, being regarded as equivalent to total transgression, and was severely punished; for such punishment was universally regarded as a religious duty incumbent upon all men. The God-fearing man was good, pious and moral, while the immoral, the irreligious and the damned, so to say, was one who was godless, and consequently in a state of excommunication. The basis of all social pursuits, work and custom and law in State and Society which go to determine the individual life, was Religion. The criterion of civilization and culture was the degree of connection between the moral, religious and individual life. The States, institutions and laws of the Greeks and the Romans were originally closely knit together with religion. The oldest books on law comprehend, in the same way as did the Mosaic Law, worship, customs and rights.

The Roman Law was the prerogative of the priests — a sacredotal law—whereof the ceremonies and teachings (if any) were the object and aim of life. A religious rite or observance was the essence of all piety, the slightest deviation from which was deemed sufficient to mar the efficacy of the whole ceremony. The rites of sacrifice and modes of worship were performed with the greatest exactitude. The high-priest alone, amongst the Jews and Hindus, could conduct such observances. So the priest was looked upon as a being of superior talent and a saviour of the people; and hence he could mould the destiny of ignorant men. It was from this same idea that the corruption of the Middle Ages sprang, when laymen placed property, life and honour at the disposal of the priest, whom they blindly followed. It was in those days of blind faith that the simple truth of Islam shed its glorious light, and encouraged the free use of the intellect and understanding which made the early followers of Islam beacons of knowledge and culture, when Medieval Europe was sunk in ignorance, darkness and prejudice, blended with superstition of the most virulent sort.

Such blindness faith in Islam has always been condemned, while, on the contrary, upholding perfect freedom of thought and action. With Islam, the sources of certain knowledge are in Reason. With reference to those whose abode shall be hell, the Qur'an says : "And they shall say : Had we but listened to the discourses of the wise, or ourselves been wise enough the tested religion and belief by reason, we should not have been among the dwellers of hell." The Qur'an is not a book which derives its force merely from the fact of its being an ancient document which has been handed down to us through a safe course of transmission; but its real power and authority lie in the sound arguments which it produces, and the clear light which it sheds.

An original inner connection between the religious and the moral duties gives a clue to the fact that, so far, Morality and Religion were united. All religious laws have everywhere the same character. All require abstinence, cleanliness, sacrifice, and the control of passions and desires. Cleanliness of mind and body, and control of the passions through moral discipline, had for their object self-purification and self-edification. Hatred of our fellow-men and pride were regarded as transgressions of the Divine law, bringing in their train Divine wrath and destruction; while humility and submissiveness found favour in the eyes of all deities. It is noteworthy that the weak, the orphan, the decrepit, were all represented as enjoying the special protection of Heaven—and any injury done to them entailed inexorable retribution.

But we can explain the connection between Religion and Morality in another way. Religion was tantamount to a belief in the transcendent power of goodness, and in the transitoriness and insufficiency of this life. This menace of the insufficiency of the present life is noticeable everywhere in every religion. Schamanism and Fetishism are attempts to accomplish by magical influence, exerted on transcendental powers and beings, that which the natural capacities of man could not otherwise achieve. Inanimate objects were worshipped for their supposed magical and mysterious attributes, that struck awe to the heart of the votary. But gradually the people came to the realization of wonders, by will-power developed through an ever-increasing intensity of concentration. If the will, on the one hand, can go to the lowest rung of the ladder of human life, when it satisfies its animal instinct, it has, at the same time, the capacity of aspiring to a beautiful and good life, realizing the loftiest ideal of humanity. It is this power not that leads life and directs thought. Thus, will once developed, the being finds itself in another atmosphere, and life is radically changed. This success can never be achieved unless one breaks definitely with the material world and its deteriorating influence on the spirit. Noble ideas begin to flash on the mind, and noble aims of life, beautiful in colour and compelling in their force, appear on the scene to guide us. This phase of will-power and its development is very scientifically dealt with in Islam, in the form of humble supplication offered to that Great Will—the Cherisher and Evolver, the Creator of the Universe, aided by the moral discipline of fast, that encourages the capacities of the mind, which would otherwise remain dormant, to work wonders. So we find that change in the direction of our will brings about a change in in the direction of our will brings about a change in our conception of the transcendental world.

The complex world of the gods in Polytheism is a creation of the higher Will. In the place of the vague, transitory, magical powers of Fetishism appear permanent, personal and historical beings. In these Polytheistic gods man found his ideal realized before his eyes, and in the forms with which his imagination had conceived of the Supreme Being. In other words, magic and Fetishism made room for human ideals, such as are represented by the Greek and Roman deities, with different powers attributed to them. The wrath and the favour of these gods brought down destruction or blessing as the case might be, and the fact that a trifling carelessness or inattention on man's part was sure to bring its consequences, was attributed to the displeasure of the deity offended.

We have, so far, traced the development of human will and consciousness. Now we come to the last and most completely developed stage of Religion, the belief in One God, with no mystery or magic about Him at all. In Monotheism the idealistic institution of the will is even stronger than it was in Polytheism. In Monotheism God is the Supreme Being with all attributes that are noble and good—Whose love pervades the universe, as inculcated by the two last religions of mankind—Christianity and Islam.

Fetishism, Schamanism and necromancy gave place to the

words of Moses (Peace be upon him!), "May you will prevail," repeatedly emphasized in the verses of the Holy Qur'an.

It is the submission of man's will to that Great Will as the goal of life that is taught in the words of the Holy Qur'an : "O! thou soul! that art at rest and restest fully contented with thy Lord, return unto Him, He being pleased with thee and though pleased with Him—so enter among My servants and enter into My paradise.

But for what reason ! For He is mighty, is holy, and has grace, so His will, by absorption, would transform a being of enfeebled will into a higher being with a will-power more developed and more majestic, that should bring contentment of mind and serenity of life. It is here that the will of man is one with God's will. "My prayers and my sacrifice, my life and my death are all for the sake of God" (vi. 163). Man sees God in his own actions. When man's love for God surpasses everything, when his life and death have no interest for himself, but are solely for the sake of god and God's creatures—mankind—then that is a phase of the life eternal that has begun on earth—when he walks in the Kingdom of Heaven on earth, and good tidings await him in the hereafter.

In short, the God of Islam is a living God, and has vouchsafed a perfect knowledge of His own self suitable to the capacity of every recipient, and according to the intensity of the love of the seeker after truth. Therefore a Muslim seeker after light concerning Him—that is to say, the favours and blessings of the Kingdom of God—repeats five times in his daily prayer, "O, Lord! Guide us in the path of perseverance, and the path of those upon whom Thou hast bestowed favours, for Thou art Beneficent and Merciful." This gives us a still stronger impetus to soar higher and higher into the spiritual realms of the life that is to come after death. So we can safely assert that the religion of a people is the reflection of its own will in a transcendental world in which it believes the reality to be existing, this life being but transitory. Belief holds the transcendental world to be the real and true world, in contrast with which the present one is worthless and unreal.

Reverting to Religion and Morality—both have the same root and aim in the aspiration of the will of man towards the Complete—the Infinite. But that which is only a demand of Morality, finds solution and fulfilment in Religion. The Complete, or the Infinite, is described in abstract terms of Morality, while in Religion it is looked upon as godly, holy, blessed, and concrete. Subjectively, Morality and Religion are two aspects of the same thing. An individual is moral when his will and his actions strive after the Complete; and religious when his feelings, his beliefs, his aspirations, and his hopes are filled with the image of the Highest—the Supreme.

**Apostasy in Islam**

Islam is the only religion that vouchsafes, expressly, full freedom of judgment and conscience in matters of faith, and condemns every kind of compulsion. It is therefore inconceivable that it should countenance, let alone encourage, the punishment of those who have strayed from its fold. The whole question, which has been quite definitely decided by the Qur'an, has, nevertheless, it would seem, involved some three years of patient toil and investigation for a writer notorious for his intentional misrepresentation of Islam. A pretentious volume of about three hundred pages under the above title, from the pen of Dr. Zwemer, seeks to refute the position taken up by the *Islamic Review* in an article bearing, the same title in the issue of October, 1922.

Islam is not without its apocryphal writings as to the traditions of the Prophets. But the Muslim divines have produced a system of criticism, unique in its quality, for the purpose of testing the genuineness of all that has been imputed to him. Not a single page of the whole record of Jesus in the Bible would stand such tests as these. Under their searchlight some four thousand traditions have been sifted as correct, from among the mass of more than one hundred thousand; but these, again, have to stand the test of the Qur'an teachings. Anything contrary to the latter, and the holy name of the Prophet, is at once dismissed as a forgery. It is this rejected stuff that supplies Dr. Zwemer material for his three years' investigation—a deplorable waste of time and energy' but that, and it benefits him. He must blacken Islam, even though his very honesty as a writer may become blackened in the attempt.

The strength, logic and cogent reasoning that have characterized our pages have unnerved the Padre. He has lost his mental uquipose, as his latest volume shows. In his own judgment he now seems to stand condemned for all the misrepresentations which he and his friends have made concerning Islam in their writings before our publications began to appear in the West. He finds himself in the plight of a person who will clutch at any straw in a vain endeavour to save an impossible situation. To write a book of some three hundred pages in reply to a pamphlet of three pages only, and to take three years to do it, relying on material unworthy of Muslim notice, speaks volumes for the admitted hopelessness of his task in his campaign of abuse against Islam. He cannot refer to a single verse of the Qur'an to support his conclusions. The black deeds of the medieval days in Christendom, of religious persecution, should have warned him against references in his book to any political adventures in Islam.

The subject has, however, now become sifted. The sad death of Maulvi Niamatullah Khan in Cabool—whether for apostasy or high treason matters not—has, however, cleared the air. It called forth a very learned controversy in the Indian Press on the punishment of apostasy in Islam, in which most of those well-versed in Islamic lore took part, among them, Al-Haj Khwaja Kamal-ud-Din and His Holiness Maulvi Muhammad Ali, the famous translator of the Qur'an. Mahatma Gandhi also took a conspicuous part in the discussion, which lasted for many months. The Khwaja now sums up the whole controversy in the pages of *Young India*—the organ of the Mahatma, who inserts this last word of the Khwaja in *Young India* "in order," as the Mahatma says, "that the readers of *Young India* may authoritatively know that the Qur'an does not countenance stoning to death in any case whatsoever, and does not punish apostasy during man's life on earth." This comes from a Hindu sage, but we wonder if it will silence Dr. Zwemer and his circle. The article was copied in almost all the leading Muslim papers in India, and for the benefit of those interested in the subject we reproduce it here:

**On "Stoning to Death"**

The Mahatma has done a piece of service to Islam by entering into the controversy regarding the penalty of apostasy in Islam. Through his instrumentality the real issue has come to the surface in a most clarified form. It has now been admitted on all hands :

(1) That the Qur'an prescribes no punishment for apostasy.
(2) That "stoning to death" is not among the penal provisions of the Qur'an.
(3) That though many cases of apostasy did occur in the days of the Holy Prophet, no one was punished solely for it.

Those in favour of punishing apostasy in Islam, however, have now taken their stand on a different ground. They allege that the Qur'an is silent on the question of the said punishment, and in such a case they would go to other sources for their authority; they would go to the *Hadith* and, failing that, to the collective judgment of the Muslim jurists of renowned piety. In the latter, they say, they find an authority for awarding capital punishment to an apostate.

The position, however, is not tenable. To begin with, the Qur'an is not silent on the issue. I read the following in the Book:

"Surely (as for) those who believe, then disbelieve, again believe and again disbelieve, then increase in disbelief, Allah will not forgive them and guide them in the (right) path."

"Whoever from among you turns back from his religion, then Allah will bring a people instead. He shall love them and they shall love Him."

"And whoever of you turns back from his religion and then he dies an unbeliever—these it is whose works shall go for nothing in this world and the hereafter, and they are inmates of the fire : therein they shall abide."

If there did exist any doubt as to the fate of an apostate in Islam, these verses—and there is no other verse in Qur'an on the subject—would dispel it at once. They are very clear and definite; they leave no room for discussion; they require no comment. The first verse speaks of one rooted in apostasy ; twice he embraces Islam, twice he recants; how could there arise an occasion for the repetition of the offence, if an apostate had to receive capital punishment on his forsaking Islam, how could he embrace it again and then forsake it? The verse goes farther : "then increase in disbelief." This occurs after the second apostasy. It means survival of the apostate even after committing the sin a second time. The verse becomes meaningless if apostasy had to meet death. The Qur'an still contains the verse, and it must have its binding force on Muslims. The punishment to be meted to such apostates, as mentioned in the Qur'an, lies exclusively in the hands of Allah and excludes human agency.

The Qur'an, therefore, is conclusive on the point. But take it, for the sake of argument, that it is not so. Are we, then, to accept every such practice, or opinion time-honoured though it may be, that insults our intelligence and perturbs our conscience? Islam does not compel us to such a condition; nay, it relieves us of it by giving us a doctrine established under the direction of the Holy Prophet, that guides all our juristic adjudications in matters not spoken of in the Holy Qur'an. No judgment—be it single or collective, and with a big name to back it—can bind us if it goes against the Qur'an and good conscience. No human authority can abrogate the tenets of the Book. The word of God is the only criterion for testing the genuineness of the *Hadith.* No word or action alleged as coming from the Prophet can be accepted as such if it controverts any thing in the Qur'an. It is not of him, as he himself says, but something forged upon him. The so-called collective judgment allowing punishment of an apostate, will be acceptable only if, firstly, it does not violate any Qur'anic tenets, and secondly, it is not contrary to reason, equity and good conscience. This, by way of implication, I say on no less authority than that of the Prophet himself.

The Qur'an admittedly allows freedom of conscience. It respects personal judgment in religion. "No compulsion in religion" is the golden rule promulgated exclusively by the Qur'an. Apostasy, after all, is a change of opinion in religion. If it is punished, it is compulsion in religion, and therefore contrary to the Qur'an. The verse, while prohibiting the said compulsion, speaks also of its *rationale*. It says : "There is no compulsion in religion; truly the right way has been made clear to reason from error" (ii. 256). "The right way" mentioned in the verse, is Islam. Its superiority over the other ways, as the Book says, has been shown on the strength of reason; but if someone is still unable to appreciate Islam's claim to his reason, he should be excused. You cannot punish any person for his defective power of reason. I agree with the Mahatma when he says that "everything has to submit to the test of reason." The Qur'an says the same thing when preaching its truth. *It gives full liberty to every man to accept or reject its message*. It is therefore ridiculous even to imagine that Islam would give countenance to the punishment of heresy or apostasy. Besides, if Islam claims to be a proselytizing institution, it must drive home its truths to others by bringing them to the anvil of reason. It would not do for us to say to Mahatma, or anyone else, that things concerning those within the pale of Islam are not of their concern; and they therefore are debarred from saying their say in the matter. It does not affect Mahatma's prestige to say what he thinks right upon the question. Islam will lose its prestige, if its adherents betray such weakness in their armoury. If Islam is the truth—and I intelligently believe it to be so—a Muslim must stand always prepared to show it so, and that exclusively on the strength of reason and logic, especially when the Qur'an itself is no authority to others, apart from any other human agency. The Book admits the situation. It therefore appeals to reason, even in teaching things that seemingly transcend reason; and if the Qur'an allows others to accept its truths only through reason and not through any coercion, a Muslim would be untrue to himself and to his God-given gift—reason—if he is called upon to accept anything in religion under compulsion, and does not spurn such a course. It is a matter of thanksgiving to the Almighty that we have been spared such a situation. There is nothing in Islam that I am called upon to accept at the mutilation of my reason and at the sacrifice of my personal judgment.

---

(Revised and edited; originally published as a miscellany in Islamic Review vol. XIII)

# 4

# The Qur'anic Theory of Riba

ZIAUDDIN AHMAD

Deals with the impact of categorical prohibition of *Riba*. Reviews the divergent views on its meaning and interpretation. Intends to discuss this point in detail with reference to the socio-economic evidence of the early and pre-Islamic period.

*Riba* was pre-Islamic business practice by which money or commodity of lender swelled out of all proportions. This caused great economic misery to people in meeting their vital needs. This is termed as *Riba al-Jahiliyya*, which will be explained later. The pre-Islamic Arab society had a number of other *Riba-bearing* dealings, especially in the *six commodities* of gold, silver, wheat, barley, dates and salt which are not covered by the Qur'anic ban on *Riba*. This is probably for the fact that economic oppression due to them was not so severe as in the case of the former. However, the *Sunna* treated all *Riba* practices relating to the *six commodities* as unlawful so that the avenue of *Riba* are totally closed. This is what may be termed as *Riba al-Sunna* and the former as *Riba al-Qur'an*.

It may be noted that the unlawfulness of the *Riba al-Jahiliyya* is absolute, i.e., established by an explicit text of the Qur'an, hence there is no scope for difference of opinion on its illegality. But due to the lack of absolute evidence, the unlawfulness of *Riba al-Sunna* is not deemed so severe. The Jurists have, therefore, sometimes differed on its scope and interpretation.

Now what has been agitating many minds is the question of

bank interest, especially the commercial one. Whether it is *Riba al-Jahiliyya* and therefore categorically prohibited, or is it to be regarded as *Riba al-Sunna*? Or is it something to be looked upon in isolation from the aforementioned classifications of *Riba*? The problem requires dispassionate consideration.

**Riba Al-Jahiliyya**

The word Riba literally means increase (*al-Ziyada*), growth (*al-Numuw*), to rise and to become lofty (*al-Irtifa' and al-'Uluw*) etc. These meanings have been amply illustrated in the Qur'anic usages.[1] So far as its technical meaning is concerned, the Qur'an does not specify any particular kind of *Riba* dealings, obviously for the reason that at the time it was declared unlawful the people concerned knew well what meant. It is generally held that the word *al-Riba* (prefixed with al) in the Qur'an connotes that kind of *Riba* dealings which had been in vogue during the pre-Islamic days. This is also indicated in the famous saying of the Prophet on the day of the conquest of Mecca: Beware! *Riba of Jahiliyya* is abolished.[2]

Although the Qur'an does not give any specific identification of *Riba al-Jahiliyya,* its characteristic features, as it would appear, have manifested themselves in the pretty large number of *Riba* verses which revealed on different occasions. Therefore, for its identification one has to study carefully the verse concerned in the light of the contemporary evidence.

Out of twelve Qur'anic verses revealed on Riba, we shall discuss the following nine only, for they explicitly contain the categorical prohibition: they are verse 130-31 of *Sura Al'Imran* and 276-82 of *Sura al-Baqara*; of the remaining three, the verses 161-62 in *Sura al-Nisa'* denounce the Medinese Jews for taking *Riba*, whereas verse 29 in *Sura al-Rum* merely condemns *Riba* in its being an economic evil.

However, when Islam triumphed after the Prophet's migration to Medina, the first revelation came in the following words of *Sura Al'Imran:*

'O ye who believe, consume not Riba, doubling and redoubling, observe your duty to Allah, that ye may be successful.'

In *Sura al-Baqara* (276-82), this prohibition was later strengthened and given an emphatic form. The *Riba* verses of *Sura Al-'Imran* were the first to be revealed in the series. We Must therefore examine them first. In this regard, Tabari records:

> A debtor being unable to repay the debt at the time of its maturity applied to his creditor for the extension of a further term with a promise of increase in the amount. And in similar terms which followed subsequently, the amount of debt used to increase manifold. This increase was in terms of cash in case of borrowed money, and in terms of age in case of borrowed cattle.[3]

From this, one might assume that the Qur'an prohibits only such kind of pre-Islamic *Riba* which, in its continued process, used to make the principal sum several-fold. Other *Riba* dealings, for example those in the *six-commodities* that supposedly did not make the principal several-fold were not regarded as *Riba al-Jahiliyya*, and, therefore, had not the same force of illegality. The prohibition imposed upon them by the *Shari'a* is due to some other evidence, i.e., the evidence of the *Sunna*, which is obviously less emphatic than the Qur'an.[4]

Analysing our sources of information, regarding the usual operation of *Riba* in the pre-Islamic days, it can possibly be held that the above distinction between *Riba al-Jahiliyya* and those of other *Riba* dealings, including bank interest for a moment, was found in the following:

(i) The celebrated statement in determining *Riba al-Jahiliyya* in the pre-Islamic days which used to swell doubly and redoubly runs as follows:

'In the pre-Islamic days, *Riba* became due when a man owed another debt; at the time of its maturity the creditor would ask the debtor: "Will you repay, or will you increase? If the debtor paid up, the amount was received. Otherwise the debtor increased the amount and the creditor extended a further term.'"[5]

This statement implies that the credit was offered free of Riba for the first term. *Riba* was charged only when the debtor failed to discharge the debt at the end of the first term. Therefore, *Riba al-Jahiliyya* is certainly different from the usual interest-bearing dealing which stipulate the increase from the very beginning.[6]

(ii) In reference to *Riba al-Jahiliyya*, the terms like *al-dayn*, *al-mal* and *al-haqq* have generally been employed to express the meaning of debt. But they do not specify whether the debt became due on account of loan or on account with interest of sale transaction. This has led some *'ulama* to surmise that loan with interest, in which case the increase is stipulated in the first term, is something different from *Riba al-Jahiliyya* in which, being a case related only to sale-purchased dealings, the increasing was imposed at the expiry of the first term.[7]

(iii) The last, is the phrase: itself in the *Al'Imran* verses. This verse has been interpreted by some contemporary scholars to the effect that the *Riba* of pre-Islamic days was an atrocious kind of dealing unlawful which caused multiple indebtedness of the poor; hence declared unlawful by the Qur'an. The present bank interest does not have the same degree of atrocity.[8]

It seems that the above notion of the *Riba* verse in Al'Imran and particularly the tendency that recently has arisen in interpreting the related evidence miss the support of *al-Baqara* verses on *Riba*. We shall see how far this is tenable. In the *al-Baqara* verses, the last to reveal in the series, the term *Riba* has found its place in opposition to both *bay'* and *sadaqa*. This clearly shows that *Riba* in pre-Islamic days did not belong to the genre of Bay'. *Sadaqa* being a term opposite to *Riba* requires no serious explanation. It is sufficient to say that *sadaqa* involves no profit motive; in its narrower sense it implies acts of benevolence and alms giving and its wider perspective it evokes in the Muslim mind a moral force to build up a system of economy based on *sadaqa,* i.e., voluntary cooperation and mutual help irrespective of private gains. *Bay'* and Riba amount to trading in capital and both involve profit motive and increase in capital investments. But *Riba* is opposed to bay' in the sense that the former amounts to making increasing in price or debt for the time involved in paying or repaying it (price or debt). *Bay'* also involves increase, but it is due transaction itself, not due to the time factor.

The Qur'an itself neither defines *Riba (Riba al-Jahiliyya)* nor does it mention the dealings that come under it. In al-Baqara verse, however, *Riba* is mentioned as diametrically opposed to *bay'*. Both *bay'* and *Riba* amount to making increase in the capital and both are prone to profit motive. Therefore, the factor of opposition between them could be nothing but the fact that Riba is related to debts stipulated with increase on the amount, which is not true in case of *bay'* (let there be post-ponement till the easing time) (Relinquish what remains from *Riba)* (for him is what of *Riba* is passed), (and for you are the principals) — all these verses clearly and unambigously indicate that it was the debt stipulated with an increase which was the basic cause for the prohibition of *Riba*.[9]

**Dayn Mu'ajjal**

An analysis of the different modes of the pre-Islamic Riba dealings, as elaborated by Ibn Jarir Tabari in great detail, leads us to the fact that it was the practice of *dayn Mu'ajjal* in which *Riba al-Jahiliyya* was embedded, *dayn Mu'ajjal,* debt deferred with the creditor's stipulation of an increase in the amount of debt against fixed terms, ultimately used to swell doubly and redoubly.[10] Tabari's treatment, however, meets with the following two deficiencies:

(i) It is not clear whether *dayn mu'ajjal* originated from sale transaction or from loan dealings;

(ii) Whether the stipulation of *Riba* increase was in the first term, or it came during the subsequent terms.[11]

This ambiguity will presently be removed.

It appears that the undermentioned two methods of transactions were the main bases from which *dayn Mu'ajjal* as a system of exchange dealing was in vogue in the pre-Islamic Arab society;

(i) *Bay'. bi'l al-Nas'ia.*
(ii) Loan with stipulation of an increase.

**Bay' Bi'l-Nasi'a**

*Bay' bi'l-Nasi'a,* i.e credit sale with a fixed term to pay up the agreed price, usually resulted in a *Riba* dealing which caused multiplication of the debt (deferred price). *Bay' bi'l-Nasi'*a and the normal sale purchase dealing resemble each other at least in the basic modes in which they are conducted. It was probably for this reason that the Arabs did not consider bay' and *riba* dissimilar, as stated in the Qur'an. Besides, in *Bay' bi'l-nasi'*a there was no specific stipulation of Riba increase for the first term.[12] This is also a reason why both appeared similiar to them. Infact there was no actual resemblance between them, as one was *Riba* and the other, the normal valid transaction, Therefore, God categorically declared the former as unlawful, and the latter as legal.

A question here arises, whether or not, *bay'l-nasi'a* actually involved any addition to the normal price value in the initial term. In a social set up such as that of the Meccan commercial society or the Medinese Jewish community, it cannot be excepted that those who were going to make their capital multiplied through bay *bay'l-nasi'*a did not speculate an increase in the normal price value of their commodities at the beginning of the deal. It may also be mentioned that the people suffering from gruelling consumption needs usually had to resort to *bay' bi'l-nasi'a.* Therefore, exploiting the situation, what the creditors-sellers used to charge as price for their commodities actually comprised the usual market value plus a *Riba* increase in exchange of the time involved.[13] Some reports related from Ibn 'Abbas and Sa'id b. Jubayr explicitly corroborate the view that in the initial term of *bay' bi'l-nasi'a,* the agreed upon price of the commodity in question itself used to be inclusive of an increase of *Riba.*[14] Subsequent accumulation over the original price with extension of terms, as a matter of fact, took effect from the beginning of the transaction.

From discussions so far, it must have become clear that *dayn mu'ajjal,* originated principally from the practice of *bay' bi'l-nasi'a.*[15] This gave rise to the growth of *Riba* in the pre-Islamic days.

**Loan with the Stipulation of Increase**

It is now clear that *bay' bi'l-nasi'a* in the pre-Islamic days worked as base for *dayn mu'ajjal* resulting into a continuous *Riba* process. This phenomenon also existed in the pre-Islamic loan dealings which stipulated an addition to the principal sum against a period of time. Under the verse: Fakhr al-Din Razi's statement on *Riba al-Jahiliyya* clearly shows that the term *Riba* in the pre-Islamic days was also applied to the increase stipulated on loans *(qard).* First, he classifies *Riba* into two kinds, (i) *Riba al-nasi'a (Riba* of debts prohibited by the Qur'an), (ii) *Riba al-fadl (Riba* of excess in case of the *six commodities* as prohibited by the sunna). Then he points out that *Riba al-nasi'a,* in fact, resulted from both the practices of *bay' bi'l-nasi'a* and leans with the stipulation of a fixed profit against the time involved.[16]

Abu Bakr al-Jassas, a famous jurist commentator of the Qur'an in the fourth century of Hijrah, appears even more categorical on the point. He states that the Arabs were accustomed to the practice of *Riba* by loaning out dirhams and dinars for a specific period of time with the stipulation of a mutually agreed upon increase on the loaned out money.[17] It is, therefore, certain that in the pre-Islamic time the practice of money lending with profit was co-existent with the practice of *bay' bi'l-nasi'a.* And both of them were characteristics of *Riba al-Jahiliyya.*

After identifying already the bases of *Riba* operation in the pre-Islamic days, we may now come to the crucial phrase of claimed to possess the central position in the series of *Riba* verses. It should be remembered here that *Riba al-Jahiliyya* is the name of a *Riba* operation through the process of which the debt used to multiply during the succeeding years. We have, however, shown that multiplication of debts through the *Riba* process, resulted, as a matter of fact, from *Dayn Mu'ajjal* which was embodied in both *bay' bi'l-Nasi'a* and loans with profit.

Therefore, it can safely be said that the phrase under consideration, in fact, refers to all kinds of *Riba al-Jahiliyya* which were characteristics of turning the principal into debt doubled and redoubled whether through the process of *Riba al-nasi'a* or by executing loans with profit. No material difference is visible, if the rate of profit was initially stipulated, as in case of loans, or the initial price value was, might be unspecifiedly, inclusive of a *Riba* increase as in case of *bay' bi'l-nasi'a* of a commodity.[18]

It is argued that the phrase under reference is purported to restrict the *Riba* ban only to such of its practices as entail multiplication of the principal sum. The ban, therefore, does not cover those of its practices which supposedly do not have the possibility of making the principal several fold. This is, indeed, a layman's assertion and must be dismissed without going into the economics of *Riba.* The reason are as follows:

(i) It is historical fact that consequent upon the Qur'anic ban on *Riba,* all the acts pertaining to it were abolished altogether, irrespective of the fact that in each and every case of *Riba,* whether of loan or of credit sale *(bay' bi'l-nasi'a)* the principal must not have increased to the extent of multiplication. This proves that all cases of *Riba,* whether of loans or of credit sale, were part of one *Riba* system, in whose nature the principal was to be multiplied. Therefore, the system was banned as whole.[19]

(ii) Since the Qur'an bans the system of *Riba,* its milder forms, viz., the cases of *Riba al-Fadl,* termed also as *al-Riba al-Khafi (concealed Riba)* by the later Jurists, were also abolished as per the *Sunna.*[20] It must be noted that in the cases of *Riba al-Fadl,* there was the least possibility of doubling and redoubling of what was to be received in exchange of the same commodity with some excess. This amply shows that in the cases of *al-Riba al-Jali (manifest Riba),* such as on loans and credit sales, the phrase: cannot be construed to exclude such *Riba* which, sometimes, may not be multiple.

(iii) The verse under discussion must also be understood in reference to the *al-Baqara* verses, the last to reveal in the series. The verse relinquish what remains due from *Riba* and (for you are the principals) leave no ambiguity as to the fact that any increase on the principal sum, whatever the quantity might be, was regarded permissible. This is also because of the fact that in such an important legislation no ambiguity on the part of the legislator could have happened. In view of this discussion, it seems a blatant distortion of the meaning of the *Baqara* verses, if the term of *Riba al-Jahiliyya* is attributed only to such *Riba* deal which made the principal multiple. It must, therefore, be held that the phrase: is intended only to point out the economic consequence of Riba dealings.

**Riba on Productive Loans**

Very often we dear of an enthusiastic proposition that the Qur'anic prohibition of Riba is restricted onlv to the case of non-productive loans rather than to the former, because, as one may argue, people of the pre-Islamic Arab society restored to *Riba* for meeting their consumption requirements only, and not for commercial needs. Therefore, the Qur'anic prohibition of *Riba,* in any case, cannot apply to such economic practices which were non-existent at that time i.e., loan for productive purposes.

Here it is not possible to go into the polemics that might arise on this problem. We, however, know that the pre-Islamic Arabs, mainly a commercial community, had been, since a very early age, in frequent contacts with the people of the surrounding regions where the system of commercial loans with interest was common. The Arabs themselves, to name particularly the merchant tribes of Thaqif and Mughira at Ta'if, the Quraysh of Mecca and the Jews of Medina, are not known to have avoided Riba on commercial loans which are indispensable for any commercial community.

The Qur'anic verse: Trading is like *Riba,* and Allah has allowed trading and forbidden *Riba* itself, the exegetical informations for example: This *Riba* with which they were accustomed in trade dealings in the Jahiliyya period and the *Riba of Jahiliyya* was that a man used to sell his commodity to another—and other texts prove that *Riba* mostly concerned commercial dealings. We have also sufficient evidence, especially in the Hadith books, that, in fact, events of loans for commercial purposes and even for the state purposes did exist in early and pre-Islamic days.

Now, in its ban on *Riba,* why has not the Qur'an dealt with the problem under sections and sub-sections, for example, one for *Riba* on consumption loans and another for *Riba* on commercial loans? The answer is simple The Qur'an aims at abolishing *Riba* as a system.

**Bank Interest**

Some 'Ulama' of recent times, probably having been perplexed by seeing that no modern society can progress by abolishing the present banking system, have very enthusiastically suggested that the coverage of the Islamic ban on *Riba* does not extend to bank interest which the present banks pay to their depositors or charge from their borrowers.

Opinions expressed by these scholars on bank interest, may be summed up as under:

(i) It is not a kind of *Riba al-Nasi'a(Riba on debts)* i.e., *Riba al-Jahiliyya* which, in the pre-Islamic days, made the principal multiple for the stipulation of *Riba* increase in the subsequent terms, and not in the first term. Bank interest for its stipulation in the very beginning of deal is not supposed to entail doubling and redoubling, hence not covered by the Qur'anic ban on *Riba.*

(ii) Bank interest should be equated with *Riba al-Fadl* is not having been prohibited by the Qur'an. Therefore, as happened in case of *Riba al-Fadl,* bank interest should be viewed leniently with regard to its lawfulness or otherwise. Precisely, bank interest falls within the scope of *Ijtihad* by the competent authority.

(iii) The present bank business is a case of *mudaraba* dealing (partnership between capital owner and working agent). *Mudaraba,* in the opinion of the classical *Fuqaha',* is lawful only when it is run on the basis of a mutual agreement to share the profit proportionately. But in the case of banking the difference is that the rate of profit is fixed for the capital only. And one has the right to go against the position taken by the classical Faqaha,' because this right does not amount to opposing any Qur'anic provisions, for the Book of God is silent over this problem.

(iv) It should be allowed under the provision of Maslaha al-*Amma,* i.e, welfare of the Muslims.

(v) It should be allowed under the legal maxim of necessity allows that which is unlawful.

We may refer back to our foregoing discussion on *Bay' bi'l-nasi'a* as well as loan with profit to see how far these notions are sufficient to make bank interest different from *Riba al-nasi'a.* However, to reassert our position it must be said that there appears no basic factor to differentiate between *Riba al-nasi'a* and the present bank interest. It will evidently appear that the factor which brings them hand into the same compartment is the time accounted for in exchange of *Riba* increase or interest. It seems to be no argument that the multiplication of the principal in the deal of *Riba al-nasi'a* in the pre-Islamic days was its characteristic because of exorbitancy with *Riba* increase during the seceding terms of the deal and that it cannot be true of the present banking in which case a moderate rate of interest is calculated from the very first term of the deal. It does not matter whether an exorbitant rate of *Riba* is imposed from one term behind or a moderate rate of interest from the beginning of the deal. Both move to the same direction. However, the burden of proof with adequate evidence that the principal sum really doubled or redoubled in all cases of *Riba al-Jahiliyya* lies with those who wish to make this a differentiating factor between *Riba al-nasi'a* and bank interest.

The question of equating bank interest with *Riba al-Fadl* with a view to forcing out a basis for taking somewhat lenient position with regard to it, does not arise at all, as must have seen so far. Similarly the present banking business cannot be construed as a case of *mudaraba* of loss and profit which is held lawful by the Muslim jurists. This demands a careful analysis of the economics pertaining to both of them. In Faqaha's *Mudaraba* entailing loss and profit for both the parties, the capital supplier loses from his capital and the working agent, the remuneration of his labour, in case of loss. And in case of profit, both gain their shares as proportionately as fixed in the agreement. But in the modern *Mudaraba* of bank business with guaranteed profit for the capital, the investor apportions his profit as fixed. And should there be any surplus, the working agent remains content with it. The crux of the matter is that in case of loss, the investor does not part with a penny from the assured percentage of his profit, while the working agent alone must be responsible to devise some means to compensate for the loss, in addition to losing what he should have earned for his labour.

It is noticeable that the arguments for legalizing bank interest from the *Shari'a* view point by a section of 'Ulama', whose opinions we have already summarized, contain an inherent inadequacy which negates the entire fabric of their propositions. In their treatment, one sees that almost all of them suppose that bank interest is not *Riba al-nasi'a,* hence lawful. They also regard it subject to *Ijtihad as Riba al-Fadl.* They do not stop here. As the position taken by them so far does not appear convincing, they invoke the principle of *maslaha,* i.e, welfare of the people, and the maxim of necessity allows that which is unlawful. Why is it that the problem should be solved with the help of *maslaha* and *darura* when it has been found that the bank interest is dissimilar to *Riba al-Jahiliyya?* A rethinking seems necessary here.

**Conclusions**

In the above pages, while analysing the notion of *Riba al-Jahiliyya,* we have attempted to determine what it meant during the pre-Islamic days, and also compared it with the practice of the present bank interest. We have also shown that *Riba al-Jahiliyya* was an atrocious kind of transaction which resulted in the heavy indebtedness of the people. We also know that, unlike older times when the lending of money was in the hands of individuals, banking in the modern times is organized and controlled by powerful institutions. And this perhaps has escalated the chances of economic exploitation of the majority of the masses. The need of imposing a check on the growth of such exploitation is being strongly felt every where in the world. And, as a matter of fact, various means are being adopted for this purpose. Nationalization of bank business in some countries appears to be a bold step towards achieving this goal.

But the resemblance between *Riba al-Jahiliyya* and the present bank interest, as we have shown in our foregoing discussion, is still a source of confusion for the Muslims who want to organize their economy strictly on the principles of Islam. Many a Muslim thinker, both modernist and traditionalist, have tried to solve this problem, sometimes by simply denouncing bank interest, and sometimes through a comprehensive approach to the entire economic system. The discussion is still continuing and this shows that the problem requires a thorough investigation especially in the context of all other socio-economic issue of the Muslim Umma.

However, it is felt that in order to eliminate the chances of economic exploitation ways and means should be devised to bring the present bank business closer to the notion of *Bay'* which is opposed to *Riba'* in the Qur'anic system. It has been suggested that the method of sharing in the profit and loss between the banks and depositors may remove the resemblance between *Riba* and bank interest.

## NOTES AND REFERENCES

1 Tafsir Tabari (ed. Shakir), Dar al-Marif, Cairo, 1374 AH., VI:7; cf. Fazlur Rahman, "Art, riba and interest," *Islamic Studies,* March 1964, pp. 1-2.

2. Tafsir Tabari, VI:27; Ibrahim Zakyal-Din Badawi, Nazariyya al-riba al-muharam fil al-shariat Islamiya al-majlis al-Ala li riayat al-furu waladab wal ulum al-ijtimaiyya, Cairo; 1383/1964, pp. 31, 46.

3. Tafsir Tabari, VIII:204-205, sura al-Imran.

4. Badawi, Nazariyya, pp. 31-32, 46-47; Fazlur Rahman, *Riba and Interest*, p. 40.

5. Malik b. Anas, Muwatta K. al-Buyu, Bab al-riba; cf. Nazariy ya, pp. 33-34ff.

6. Badawi, Nazariyya, pp. 31-32.

7. Ibid.

8. Fazlur Rahman, *Riba and Interest,* p. 7.

9. Badawi, Nazariyya, pp. 31-32.

10. Ibid., pp. 33-34.

11. Ibid.

12. Ibid., pp. 34-35.

13. Ibid., pp. 36-37; Fazlur Rahman, *Riba and Interest,* p. 5.

14. Ibn Abbas, Tanwir al-Maqais on the margin of al-darr al-manthur, I:143; II:71;

15. Cf. Nazariyya, op cit.

16. Tafsir Kabir, Matba al-Khayriyya, Cairo, II:357.

17. Ahkam al-Quran I:465.

18. Nazariyya, pp. 40-42.

19. Cf. Riba and Interest, p.7.

20. See Ibn al-Qayyim, Ilam Muwaqqin, Delhi, 1313AH., I: 200-201.

---

(Revised and edited; originally published in Islamic Quarterly).

# 5

# The Qur'anic Adam: The First Man and the First Prophet

MUSTANISR MIR

Adam is much more than the biological father of humans, besides being the first Prophet he is also the spiritual-moral progenitor of all humanity. Compares the similarities and dissimilarities in the Quranic and Biblical references on Adam.

Too often the study of the Qur'an has begun and ended with an investigation of the "sources" of the Qur'an. Too often, the Bible has been regarded as the source of this or that Qur'anic statement, idea, or story. While there certainly are a great many parallels between, the two books, parallels that form a legitimate subject of study, it is a mistake to take the reductionist approach beyond a certain point. The Qur'an, after all, is a unique scripture, and its uniqueness needs to be explained rather than explained away. In order to gain a deep understanding of the Qur'an, questions like the following must be asked: What perspective does the Qur'an place on its materials — whatever those materials may happen to be? how does it handle those materials? And what conclusions does it draw from its treatment of them? In other words, there is need to study the characteristic approach the Qur'an takes to its subject-matter.

The Qur'anic story of Adam is a good illustration of that approach. The main thesis here is that the Qur'an differs from the Bible not only in respect of factual detail, but, more important, in respect of notional framework as well. To be sure, there are a number of parallels between the two accounts. In both, Adam is the first man, is placed in Eden after his creation, is instructed not to eat fruit of a certain tree in Eden, it eats, is made to leave Eden, and so on.

**Adam's Place**

In the Bible[1], Adam belongs to primeval history. The story of Adam forms a background for the narration of patriarchal and Israelite history. Here history proper begins when Abraham is charged with a great mission.[2]

The Qur'an seems to say that patriarchal and Israelite history cannot be disjoined from the times of the first man, Adam. In Chapter III Adam is mentioned with other prophets who were elected to guide mankind,[3] and the implication is that the institution of prophecy began with Adam, the prophets coming after Adam being only continuators of a tradition that started with him.[4] In verse 58, these prophets are called the "progeny" *(dhurriyah)* of Adam. Here he is also the spiritual-moral progenitor of mankind. In a number of verses[5] mankind are exhorted to certain kinds of moral action, and are for this purpose addressed as "children of Adam" *(ya bani Adam),* with the implication that, being the progeny of Adam, they are to have the same status of honour as did Adam and are to be placed under the same kind of religio—moral obligations, as, according to the Qur'an, was Adam. 17: 70 refers of the position of preeminence God has given to the progeny of Adam. VII 7: 172 gives an account of the primordial covenant in which the progeny of Adam were bound to serve God. Verses 26-27 of the same chapter admonish men to wear modest dress and be on their guard against Satan, who caused their parents Adam and Eve to be deprived of their clothes by persuading them to eat of the forbidden tree. But particularly instructive is the incident of the offerings of "the two sons of Adam," namely, Abel and Cain.[6]

From the Qur'anic narration of the incident of Abel's murder by Cain, one gathers that even in the earliest times murders was considered not only a sin, to be punished in the hereafter, but also a crime, to be punished in this world.[7] It is probable that the law declaring murder a crime was given to his sons by Adam. If so, then the fact that men have always regarded murder as a crime establishes a clear connection between the age of Adam and the later ages of mankind. That the Qur'an affirms the existence of such a connection is made clear in the verse immediately following. The verse reads: "It was *on account of this* that We imposed upon the Israelites the law that whoever kills a person without [that person's having killed] someone or [having caused] corruption in the land — it shall be as if he has killed all mankind; and whoever gives life to [i.e. saves the life of] a person — it shall be as if he has given life to all mankind...."[8] The italicized words establish an intimate connection between the incident of Abel's murder by Cain and the declaration of murder as a crime in Mosaic law.

**Image of God and Caliph of God**

In Genesis man is called the "image" of God,[9] in the Qur'an the *Khalifah* ("vicegerent") of God.[10]

As the image of God, man is given authority: "... Be fruitful and multiply, and fill the earth and subdue it; and have dominion over the fish of the sea and over the birds of the air and over every living thing that moves upon the earth."[11] The dominion that man is given is not made subject to any moral checks. In fact the Biblical account raises the question whether man was endowed with the *capacity* to act morally. Moral action involves and presupposes some understanding of good and evil, but, in the Bible, the forbidden tree is the tree of the knowledge of good and evil, which means that man is not supposed to acquire the knowledge of good and evil. But if man is not to acquire that knowledge, then the notion of "man as the image of God" becomes a little problematic. Further problems arise when we note that, after Adam and Eve have eaten of the tree. God is "afraid" that man might now eat of the tree of life. For if man will neither partake of divine knowledge of good and evil nor enjoy immortality, then in what sense can he be called the image of God? And if he is to be expelled from Eden for fear that, having eaten of the tree of life, he might become like God, then may not one say that, far from being the image of God, man becomes the rival of God?

The Qur'an avoids these problems by using the word *Khalifah* instead of *image. Khalifah* means "successor, deputy, vicegerent" — and hence "caliph" — and while some commentators have speculated whether man was made a successor to another species which held the title of *Khalifah* before him, we can safely accept the majority opinion that man was made the caliph of God. Of course by making man His *Khalifah,* God did not mean to retire into inaction Himself. The only reasonable interpretation (and one that is amply supported by the Qur'an) can be that God wished to put man to a certain test: by entrusting His vicegerent with certain powers, He wanted to see how those powers would be used by man. Now a test can be meaningful only if the person to be tested has been informed of its nature and scope and endowed with the potential to succeed on the test. Since it was going to be a moral test, the Qur'an says that man, or Adam, was apprised of good and evil. It narrates how, upon learning that God is about to create man, the angels become curious[12] : a *Khalifah* is one who has authority, but might not man, the would be *khalifah,* misuse that authority, causing disorder and bloodshed? At the behest of God, Adam informs the angels that man shall have the power to do good as well.[13] In other words, man shall have an awareness of god and evil. In Chapter XX Adam and Eve are forewarned against being misled by Satan,[14] and in Chapter VII they are rebuked by God for having eaten of the forbidden fruit and are reminded that god had already warned them about Satan, their enemy.[15] The two verses imply that Adam and Eve had been instructed to take the right path and shun the wrong path. In other words, Adam and Eve were possessed of the knowledge of good and evil *before* they succumbed to the inducements of Satan.

**Earth as the Constitutive Element of Man**

Adam was so named because he was formed of "dust from the ground,"[16] *'adamah* in Hebrew.[17] The Qur'an uses the word *turab,* which also means "earth, dust." The Qur'an, unlike the Bible, is not concerned with providing the etymology of Adam's name. But it consistently uses the word *turab* in order to drive home certain points. Like Adam,[18] all men have been created from *turab*[19], a lowly thing. It does not thus behove man to become arrogant and deny his Creator. Furthermore, if God created man from *turab,* then it is unreasonable to suppose, as some people do, that He will be powerless to re-create man at a later time for the purpose of judging him.[20] The word is thus made a basis for vindicating certain recurrent Qur'anic themes. In Chapter III it is used to deny the deity of Jesus. The verse runs: "Indeed the likeness of Jesus is as the likeness of Adam; He created him from *turab,* then said to him, 'Be,' and he came into existence."[21] In other words, Jesus may not partake of divinity on the grounds that he was born without a father, for them Adam would have a prior claim to godhead since he was born without any parents at all.

**Adam and Eve**

According to the Bible, Eve was created from Adam's rib.[22] In the Qur'an, Eve is described as having been created "from" Adam.[23] The Arabic word for "from" is *min,* which, grammatically, is "generic" (li *al-jins).* Eve thus belonged to the same "genus" as Adam, which is to say that she partook of Adam's humanity. It may be argued that the only difference between the Biblical and Qur'anic statements is that the former is more metaphorical whereas the latter is more literal. But the different modes of expression used in the two books are perhaps not entirely without significance, especially when we note that while the Biblical statement stresses the importance of conjugal bond to the exclusion of other types of bonds,[24] the Qur'anic statement appears to stress the importance of the bond of humanity as such.

Furthermore, according to Genesis[25], Adam was placed in Eden before the creation of Eve: "... but for the man there was not found a helper fit for him. So the Lord God caused a deep sleep to fall upon man, and while he slept took one of his ribs and closed up its place with flesh; and the rib which the Lord God had taken from the man he made into a woman..."[26] Also, it was *before* the creation of Eve that Adam had been instructed not to eat of "the tree of the knowledge of good and evil...for in the day that you eat of it you shall die."[27] The Qur'an does imply that Eve was created *after* the creation of Adam,[28] but says expressly that Adam and Eve were placed in Eden *together* and that both were commanded not to eat of the forbidden tree.[29] Since both were forbidden to eat of the tree, it follows that neither could shift responsibility for violating the command, which in turn means that the Biblical incident in which Adam blames Eve for tempting him to eat of the tree and Eve in turn blames the serpent[30] would have been out of place in the Qur'an, and, consequently, finds no mention in it.

Finally, in the Bible, it is Eve who is successfully tempted by the serpent. After eating the fruit herself, she offers it to, Adam, who then eats it. In the Qur'an Adam and Eve are both tempted by Satan, both eat the fruit, and so are equally guilty. In fact there are some verses[31] which, if they do not state clearly that Adam was the first to eat the fruit, suggest that Adam bore greater responsibility for the infringement of the divine commandment, possibly because, being the "head" of the "family unit" in Eden, he failed to ward off Satan's attack.

**Satan's Motive**

The Bible does not explain the serpent's motive for his attempt to mislead Adam and Eve; it only says that he was "more subtle than any other wild creature."[32] The Qur'an gives Satan's envy as the motive. After their query about the creation of man has been answered, the angels are commanded by God to bow to Adam, and all obey except Satan."[33] Made of fire, Satan would not bow to a creature of dust.[34] He is expelled from heaven.[35] Swearing revenge, he asks for, and gets, respite until the Last Day to misguide mankind, and is told by God that those who follow him will end up in hell, and that he shall have no power over God's true servants.[36] Envy leads Satan to plot against Adam and Eve.

**Loss of Heavenly Robes**

In the Bible, Adam and Eve "were both naked, and were not ashamed";[37] in fact, only after they had eaten of the tree that they realized nakedness, i.e., "the eyes of both were opened, and they knew that they were naked."[38] In the Qur'an Adam and Eve, when they are placed in Eden, have heavenly garments on; they lose these garments as a punishment for following the Satan.[39]

## Adam's Repentance

In the Bible, when Adam and Eve are accused by God for having eaten of the forbidden fruit, they react, as we have seen, by trying to shift responsibility for the act. In the Qur'an they become repentant, seek the forgiveness of God, are forgiven, and are furnished with guidance[40]. This means that man no longer remains "fallen" but is reconciled to God. Here a major difference between the Bible and Qur'an is noticeable.

In the Old Testament, man remains unreconciled to God for a long time. As a result of this lack of reconciliation, man ever increases in wickedness, so that even after the Deluge, he would build the Tower of Babel in his presumptuousness. Not until many generations latter, when Abraham is called upon to migrate from Harān to Canaan[41] and a covenant between him and God is made,[42] is this moral descent of man arrested. In the New Testament, according to Paul's interpretation of Christian doctrine, man's fall remains unredeemed until the advent of Jesus, the "last Adam."[43]

## Departure from Eden

Adam and Eve's departure from Eden is differently described in the Qur'an and in the Bible. In the Bible, Adam and Eve are expelled from the garden. Man is driven out of Eden "lest he put forth his hand, and take also of the tree of life, and eat, and live for ever."[44] Also, arrangements are made to prevent man's return to Eden: on the east side of Eden are placed angels, and also "a flaming sword which turned every way."[45] And not only the serpent, but Adam and Eve too are put under a curse.[46]

In the Qur'an, Adam and Eve leave Eden for earth simply because the purpose of their stay in Eden has been fulfilled and they must move on to their proper abode, the earth, until their death. For it is on earth that they will be put to the moral test.

This brings out another important difference between the Biblical and Qur'anic accounts. One might say that, according to the Bible, Eden was meant to be the permanent home of Adam, but that man's eating of the fruit of the forbidden tree caused that plan to be altered, with the result that man was despatched to earth. According to the Qur'an, it was part of the original plan to send man to earth. When God announced to the angels that He was about to create man, He said that He was going to station him *on earth.*[47] This means that the stay in Eden would be temporary. But the question arises: Why place man in Eden at all? The answer would seem to be that Eden was meant to be a place for a trial performance, a kind of laboratory where man could assess his strengths and weaknesses before taking the real moral test on earth. Life in Eden was thus to be a"rehearsal", and once the rehearsal had served its purpose, man was ready to be sent to earth *in accordance with the original plan.*

**Conclusion**

My treatment of the Qur'anic story of Adam is not exhaustive. But I think it sufficiently brings out my main point, namely, that to look at the Qur'an only in terms of the "sources" from which it may have been derived is not always the best way of approaching this book. The Qur'an needs and deserves to be studied in its own right and on its own terms, and the most fruitful way of approaching it is by examining the perspective it places on its materials and the use it makes of these materials in order to achieve objectives peculiar to it. The discussion of the story of Adam in this article should have made it clear that the significance of the story is conceived very differently in the Qur'an than it is in the Bible, and that a more listing of "Parallels" between the Bible and the Qur'an will not only not do justice to the Qur'an, it will be an impediment to a proper understanding of that book.

## NOTES AND REFERENCES

1. The revised Standard Version is used for purpose of citation. The translations of the Quranic verses cited is my own.
2. Genesis, XII: 1-3
3. Al-Quran, III:33
4. Genesis, V:3; Gen. IV: 26; cf. Exodus, III:13-15 and VI:2-3.
5. Al-Quran, VII: 26-27, 31, 35.

6. Ibid., V:27-31.
7. V:27-31; Amin Ahsan Islahi, Tadabbur-i Quran [8 vols; Lahore, 1967-1980], vol. ii, pp.271-72; see also idem, Islami Qanun ki tadwin [Lahore, 1976], p. 13).
8. Al-Quran, V:32.
9. Gen, I: 26-27; V:1
10. Al-Quran, II:30
11. Gen, I:28.
12. Al-Quran, II:30-39
13. Islahi, vol.i, pp. 116-17.
14. Al-Quran, XX:117.
15. Ibid, VII:22
16. Gen, II:7.
17. In Arabic adamah.
18. Al-Quran, III:59.
19. Ibid., XXX:20; XXXV:11; XL:67.
20. Ibid., XXII:5.
21. Ibid., III:59
22. Gen., II:21-22.
23. Al-Quran, IV:1; VII:189; XXXIX:6.
24. Gen., II:24.
25. Gen., II:18-23
26. Gen., II:20-22.
27. Ibid., II:17.
28. Al-Quran, IV:1; VII:189; XXXIX:6.
29. Ibid., II:35.
30. Gen., III:12-13.
31. See also, al-Quran, XX:121-122.
32. Gen., III:1
33. Al-Quran, II:34; VII:11; XX:116.

34. Ibid. VII:12.
35. Ibid. VII:13.
36. Ibid. VII:14-17; XVII:62-65.
37. Gen., II:25.
38. Ibid., III:7.
39. Al-Quran, VII:20, 22; XX:121.
40. Ibid., II:37; VII:23; XX:122.
41. Gen., XII
42. Ibid., XV.
43. See Romans, V:12-19 and I Corinthians, XXV:42-50.
44. Gen., III:22.
45. Ibid., III:24.
46. Ibid., III:14-19.
47. Al-Quran, II:30.

---

**(Revised and edited; originally published in Islamic Culture, January 1988).**

# 6

# An Inquiry into the Earliest Collection of the Qur'an

MAJMAL KHAN

Deals with Meccan writers of the revealed verses; the writers of Medina; other writers; the method of compilation; etc.

Qur'an, a collection of inspirations, which Muhammad received from Allah during a period of twenty-three years (609 to 632 A.D.). The whole of the Qur'an was collected in the lifetime of Muhammad, and there are no two opinions about the authenticity of the collection. The authenticity of the contents of the Qur'an is above suspicions, and this is the main difference between the Qur'an and other scriptures. Dr Leitner thinks that "there are instances of eminent scholars who, for want of sympathy, have greatly misjudged Muhammadanism. Sir William Muir, *e.g.*, has been led into very serious mistakes in dealing with this religion."[1] Yet even Muir is forced to admit that "we may upon the strongest presumption affirm that every verse in the Koran is the genuine and unaltered composition of Muhammad himself, and conclude with least close approximation to the verdict of Von Hammer: That we hold the Koran to be as surely Mohammad's word, as the Mohammadans hold it to be the word of God."[2]

The Qur'an is not a large book. "Reckoned by the number of verses, the Koran is only two-thirds of the length of the New Testament, or if the stories of the Jewish patriarchs are omitted, it is no more than the Gospels and Acts. But the real permanent contents of the Koran may be taken at far less even than this estimate."[3] It contains prayers, moral precepts, temporary exhortations, stories, fables, principles of law and such other things as were necessary for the guidance of a people who possessed neither law nor any kind of government. The Qur'an was given to the people piecemeal by Muhammad.

The Qur'an is in prose, sometimes in rhymed prose; but certainly it is not poetry, and its *ayat* (sentences) should not be called verses, as is done by most European writers. Several *ayat* make a discourse, and sometimes one, and often more than one, discourse makes a complete chapter of *sura.*

The different passages of the Qur'an were arranged in complete *suras* by Muhammad himself, and these were used in public prayers till his death. The different chapters or discourses of the Qur'an were learnt by heart by the zealous followers of Islam, because memory was the safest repository for all they cared to remember. Very few persons knew how to read and write. But owing to the constant exhortations of the Apostle to learn to read and write, many Muslims learnt it, and some of them were employed as his amanuenses. His zeal for promoting literacy is best shown in the fact that those captives of the Battle of Badr who were unable to pay ransom owing to their poverty were allowed to purchase their freedom by teaching the art of writing to at least 10 children.[4]

### A. The Writers of Mecca

The life of the Muslims at Mecca was not peaceful. They were constantly being harassed and persecuted by the non-Muslims. Hence it was not possible for them to commit the Qur'an to writing. Moreover, the Meccan discourses of the Qur'an were couched in such a beautiful language, containing rhyming sentences, that the people could remember them without an effort. No reference is given to the written *suras* of the Qur'an in the traditions or the history of the Meccan period. Twice the Muslims emigrated to Abyssynia, but there is no mention of their carrying any written passage of the Qur'an. No mention is made of an amanuensis in the quarter of Abu Talib, where the Apostle lived for three years with his tribe when they were excommunicated by the Meccans. The most important event of Islamic history is the emigration of Muslims to Medina (*hijra*). At that time they left Mecca secretly, and must have carried all the valuables belonging to them along with them. Even at such a critical juncture not a single individual is mentioned to have carried the written discourses of the Qur'an. Details of how Abu Bakr made an arrangement for two camels before their departure, and how he took all his wealth amounting to 5,000 dirhams, are found in chronicles. It is also mentioned that the Apostle gave all the deposits of the people of Mecca to 'Ali, to be handed over to their owners, one day before his departure. The camels on which they travelled were brought by a pagan guide on the third day of their secluded sojourn in the cave of Hira. Surely, the guide could not have been entrusted with bringing the manuscript of the Qur'an along with the camels. Everything has been recorded in the minutest details, such as the binding of the food wallet by Asma, daughter of Abu Bakr, by tearing her scarf. But it is not mentioned that any one carried the manuscript of the Qur'an along with him to Medina.

However, a doubtful story about some written leaves of the Qur'an is related in connexion with the conversion of 'Umar. It is said that Khubab was reciting the discourse of the Qur'an beginning with *ta ha* to his sister and brother-in-law. When 'Umar entered the house to know the truth of their conversion of Islam, the teacher hid himself, and the sister hid the *sahifa* under her knee[5]. But Abu Nu'aim Isfahani (330-430 A.H) gives the word *kitab* also along with *sahifa* in a tradition with the following chain of narrators[6]:

(i) Ahmad b. Muhammad b. al-Hasan.
(ii) Muhammad b. Uthman b. Abi Shiba.
(iii) Abd Hamid b. Salih.
(iv) Muhammad b. Aban.
(v) Ishaq b. 'Abdulla.
(vi) Aban b. Salih.
(vii) Mujahid.
(viii) Ibn 'Abbas.

Now, the last named narrator, *i.e.* Ibn 'Abbas, is said to have asked 'Umar about the story of his conversion of Islam. 'Umar related that he entered the house and beat his brother-in-law and sister, and drew blood from both. He was then ashamed to see the blood of her sister and wanted to see the book which was being read. Then his sister read a passage of the Qur'an from Discourse 46 bearing the title *al-Waqi'a* (The Inevitable): "Let none touch it but the purified"[7] and asked 'Umar to take a bath and purify himself. He did it, and then read the Chapter *Ta Ha* which began by the usual formula, "In the name of Allah, Rahman, the Merciful".

According to Ibn 'Abbas himself Discourse No. 20 is earlier than Discourse No. 66. It was, therefore, impossible for the lady to quote from a discourse which she did not know, because perhaps it was not revealed up to that time. Moreover, the formula *bi'smillah* was written to differentiate between different *suras* of the Qur'an in Medina. It was not done in Mecca and the formula itself was not yet announced by the Apostle. However, under the circumstances one cannot believe Umar taking a bath, although he was not soothed by any arguments and his fury had not abated.

But Ibn Hisham relates two other anecdotes about the conversion of Umar which are quite reasonable, and totally differ from the above-mentioned story. It is, however, strange that many writers of the life of Muhammad have not mentioned these stories, as perhaps they were not sensational or extraordinary.

Mujahid and 'Ata are the relators of the story in which 'Umar is described as hearing himself the Qur'an from the lips of Muhammad. He hid himself behind the curtains of the Ka'ba and heard the simple and sincere prayers of Muhammad, and after a short time was converted to the mission of peace.[8] There is no mention of written Qur'an here.

Another story is related by Nafi, the client of Abdulla b. Umar, who does not mention the march of Umar to the Ka'ba along with Hamza and other Muslims, to announce that he had become a Muslim, and thenceforth they will preach and pray in public. He only relates that Umar announced his conversion to Jamil in the beginning. He was famous as a gossip-monger, and Umar believed that his Islam will be known to all by this means. Jamil then and there announced the fact to the people, and people began to beat Umar and he fought with them till noon when As b. Wa'il appeared on the scene and stopped the men from fighting.[9]

From the above accounts it is quite clear that the story of hiding the *sahifa* is merely a fabrication. There were few men who could read and write and perhaps no woman. We may conclude that they did not write down the discourses of the Qur'an in Mecca. It was in Medina that the writing of Qur'an was introduced by Muhammad.

**B. The Writers of Medina**

There were many writers among the Muslims, but only a few were appointed to perform the different kinds of writing. Some were specially fitted to write diplomatic dispatches, owing to their experience of good hand-writing. Others, who constantly remained near the Apostle and had a good memory, were selected to write down the Qur'anic inspirations of the Apostle. Following is a list of various kinds of writers[10]:

(i) *Ubai b. Ka'b Ansari*. He was a native of Medina who was present at the second pledge of Aqaba near Mecca, and had submitted to the Apostle there. The Apostle said that he was the best reciter of the Qur'an. He used to write then inspirations before Zaid b. Thabit. He also wrote the Qur'an along with Zaid. According to Ibn Sai'd he was the first man who wrote the inspirations of the Apostle of God after his advent to Medina. He was also a writer of the letters of the Apostle to the people. There is difference of opinion about the date of his death. It is said that he died during the Caliphate of Umar I in 19 A.H., others say that the year of his death was 20 A.H. or 22 A.H. or even 32 A.H.

(ii) *Zaid b. Thabit Ansari*. It is said that Zaid was eleven years old at the time of the advent of the Apostle at Medina, and at the time of the battle of *Buwat* (616 A.D) he was only six years old.[11]

He learnt reading and writing after the battle of Badr (624 A.H.) from the prisoners of the Meccan army. Historian *Zarqani says* that he had learnt the Hebrew language by order of the Apostle, as it was the religious language of the Jews of Medina.[12] But it is related that he had learnt Syrian (not Hebrew), as many letters used to come to the Apostle in that language[13]. He was present at the battle of Uhud, (625 A.D.) and at the Battle of the Ditch (627 A.D.) he was removing earth from the ditch and the Apostle praised the boy for his good work[14]. So at this time his age was 17 years, and he must have begun writing the Qur'anic inspirations at about this time, or even after this time, as a boy of 17 might not have been selected for such an important work.

Yet it is known that he had learnt much of the Qur'an by heart at the time of the battle of Tabuk, as the Apostle transferred the banner of war from Amara to him, and on the protest of Amara the Apostle replied that the Qur'an should be given preference, and "Zaid knows more Qur'an than you do."[14] But according to the author of Isti'ab this report is not correct. So we may only infer from it that as a boy he must have been given to reading and writing of the Qur'an, and other things also, and that his memory was greater and fresher as compared to older Muslims. Still the tradition of Anas b. Malik is said to be correct, in which he reports that Zaid was one of the persons who had collected (learnt by heart) the whole of the Qur'an in the lifetime of the Apostle. This means that he was one of the Helpers (*ansar*) who knew the whole of Qur'an by heart. This statement is, however, challenged by people on the basis of Ibn Shahab's tradition that Zaid himself collected the Qur'an in the days of Abu Bakr. They assert that if Zaid had collected the Qur'an in the lifetime of the Apostle he could have written it from his memory, and could not have taken the trouble of compiling it from the pieces of leather, parchment, and memories of men, and even then he did not know the last sentence of the 9th Chapter, which was with Khuzaima or Abu Khuzaima alone.[14] This fact only leads us to think that he was not present at the time when this sentence was dictated by the Apostle. We may also say that the passages of the Qur'an were mostly remembered by heart, as no tradition is found to the effect that whole of the written Qur'an by Ubai or Zaid was kept in order in one place. This will be discussed further.

In the days of Abu Bakr he was entrusted with the collection and compilation of the Qur'an. It was he who was also entrusted in the days of Uthman to edit the Qur'an in such a way that the people may not differ in reading it.

He was an important person, and as he knew most of Qur'an he was appointed Governor of Medina by Umar and Uthman, whenever they went to the pilgrimage to Mecca. Hamid b. Al-aswad relates a tradition from Malik b. Anas that Zaid was the Imam (of Medina) after Umar, and Abdulla b. U'mar was the next Imam. He was also the governor of the *bait al-mal* in the Caliphate of Uthman. He was much loved by Uthman, and he was a partisan of Uthman, yet he loved Ali and honoured him, although he never fought along with 'Ali any of his battles.

The date of his death is not known for certain. It is said that he died between the years 45 and 55 A H. Mada'ini says that he died in 56 A.H.

(iii) *'Abdulla b. Sa'd b. Abi Sarah.* According to Waqidi he was the first man from among the Quraish who wrote the Qur'an for the Apostle in Medina. He was a foster-brother of Uthman. He said that he himself received inspirations from God, and tried to interpolate them in the Qur'anic text, but he was caught in this attempt, and ran away to Mecca, and joined the heathens. It is perhaps to him that the following verses of the Qur'an (see chapter VI) refer:

> But is any more wicked than he who deviseth a lie of God, or saith, "I have a revelation", when nothing was revealed to him, and who saith, "I have had a revelation", when nothing was revealed to him, and who saith, "I can bring down a book like that which God hath sent down"? But couldst thou see when the ungodly are in the floods of death,

> and the angels reach forth their hands, saying, "Yield up your soul: this day shall ye be recompensed with a humiliating punishment for your untrue sayings about God, and for proudly rejecting his signs!"

The crime of fabricating false inspirations and his apostasy were punishable by death, and hence when Mecca was conquered by the Apostle the blood of Abdulla was made lawful and his life was forfeited. Uthman gave him refuge, and brought him to the Apostle so that he may take an oath of allegiance. The Apostle, however, was not prepared to admit his apology and allegiance until he had taken the hands of three other persons. He later on asked: "Was there no wise man amongst you, who could have killed him, when I had delayed in accepting his allegiance?" The men replied that the Apostle should have winked about it, but the Apostle said it was not befitting a prophet to wink. There is another report which states that as 'Uthman had given him refuge, the Apostle also forgave him.

Uthman was very kind to him during his Caliphate also and had appointed him the governor of Egypt, and he conquered some parts of Africa. He died in 'Asqalan in 36 A.H.

**Other Writers or Secretaries**

There were many persons who wrote letters and diplomatic documents such as treaties, letters of appointments etc. The need for such persons arose mostly after the conquest of Mecca, when the Islamic State began to extend its citizenship to other peoples and nations. A list of secretaries with special mention of the work allotted to them, as given in *kitab al-Isaba* and *Kitab al-Isti'ab,* follows.

(i) *Abdulla b. Arqam al-Zuhri* : It was a permanent writer of the letters of the Apostle. He was the nephew of the Apostle, as this grand-father Abd Yaghuth was the maternal uncle of Muhammad. He became a Muslim on the day of the conquest of Mecca. He wrote for the Apostle, Abu Bakr and Umar. He was the keeper of the treasury during the Caliphate of Umar. Baghawi says that the

Apostle asked him to answer the letters of kings on his behalf. He was an honest man, so much so that the Apostle did not ask him to re-read the letters, and he used to affix the seal.

(ii) *'Ali b. Abi Talib* : It was the writer of treaties and truce agreements. He was brought up by Apostle Muhammad, and remained always with him. The Apostle made him his brother. He was famous for horsemanship and courage. He did his utmost to propagate learning after the death of the Apostle. He was sent to the Quraish to recite to them Chapter IX of the Qur'an declaring "the annulment of agreements with the unbelievers, excepting those who were true of their word". Ali used to invite questions about the Qur'an from the people, as he said that he knew the time of revelation of every passage of the Qur'an, and he could tell whether it was revealed to the Apostle at night or in daytime.

(iii) *Abu Bakr b. Abi Quhafa* : It was also a secretary of Muhammad. He was born two years and a half after the event of the Elephant, *i.e.* in A.D. 573. He was the first man to accept Islam, and remained along with Muhammad in Mecca throughout his stay there. He was the greatest authority on the pedigrees of the Quraish. He was a rich merchant, and a generous man with good manner. He converted Uthman Talha, al-Zubair, Sa'd and Abd al-Rahman b. Auf. He purchased seven slaves who were being tortured for becoming Muslims and set them free. They were Bilal, Amir, Zunaira, Nahdiya and her daughter, Umm Uwais and a slave girl of Bani Mumal. He used to prescribe blood money in the days of arrogance. He died in A.H. 13 after remaining a Caliph for 2 years, 3 months and 20 days.

Along with Abu Bakr some more names of writers are given in *Kitab al-Kuttab,* which are noted below. It is, however, not mentioned whether they wrote the Qur'an or not.

(iv) *Umar b. Al-Khattab*. He was ten years younger than the Apostle. During the days of arrogance he used to hold the office of an ambassador in Mecca. He was Abu Jahl's nephew. It was after his becoming a Muslim that people could pray to God openly.

(v) *Uthman b. Affan.* His maternal grand-mother, al-Baida, was the daughter of Abd al-Muttalib, aunt of Muhammad. He was six years younger than the Apostle. He was the first emigrant to Habsha with his wife Ruqaiya. He was the cause of the pledge of Ridwan in which the Apostle put one of his hands over the other to take the oath and said, "This is the hand of Uthman."

(vi) *Ali b. Abi Tailb.* He has been mentioned as a writer of treaties.

(vii) *Al-Zubair b. al-Awwam.* His mother, Safiya, was the aunt of the Apostle. He accepted Islam at the age of 12 or 15. He and Abdulla b. Mas'ud were made brothers by the Apostle in Mecca. He was murdered by Ibn Jurmuh near Basra in 36 A.H.

(viii) *Khalid b. Sa'id b. al-'As Umawi.* He accepted Islam after Abu Bakr, so he was the third or the fourth Muslim. Damra says that Khalid and Abu Bakr became Muslims at the same time. He emigrated to Abyssynia with his wife and children and returned to the Apostle after the conquest of Khyber in A.H. 7 (A D. 623). The daughter of Khalid (Umm Khalid) says that it was her father who first wrote *bi'smillah al-Rahman al-Rahim.* He was appointed the governor of Yemen by the Apostle, and remained there till the death of the Apostle.

(ix) *Aban b. Sa'id b. al-'As Umawi.* According to Waqidi, he accepted Islam in the days of Khyber, but Ibn Ishaq says that he emigrated as a Muslim to Abyssynia with his wife Fatima b. Safawan. Khadija b. Zaid b. Thabit says that he wrote the Qur'an with Zaid in the Caliphate of Uthman. But this is not correct as he died previously during the caliphate of Abu Bakr.

(x) *Hanzala As'adi.* He was the nephew of Aktham b. Saifi. He was a secretary of the Apostle and has reported sayings from him. He lived in Kufa and did not fight with Ali in the battle of Camel. He died during the days of Mu'awaya. It is also related by Tirmidhi that he was a writer of the Apostle.

(xi) *Al-'Ala b. al-Hadrami.* The cause of the Battle of Badr was the murder of his brother 'Amr b. al-Hadrami. The Apostle appointed him as a governor of Bahrain, where he remained up to A.H. 14, in the Caliphate of 'Umar. He was a man whose prayers were said to be accepted by God. He died in A.H. 14.

(xii) *Khalid b. al-Walid.* The mother of Khalid was Lababa the younger; the wife of 'Abbas was Lababa the elder, and the wife of Muhammad was Maimuna. All these ladies were the daughters of al-Harith b. Harb. Harith was the keeper of the reins of horses in the Days of Arrogance. Khalid accepted Islam in A.H. 7. He was a great general.

(xiii) *'Abdulla b. Rawaha Ansari.* He is the famous poet who was appointed as one of the Naqibs in the night of pledge of 'Aqaba. According to Ibn Sa'd, he used to write for the Apostle. It is he who first announced the news of the victory of Battle of Badr to the people of Medina.

(xiv) Muhammad b. Muslima Ansari was born in 587 A.D. and was one of those who were named Muhammad before Islam. He was a learned companion of the Apostle. He did not join the battles of Camel and Siffin. He died in A.H. 64 (A.D. 663) at the age of 77.

(xv) *'Abdulla b. Sa'd b. Abi Sarah* (see above).

(xvi) *'Abdulla b. 'Abdulla b. Ubai b. Abi Salul.* (Salul was a woman of Khuza'a tribe). The father of 'Abdulla was the leader of hypocrites in Medina, so he asked permission of the Apostle to kill him but was not allowed to do so. He was one of those who fought in the Battles of Badr and Yamama.

(xvii) *Al-Mughira b. Shiba.* He accepted Islam before the truce of Hudaibia. He was a famous warrior of Arabs and was appointed the Governor of Basra by 'Umar, where (according to Baghawi) he first intalled the government secretariat. He was dismissed by 'Umar on the complaint of Abu Bikreh.

(xviii) *'Amr b. al-'As.* He accepted Islam in A.H. 8 and came to Medina along with Khalid b. Walid. He was the leader of the deputation to Negus, against the Muslim refugees. He was appointed as a governor of 'Uman by the Apostle where he remained till the death of the Apostle.[15]

(xix) *Mu'awiya b. Abi Sufyan*. According to Waqidi also, he wrote for the Apostle after becoming a Muslim in A.H 8 (A.D. 630). Abu Nu'aim says that he was a beautiful writer, and wrote for the Apostle. Mada'ini says the Zaid b. Thabit used to write the inspirations, and Mu'awiya used to write letters from the Apostle to the Arabs. His sister Umm Habiba was the wife of the Apostle.

(xx) *Juhaim b. Salt b. Mukhrima b. Muttalib b. 'Abd Manaf.* He became a Muslim in the year of Khyber A.H. 7 (A.D. 628), and the Apostle gave him 30 camel-loads of provisions from the booty of Khyber.

(xxi) *Mu'aiqib b. Abi Fatima Dausi*. It is said that he was one of those who emigrated to Abyssynia. He was an old Muslim. He suffered from leprosy, and was medically treated by order or 'Umar. He was the keeper or treasury in the days of 'Umar, and kept the seal of 'Uthman also. He died during the caliphate of 'Uthman.

(xxii) *Shurahbil b. Hasana*. Hasana was his mother, and his father was 'Abdulla b. Muta.' He emigrated to Abyssynia and afterwards to Medina. He died in the Plague of 'Amwas (A.H.18) at the age of 67. Some say that the Apostle sent him to Egypt where he died.

It is quite clear from the lives of the above-named writers that they were not systematically engaged in writing the Qur'an, but they wrote letters and treaties, and sometimes the Qur'an also for their private use, or to transfer it to such persons who wished to learn it by heart. Many of them accepted Islam very late; some had emigrated to Abyssynia, others were appointed as governors and collectors of taxes, and some were sent on holy war against the unsubdued people. The two persons who are said to be the constant companions of the Apostle were Ubai and Zaid, both helpers and natives of Medina. "In the absence of Ubai, Zaid was called to write by the Apostle"[15] who learnt writing after the Battle of Badr.

Thus it can reasonably be concluded that the writing of the Qur'an began late even at Medina.

"No sooner had it become noised a broad that the Prophet was dead than the unruly spirit of the Arab broke forth; whilst a great fear fell upon the earnest followers of the new Faith. Some of the tribes who had only recently abandoned idolatory, reverted at once to *their evil ways,* and *several* imposters who had appeared in distant provinces in the life-time of the Prophet began harrying the Muslims. Within a little time the Faith had become almost confined to the city of Medina, and again a single town had to contend against the idolatrous hordes of the peninsula.

"The principal work of subjection was entrusted to Khalid; son of Waleed, a ferocious soldier but a skilled general. At the battle of Yamamah (A.H. 11) the formidable tribe of the Banoo Haneefah were thoroughly defeated, and their leader the imposter Mosailimah was killed."[16] It was a terrible battle in which numerous persons were killed. According to Baladhuri there is a difference of opinion about the number of Muslims who were killed there, ranging from 700 to 1,700 men. But Ibn al-Athir says that 360 refugees and helpers of Medina and 300 refugees from other places than Medina were killed in this battle.[17] He mentions further that in this year, after the battle of Yamama Abu Bakr ordered the collection of the Qur'an, when he says the slaughter of so many companions of the Apostle, so that the Qur'an may not be lost.

The men (numbering 700) who were killed at Yamama were all *hafiz*. Among the companions of the Apostle who fell in this engagement were Abu Hudhaifa b. 'Utba, 'Abdullab. Sahl, Yazid b. Qais, Abu Dujana, Zaid b. al-Khattab (the brother of 'Umar I) and others numbering seventy.[18] This naturally aroused the fears of 'Umar about the loss of much of the Qur'an, as there were few men who knew the whole of the Qur'an by heart. So he persisted that the whole of the Qur'an should be taken down in black and white from the oral recitations of the persons who knew the different passages by heart. The following tradition proves this fact to a certainty that no written copy of *the complete Qur'an existed with any* one after the death of the Apostle; hence the need of a written copy. Al-Bukhari records the Zaid b. Thabid said:

"Abu Bakr sent for me after the slaughter of the people at Yamama. 'Umar b. al-Khattab was also sitting there. He said: 'Verily 'Umar hath come to me saying that the slaughter of the men at Yamama was great and he fears lest the loss in battles of the readers (i.e. those who remember passages of the Qur'an by heart) of the Qur'an may be lost unless they collect it together, and he emphatically wishes that the Qur'an should be collected".[19]

It should be noted here that the Qur'an was not collected in one place until the suggestion of 'Umar. Moreover, the reply of Abu Bakr, further on in this tradition, corroborates this view. He replied to 'Umar: "How shall I do a thing which the Apostle of God has not done?"[20] Certainly, the whole of the Qur'an was not collected in writing in the life-time of Apostle Muhammad, in one place. Zaid b. Thabit also asserts: "The Apostle of God passed away and the Qur'an was not collected in one place." This confirms the above concern of 'Umar for the collection of the Qur'an.

An attempt at writing down the Qur'an was made three times according to al-Hakim who says in Mustadrik on the authority of Zaid b. Thabit: "We compiled the Qur'an from small pieces of notes in the presence of the Apostle."[21] on this, al-Hakim says further on that this proves that the collection of the Qur'an was not done only once because some of it was collected in the presence of the Apostle of God, and the rest was collected in the presence of Abu Bakr. The third collection—the arrangement of the *suras*—was done during the Caliphate of 'Uthman b. 'Affan.[22]

However, after the exhortations of 'Umar, Abu Bakr consented "to do a thing which the Apostle himself had not done." 'Umar said: "By Allah, it is a good work (to collect the Qur'an)," and he did not cease to persist with Abu Bakr until God enlightened his mind concerning it, and he began to think as 'Umar thought. Zaid adds: "Umar was meanwhile seated by (him, not speaking; then Abu Bakr said to Zaid: 'Thou art an intelligent youth, and I have no doubts regarding thee, and verily thou wast he who recorded the revelations of the Apostle of God; *search* therefore the Qur'an and collect it." Zaid was unnerved on this commission and said, "By Allah, had he charged me with the carrying away of a hill from out of the mountains, it would not have been weightier upon me than that which he commanded me in the collection of the Qur'an." Zaid, therefore, said: "How can you two undertake to do a thing which the Apostle of God hath not done?" Abu Bakr replied: "By Allah, it is a good work." Zaid did not cease discussing it with him, until God enlightened his mind in that towards which He had already disposed the minds of Abu Bakr and 'Umar. "Then Zaid *searched* for the Quran and collected it from leafless palm branches, and tablets (of wood, stone, or shoulder blades) and minds of men; until he found from the Sura of Repentence (IX) two verses in the possession of Khuzymah b. Thabit only which he found with no one else, *viz*—'Now hath an Apostle come to you of your own nation' to the end."[20]

No comment is necessary on this tradition. It is clear that the former tradition of Zaid about his collection of the Qur'an in the lifetime of the Apostle only lays down the fact that they collected *some* of the Qur'an at that time, and that too from the written scraps. On the previous occasion no attempt of collecting Qur'an from the "minds of men" is mentioned. This was also unnecessary, as the *suras* of Meccan period were mostly in rhymed prose and were memorized by numerous Muslims. The only part of the Qur'an which they had to collect was that which was given in Medina. The inclusion of Zaid among the collectors (whose names are not mentioned) also proves that Zaid had grown up and had learnt writing, which he did from the prisoners of Badr, and the first collection must have taken place much later than the Battle of Badr. The collectors were making collections for their personal use only, as the Apostle is stated, both by Abu Bakr and Zaid, not to have done or ordered it, and hence they wanted to desist, from what the Apostle himself had not done. Zaid relied mostly on the *memory of the people*, which is the safest repository of all unlettered and primitive peoples, and he also took the aid to scraps of writing on papyrus and tablets, but no mention is made at this time of the *suhuf* of parchments which were written down at the time of the first collection in the lifetime of the Apostle. These might have proved very useful in giving an idea of the chronological order of the *suras*.

There is also a tradition that 'Umar was also ordered by Abu Bakr to sit along with Zaid to write the texts of the Qur'an after first taking two *witnesses*. Ibn Hajar thinks that by *witnesses* is meant memory plus the written copy of the text brought by a person.[23] Here also no mention is made of the *suhuf* or parchments which were collected by Zaid himself in the lifetime of the Apostle. This clearly shows that these traditions are weak, and were fabricated later on by interested persons, as they contradict each other.

*The method of compilation.* After consulting 'Umar, Zaid collected the Qur'an on *qaratis* (pl. of *qirtas*, thin leather used for writing).[24] Ibn Ashta says that people came to Zaid and he did not write any passage unless two just witnesses attested the athenticity of the passage according to the orders of Abu Bakr. The last portion of *sura ix* was found only with Abu Khudhaima b. Thabit, which Zaid ordered to be written down, because the Apostle of God had counted his evidence equal to the evidence of two men; so it was noted down. But 'Umar came with the passage relating to *rajm* (stoning do death) and it was not written down, on the single evidence of 'Umar, as no one else corroborated him.[23]

The tradition, if correct, proves:

First, that the whole of the Qur'an was *not memorized* and collected even by the great companions of the Apostle. Had it been done so, there would not have arisen the occasion of so much fuss about its collection.

Secondly, that no complete passages on different materials written by Ubai, Zaid and other secretaries of the Apostle were produced from the house of 'A'isha or any of the wives or companions of the Apostle. It is only al-Harith al-Muhasibi who testifies to the collection of the Qur'an from written material. He says in his book *Kitabu fahm al-Sunan*, that the writing of the Qur'an was not an innovation (bid'a), as the Apostle of God used to order it to be written down. But these writings were separately written on scraps of palm branches and shoulder blades of animals. When Abu Bakr ordered their copy to be made, these scraps were found in the house of the Apostle of God. The collector collected them and bound them with a cord, so that nothing may be lost.[23]

This and other such explanations of the Qur'an from written passages are given by various persons, who think that writing can only be a sure method to keep a literary piece in its purest form. However, such unnatural explanations prove, firstly, the fact that after two hundred years of the death of the Apostle, there had arisen a strong suspicion about oral traditions, and people's memories had become weak owing to the use of writing. Secondly, that it was not the written copies of the Secretaries of the Apostle but the writings or *memories* of only two just witnesses, which were consulted at the time of the compilation. Thirdly, that many of the Medinian *suras* were not completely compiled in the lifetime of the Apostle, as they were not only collecting them from scraps of writings, but also compiling them as they pleased. This requires further elucidation.

The *suras* of the Meccan period were short and comprised of small rhyming *ayat*. When the number of Muslims grew, they began to recite these passages of the Qur'an, and as no special method of prayer was set forth by the Apostle till the 10th year of his mission, it was usually the custom to recite the Qur'an only. Sometimes it was done standing near the sanctuary of Ka'ba, sometimes in the house of Arqam (near the Safa hill) and sometimes in one's own house, as did Abu Bakr after he was given amnesty by a heathen friend and he was stopped from emigrating to Abyssynia.

So, the reading of the Qur'an itself was considered to be a form of prayer.

As the passages of the Qur'an grew in number, it became necessary to differentiate one passage from another, and certain names were attached to different passages. It so happened that no name or place was allotted to a passage which was dictated by the Apostle nine days before his death, and no one could tell where to place it. The least number of *ayat* which made a complete *sura* was considered to be three.[25] Abu Da'ud says that Harith b. Khudhaima recited two *ayat* and said that he had heard them from the Apostle. 'Umar corroborated him and said that had there been three *ayat* it would have become a complete *sura*, but as there were only two, they could be added to the *sura* which was last in order of time. They were, therefore, appended to *sura ix.*[26] These two *ayat* were accepted on the authority of Abu Khudhaima Ansari, as his evidence was considered to be equal to two persons. However, this only proves that the compilers had collected every text of the Qur'an, and they only hesitated to place two *ayat* of the Qur'an in a *sura* other than the last one, as they had no injunctions of the Apostle to the contrary. It was the only correct procedure which could have been adopted, when not a single companion of the Apostle came forward to oppose it. The statement of 'Umar, that they could make it a new *sura*, is also important. It means, perhaps, that the Muslims by common consent have a right to make new *suras* out of the existing texts of the Qur'an. They have already subdivided a *sura* into many parts called a *ruku* for the the purpose of recitation in prayers, and the whole Qur'an is divided into seven parts (each called a *hizb*), and also into thirty equal parts, irrespective of the fact whether a chapter ends after every part or not.

It is admitted by all the learned divines and the oldest authorities on the Qur'an that the place of the *ayat* in different *suras* of the Qur'an was allotted by the Apostle himself.[27] It means that the names of different *suras* were already known to the people. Sometimes a *sura* was known by many names, *e.g. surat al-fatiha*, which had more than twenty names.[26] The names or headings of the various *suras* referred sometimes to the introductory words or letter or the heading itself occurred somewhere in the *sura*. Such names or titles were given to the *suras* to differentiate one from the other. It was not necessary that a discourse should contain material relevant only to the title given to it. As a title was given after the revelation of a passage of the Qur'an, it only referred to the most important feature of the passage. Thus *sura iv* is named *al-Nisa* and *sura xi* is called *Hud*; the former contains much about women in addition to other things, but the latter contains more of the story of Noah than that of Hud. As an explanation of this anomaly, it is asserted that the story of Noah has been told in many other *suras*; and the reference about Hud is specially made in *sura xi,* therefore it is fitly named *Hud*.[28]

So it is clear that the names of all the *suras* of the Qur'an were already fixed and known to the reciters of the Qur'an in the very life-time of the Apostle. However, it is not certain which names were given by the Apostle himself. The traditions give most of the *suras* as being either recited by the Apostle himself in various congregational prayers, or his giving instructions about certain texts to be inserted in certain *suras* by name. A Muslim is, therefore, at liberty to use any of the many names of the *suras*, so long as he does not mistake one for the other.

There are certain persons who assert that although the exsiting Qur'an contains nothing but the Qur'an, there might have been some passages which are not included in it. They also say that the different texts of the Qur'an are placed haphazardly in the various *suras*, and their arrangement is contrary to the original arrangement of the Apostle. We shall now discuss these problems.

A Shi'a divine says: "The method of collecting the Qur'an shows that great precaution was taken against any interpolation of a passage in the Qur'an, which was not in reality a part of it. But this precaution could not tend to include every *ayat* of the Qur'an (in the compilation of the Qur'an). Had this been the case, no single companion of the Apostle would have been refused his say owing to the want of another witness." He further on thinks that there were many companions of the prophet, who believed every word of the present Qur'an to be the word of God, yet they thought that some *ayat* were missing here and there. They do not believe in excess, yet they believed in the defect of the Qur'an. In his opinion, the condition of accepting a text of the Qur'an on the evidence of two just witnesses was the cause of this defect and this creates a doubt in the completeness of the Qur'an.[29] This is made clear further on.

*Jam, talif* and *qir'at.* Certain Arabic words have lost their original meaning, causing a great deal of confusion. The traditionists and other writers about the Qur'an have constantly used several words about the collection and compilation of the Qur'an, which should be clearly understood at the outset.

*Jam'* ordinarily means a crowd or multitude of men, an army, a flock. It also means addition or collection. In reference to Qur'an, it generally means to collect it in one's memory or to remember it by heart.[21]

*Talif* means to *compile or collect together in a certain order.* In connexion with the Qur'an, it is sometimes used as a synonym of *jam* and sometimes it means writing down together.

*Qir'at* is a noun from the verb *qur'a.* This means *reading* nowadays. But in earlier days when written things were very uncommon this meant oral recitation only.

Now, the whole of the Qur'an was collected and written by order of Abu Bakr, and with the active help of 'Umar and other companions of the Apostle in the first year after the death of Muhammad. The turbulent history of the times is well-known, and this work was done under very hard conditions even at home. Yet it saved the holy text from the interpolations of interested political parties, which in later days fabricated so many traditions about their sects. A mass of traditions has been separated from the genuine material by later scholars under the title *maudu'at.* This fate was saved of Qur'an, and it remained with the first Caliph till his death. Then 'Umar kept it in his custody till his death, and after him it remained with Hasfa,

No copies of this collection were published by authority of the Caliphate. As it was usual that some *sura* or other was necessarily to be recited orally in prayers by Muslims, it had become a custom since the days of the Apostle to remember the Qur'an for this purpose. There are so many injunctions in the Qur'an itself about learning the Qur'an that every Muslim had to do it, and it is done up to this day. Yet the ordinary soldier who went out to conquer the domains of Roman and Persian Emperors could not have learnt much of the Qur'an. Hence it was written down on skins, stitched together or rolled and kept by many pious Muslims. Paper was then unknown to the Arabs. It was manufactured by them after the conquest of Samarqand, where they learnt its manufacture from the Chinese prisoners of war in A.D.751. So the rolls of skins or volumes in book form must have been sometimes very unwieldly. It was, therefore, easier to remember by heart than to carry an unwieldy volume. However, the Qur'an was written down by other Muslims also who were not present at the time of the official collection. The order of the *suras* of many compilers must also have been according to their choice.

Neither the Qur'an collected or remembered in the time of the Apostle nor the collection of Abu Bakr was given publicity by authority in a systematic form. It could not have been done in the days of the Apostle, because the Qur'anic texts were every now and then being added to various *suras* by the order of Muhammad. So it is unanimously believed by the Sunnis that the different *ayat* of the Qur'an were placed in different *suras* by the definite orders of the Apostle.[27]

The present-day Shi'as quote some traditions of Imams that the *ayat* of many *suras* have been misplaced in the existing version of the Qur'an. This is, however, a serious allegation against the order of the *ayat*, as it makes the Qur'an a jumble of sentences haphazardly put together. This also means that in its present form, it is fairly difficult, if not impossible, to understand the meaning of the Qur'an. The Shi'a traditions on the point are not many, yet they are enough to create doubts about the original order of the *ayat* of the Qur'an. It should also be noted here in all fairness that only the later Shi'a writers have begun to create such doubts, basing their theories on some weak saying: the earlier authorities never doubted the authenticity of the order of the *ayat*. Whatever they say pertains only to the chronological order of the *ayat*, which does not prove any defect in the Qur'an, viz:

(i) Abu Hamza Isama'ili quotes from Imam Abu Ja'far that no one has collected (or learnt by heart) the Qur'an from among the people, according as the Gabriel had brought it down upon Muhammad. But this was done by the testator of Muhammad, *i.e.* 'Ali.[30]

(ii) Another tradition from *Kafi* and *Basa'ir al-Darajat* is: "Jabir says that he heard Abu Ja`far saying that no one will dare say that he has collected (or learnt by heart) the whole Qur'an as it was sent down (chronologically). If anyone asserts this then he will be called a great liar. The Qur'an has only been collected and learnt by heart, in the chronological order, by Ali b. Abi Talib, and the Imams after him."[30] One of the authorities of this tradition is Ahmad b. Muhammad Saiyari, who, according to Shi'a critic Shaikh al-Tai'fa is unreliable. This tradition is, therefore, not of much value. Moreover, it is absurd to think that `Ali could not have made public what he thought to be right, even in the days of his own Caliphate.

But, the Sunnis also hold the same view as the Shi'as, with, of course, a minor difference. They say that the arrangement of the texts in various *suras* is the same as dictated by the Apostle himself. Not only all the authorities concur on this point, but there are traditions which clearly point out that the arrangement of texts was done by the Apostle and was known to the numerous reciters of the Qur'an in his lifetime. For instance, the names of many *suras* were mentioned by the Apostle in which he pointed out certain passages to be read for special purposes. It means that many passages had already definite places fixed in different *suras*. This was the reason why 'Uthman said to Ibn al-Zubair that he had no authority to change the fixed position of the *ayat.*[27] Moreover, there are many books of learned divines who have tried to prove the present arrangement of the *ayat* to be a marvel of literary art. Zarkashi's *al-Burhan,* Shah Waliullah's *Fauz al-Kabir,* Razi's *Commentary* and other books have paid special attention to the mode of expression in the Qur'an. These, and other books on grammar, rhetoric and miraculous beauty of language (*i.e.* i'jaz) of the Qur'an invariably eulogize the present arrangement of the *ayat* in different *suras*. But it is admitted by the Sunnis that the *ayat* are not placed chronologically in the Qur'an. This does not mean that they are placed haphazardly in different passages. In fact, they prove it to be the best arrangement possible.

The second compilation was done a few months after the death of the Apostle. In this, 'Abdulla b. Mas'udi was not given a preference to Zaid. He naturally resented this action of the Caliph and *openly announced his disapproval* of the appointment.

Ibn Mas'ud was one of the oldest Muslims. Some say that he was the sixth Muslim. He had accepted Islam before the entry of the Apostle in the house of Arqam. He was a personal friend and servant of the Apostle, and kept his tooth-brush, water-pot and the sandals in the custody. He was one of those who had emigrated to Abyssynia, and later on took part in all the battles. The Apostle had announced to him the good news of his being a saved man whose abode will be Paradise. He also said: "I like what he likes for the Muslims, and I hate what he does not like for them." He was appointed the Qadi of Kufa during the Caliphate of `Umar. He was also the keeper of the public-treasury there. He remained at his post during the period of 'uthman also. He returned to Medina, and died there in A.H. 32.[31] Abdullah b. `Umar heard from the Apostle: "Take the Qur'an from four persons: Ibn Mas`ud, Mu`adh b. Jabal, Ubai b. Ka`b, and Salim, the slaves of `Abu Hudhaifa. And whosoever wishes to recite the Qur'an as it was revealed, he should recite according to the pronunciation of Ibn Mas'ud."[31]

"His claim that he knew every chapter and verse of the Qur'an, and the occasion and time of its revelation, was never questioned by anybody," says Abu Wa'il.[31] He was present also at the *last recital* of the Apostle, *i.e.*, in the year in which the Apostle died. So he knew every abrogation of the Qur'an[31, 32]

The preference of Zaid over Ibn Mas'ud was based on the fact that Zaid was one of the writers of the inspirations in the lifetime of Muhammad. He, therefore, knew more about the written fragments of *suras*, and he could compile them more easily. Moreover, he was very young, and the memory of youth is always preferable to the memory of old age.

It is not known whether Ibn Mas'ud could write in Mecca as in his early life he led a poor shepherd's life, tending the sheep of "Uqba b. Abi Mu'it, the arch-enemy of Islam. He was, no doubt, the oldest believer; but he had emigrated to Abyssynia, and it is certain that during this period he could not have learnt that part of the Qur'an which was revealed in his absence. He was present at the Battle of the Badr, and since then he must have taken a keen interest in learning the Qur'an. So the compilation from the written fragments could not be entrusted to one who perhaps wanted to dictate his memorized Qur'an to the compilers. If he knew writing, as can be gathered from the traditions about his written copy of the Qur'an, he was at liberty to write down his own version about the order of the *suras*. But so far as the arrangement of the *ayat* in different *suras* is concerned, we hear not a single word from him. He seems to have given his consent to the work done by Zaid, and he surely did not differ from the arrangement of *ayat*, as it was done according to the statement of the numerous oral reciters present at the occasion.

Later on we find him in a high office at Kufa, from where he was called back by *'Uthman* during his Caliphate. During all these years (A.H. 11 to A.H. 32) he had the fullest liberty to preach his system of reading of the Qur'an. He even had the backing of his office for his pronouncements.

Until A.H. 21, Ibn Mas'ud was in the city of Hims in Syria. After the resignation of Ziyad b. Hanzala, 'Ammar b. Yasir was appointed the Governor of Kufa. He was given a written order to the people of Kufa, which said that 'Ammar was being appointed governor, and 'Abdulla b. Mas'ud was being appointed teacher of religion. The basis of Islamic jurisprudence was the legal interpretations of Ibn Mas'ud. These were compiled by Imam Abu Hanifa and his companions, in the form of Hanafi Jurisprudence, later on. So he could promulgate his readings of the Qur'an in Syria, Hijaz and Iraq without any hindrance till that time.

Still later, we find him not only a judge, but also the Keeper of the *Bait al-mal* of Kufa. In A.H. 25 a quarrel arose between him and Sa'd b. Abi Waqqas, the governor of Kufa, about the return of a certain amount which Sa'd had borrowed from the public treasury. This was the beginning of the dissension of the people of Kufa. Half of them sided with the Qadi and another half with the Governor. Sa'd was later on relieved of his office by Caliph 'Uthman, but Ibn Mas'ud remained where he was.

After the death of Muhammad, the most important question was that of the election of his successor. The *ansar* of Medina had given the most vital support to the Apostle, when he was hard to find support in Mecca. Naturally, they thought that one of them should either become a ruler of the faithful, after the death of the Apostle, or at least a joint Caliph with a *muhajir* (emigrant). A disruption between the *ansar* and *muhajirun* was averted by the tactful and prompt handling of the situation by Abu Bakr, 'Umar and Abu 'Ubaida b. al-Jarrah. The conciliatory speech of Abu Bakr (quoted by Tabari) created the desired effect. Zaid b. Thabit and Bishr b. Sa'd, who were the leaders of the *ansar*, were converted to the views of the *muhajirun*, who supported them in their speeches and exhorted the *ansar* to follow their lead, and not to create difference in Islam. Abu Bakr then asked the people to swear allegiance to either 'Umar of Abu 'Ubaida. But they refused, and preferred Abu Bakr to this office. Bishr b. Sa'd Ansari was the first to swear allegiance to Abu Bakr, who was followed by the rest of the people present there.

'Ali b. Abu Talib could have created a havoc, if he so liked.

But he had lived all along with the Apostle, and no worldly avarice could lure him to aspire for the thorny leadership of the unruly Arabs. He wanted to serve the cause of Islam and kept quiet over this election.

"Abu Musa b. Uqba in his Maghazi (battles) records (likewise al Hakim verifies it on the authority of Abdur Rahman b. Auf) that Abu Bakr preached and spoke saying, "By Allah, I was never covetous of this authority, neither by day nor by night, nor desirous of it, nor asked it of God either in secret or openly, but I was in fear of sedition. I have no response in this authority. Verily I am invested with a mighty office, the power and capacity for which are not in me, save by the assistance of God." Then 'Ali and Al-Zubair said, "We were not incensed but for this, that we were put aside from consultation, yet we think Abu Bakr the most deserving of that authority among men, for he was the companion in the cave, and we indeed recognize his superiority and his excellence, and verily the Apostle of God, while he was yet alive, commanded him to lead the prayers".[33]

However, the later conduct of 'Ali shows that he did not take active part in any political or religious movement after the election of Abu Bakr. He began to learn the Qur'an by heart and kept to his house only. Suyuti says that Abu Bakr was told that 'Ali did not like his allegiance. So Abu Bakr sent for 'Ali, and asked him whether he disliked the allegiance. But 'Ali, said: "I do not come out of my house simply because I think that the Book of God will be added to, so I decided not to put on my toga, till I remember (or collect) the whole of the Qur'an". Abu Bakr praised him for his resolve.[34]

At the time of the collection of the Qur'an by Zaid, we do not hear the name of 'Ali as a helper to or a dissenter from the work. This would be a serious allegation against him, if we say, that he knowingly desisted from helping Zaid and 'Umar from the collection, as the future of Islam depended much on a proper collection of the Qur'an. Moreover, it was the injuction of the Apostle on his death-bed to follow the *kitab Allah*, This could not be done unless the Qur'an was collected in one place.

It is strange that some Shi'a authorities try to establish that although there are no interpolations in the Qur'an, yet the Qur'an of 'Ali was different from the present Qur'an.[35] The order of 'Ali's Qur'an is said to be chronological. This is unbelievable for the following reasons:

(i) All the texts were placed in different *suras* by the order of Apostle himself, and in that order they were memorized immediately by many Muslims. There was a special class of people devoted to this purpose only. They were called *ashab-i suffa*.

(ii) 'Ali was one of the bravest and the most honest persons of his time. He had lived long enough with the Apostle himself and he knew that dissembling of truth, specially in relation to the Qur'an, was more than blasphemy. In such a case it was not the fear of any opponents or fear of bloodshed, as some Shi'as have asserted,[36] but a genuine belief in the validity of the action of Abu Bakr, and the collection of Zaid.

(iii) There is a difference of opinion among the Sunnis themselves about the order of the *suras*. Some say that the present order was dictated by Muhammad himself, others deny it. Hence it is quite reasonable and probable that 'Ali had learnt the different *suras* chronologically. Yet that order is not followed even by the Shi'as. Ibn Hajar, in *Fath al-Bari (vol. ix, p.* 38), gives the order of the *suras* as read by 'Ali. Similarly Suyuti has given a list of *suras* as read by Ibn 'Abbas. But we do not find anything about the order of *suras* by 'Ali, much less of the *ayat*, in any of the Shi'a works. Ibn al-Nadim belonged to the Shi's sect, and he had seen the Qur'an written by 'Ali himself in the 4th century, which was in the possession of Abu Ya'la Hamza Husaini (*Fihrist, p.* 26). But he does not say in what the Qur'an of 'Ali differed from the present Qur'an. A real manuscript of 'Ali's hand exists in Meshhed. Some leaves in his handwriting are also in the archives of Shahi Masjid of Lahore.[37] These are not chronologically arranged.

(iv) 'Ali was all along helping his predecessors during their Caliphate. Sometimes he had to be critical, as when he resented the action of the electors in not calling him at the time of Abu Bakr's election. Later on he *rebuked* 'Uthman for an innovation in prayer during the pilgrimage, and 'Uthman apologized for not having curtailed the prayer as was the wont and precedent of the Apostle. Yet it is said that he kept silent at a time when the *ayat* of Qur'an were being misplaced or transposed by Zaid. It is unbelievable.

(v) Most of the Shi'a traditions, and a whole book, *viz., Nahj al-Balagha,* is stated to have been written or pronounced by 'Ali. This book which has been printed in two big volumes in Egypt, does not contain a list of the chronological order of the *suras* as collected by 'Ali. This is a further proof of the fact that 'Ali had not only consented but had given his active help in propagating the collection of Zaid.

(vi) Just as 'Abdullah b. Mas'ud, Abu Musa 'Ash 'ari, and every other Muslim had his own way of reading and writing the Qur'an up to A.H. 30, 'Ali also had the fullest opportunity to do so. Nay he had the advantage of being a Hashimi, and a very near relative of the Apostle. He could dictate his own chronology of *ayat* in different *suras* for more than 30 years. He himself was the Caliph from A.H. 34 to A.H. 40. During these years he could have done the greatest service to Islam by publishing his version of the Qur'an, if he had any.

But we, in all fairness to 'Ali, are bound to admit that the mud-throwing of later years has much to do with false traditions and stories about him. At the most he might have differed as to the order of the *suras*. This we shall discuss further. But so far as the order of the *ayat* in differents *suras* is concerned, it is certain that neither 'Ali nor Ibn Mas'ud could have done so against the established reading of various *suras* from the time of Muhammad.

The third official compilation was done during the Caliphate of 'Uthman. He was elected Caliph on Muharram 1, 24 A.H. (7th November, 677 A.D.) Muslim conquerors led their victorious men to distant countries, and a combined army to Hudhaifa b. Yaman, 'Abd al-Rahman b. Rabi's and Sa'id b. 'al 'As penetrated upto

Caucasus (Qafqaz). It was on his return from *Azerbaijan* (A.h. 22) that Hudhaifa marked the difference in pronunciation and readings of the Qur'an. He talked the matter to Sa'id b. al-'As who was the governor of Kufa. He said that the natives of Hims, Damascus, Basra and Kufa all differed in reading the Qur'an, and all of them thought that they only recited the Qur'an correctly. The people of Kufa rightly said that they had learnt the reading of the Qur'an from no less a man than Ibn Mas'ud. The people of Basra had learnt it from Abu Musa Ash'ari, whose Qur'an was called *Lubab al-Qulub* (Core of the Hearts). His reading must have been similar to that of 'Ali, as he was a staunch follower of 'Ali.

At this time, says Suyuti, the people of Kufa, and Ibn Mas'ud himself, declared that he was not ready to follow the readings of Zaid, who was a mere child when he had already leant more than 70 *suras* from the Apostle himself.[32]

Hudhaifa, however, came to Medina, and warned the Caliph against the threatening calamity, and asked him to save the nation before they began to differ like the Jews and Christians about their scriptures.

The sheets which were written during the Caliphate of Abu Bakr were sent for from the custody of Hafsa, the daughter of 'Umar, and the widow of the Apostle. A committee of four persons was appointed to copy the Qur'an from the sheets (*suhuf*) by Caliph 'Uthman.

According to al-Hakim, the third compilation was only an arrangement of the *suras*.[24] Till then the written copies of the different *suras* were only on loose sheets of skin (*suhuf*). This clearly shows that there was no order in the sheets so put together. The arrangement was done after the conquest of Armenia, i.e., in A.H. 29.

The basis of arrangement was, perhaps, the length of the different *suras*. The lengthier ones were put in the beginning and the smaller ones at the end. They were divided into four groups, according to their length:

(i) *Tiwal*, the seven lengthy *suras*. They are seven in number and are placed in the beginning, from No. 2 to No. 9.

(ii) *Ma'in*, or the *suras* containing more than hundred *ayat*. These were placed after the *tiwal*. They are twenty-six, from No. 10 to No. 35

(iii) *Mathani* are placed in the third group. They are the *suras* which are repeatedly recited in prayers and at other times. They are fifteen, from No. 36 to No. 50.

(iv) *Mufassal* is the name given to *suras* which are separated from each other very often. Mufassal also means an ornament or necklace strung with beads and pearls interlaced. These *suras* are, therefore, those which have a more ornamental or poetic style than the rest. They begin with *sura* No. 55, which is called the 'Bride of the Qur'an', and end with *sura* No. 114. Their total number is fifty.

Thus the different *suras* were arranged according to their length in four groups. This was done by a group of experts by order of the Caliph 'Uthman in A.H. 29-30. "Bukhari relates a tradition from Anas that Hudhaifa b. Al-Yaman came to 'Uthman from the front of Armenia and Azerbaijan and complained to the Caliph about the differences of the people in the reading of the different passages of the Qur'an. He exhorted 'Uthman to save the nation from this calamity before it was too late, as the Muslims differed regarding their scripture like the differences of Christians and Jews about theirs. *Then from the pieces of skin (suhuf), which were kept in the custody of hafsa, several copies of the Qur'an were compiled and put together as a book (mushaf).* The committee of transcribers consisted of four men: Zaid b. Thabit, 'Abdulla b. al-Zubair, Sa'id b. al-'As and 'Abdurrahman b. al-Harith b. Hisham. They were asked to write according to the dialect of the Quraish in case of difference about the pronunciation of a word among themselves. The latter three persons of the Committee belonged to the Quraish tribe, and this is significant that their motive was to rewrite the variants of pronunciation only according to the standard speech.[24]

"This version was copied in several volumes and sent out to important Muslim centres, viz., Kufa, Basra, Bahrain, Yemen, Syria, and Mecca. Only copy was kept at Medina by the Caliph himself. This was called Imam. It is said that some of these Qur'ans exist, even upto this day in Mecca, Medina and Damascus. According to Muir, the Imam of `Uthman was removed from Cordova to Fez, after the fall of the Muslim empire in Spain. Ibn Buttuta mentions this Qur'an to exist in the Mosque of Basra. Now it is said to belong to a Moscow Muslim, where it was brought in 1904 from Bokhara."[37]

*The suras of the Qur'an were divided into four groups, as noted above.* These groups do not conform to the title given to each group. It seems probable that the four writers wrote a group of *suras* each, and then they stitched them together in a form of book. What group was allotted to each of the writers cannot be conjectured with certainty. It may be said that Zaid had been specially assigned to write the *ma'in, i.e.,* the *suras* of the second group. This can be inferred from a tradition in which Zaid says that he lost one, *ayat i.e.*, No. 23 of *sura* No. 33 at the time of the transcription (from the MSS), which they found in the Qur'an of Khudhaima b. Thabit, and placed it in its proper place in the *sura.* Hence, he must have been specially interested with the second group, which contains *sura* No. 33. This conjecture also may explain the fact that the *suras* of different groups do not contain the number of *ayat* in descending order. In fact, some of the longer *suras* are contained in groups which should contain shorter *suras*.

The difference between the second and the third compilations is that Abu Bakr ordered the second compilation to be simply collected together (one loose sheets of skin) so that no portion of it may be lost, as it was not collected in one place. So he arranged the different texts and *suras* according to the orders of the Apostle.

"`Uthman corrected the different pronunciations, and preferred the known readings of the Apostle," says Qadi Abu Bakr in *al-Intisar*.[27] Al-Harith al-Muhasibi also says that it was current among the people that `Uthman was the *Collector of the Qur'an, whereas he only caused men to follow one reading*.[27] He also followed the arrangement of the *suras* by the official committee.

There were some dissenters from the view of the committee as to the order of the *suras*, as well as from the various readings of the Qur'an which the official committee had recommended. But, as the weight of the official committee was greater in respect of the pronunciations, the majority of Muslims followed it, and no one demurred when an order of burning away the copies containing the unauthorized readings of the Qur'an was given by the Caliph. Some important *supporters of* this version of the Qur'an could have been the followers of 'Ali, and Ibn Mas'ud. Their conduct is noted below.

(i) "'Ali," says Ameer Ali, was "endeavouring in Medina to give an intellectual turn to the newly developed energy of the Saracenic race, whilst Islam was extending its sway in distant parts (31 A.H./652 A.D.). In the public mosque at Medina, 'Ali and his cousin, 'Abdullah ibn 'Abbas delivered weekly lectures on philosophy and logic, the traditions (history), rhetoric and law, whilst others dealt with other subjects. Thus was formed the nucleus of that intellectual movement which displaced itself in such great force later times at Baghdad."[38]

He is not heard of dissenting from the collection of 'Uthman. He might have had his own arrangement of the *suras*, but that is not found anywhere. Ibn Hajar says that he had collected (or learnt by heart) the Qur'an, according to the chronological order, after the death of the Apostle. The conduct of his Shi'as (or partisans) also confirms the view that he allowed the 'Uthmanic arrangement to be followed by all.

(ii) *Ibn 'Abbas* was another famous interpreter of the Qur'an. He knew the chronological arrangement of the *suras* which is described by Suyuti in *al-Itqan*. A copy of the Qur'an, according to the order of the *suras* by Ibn 'Abbas, can be seen in manuscript in the Khuda Bakhsh Oriental Library of Patna. This copy contains some spurious *suras* in praise of 'Ali and his family which according to Shi'a authorities are later compilations and interpolations.

(iii) *Ibn Mas'ud*. Important differences of readings are marked on the margins of every Qur'an. Some of them are Ibn Mas'ud's. He had also arranged his Qur'an differently—as regards the *suras*—from that of the official compilation. But this arrangement is not chronological (see further). He is also said to have included *tashahhud* in the Qur'an. This is a small passage read in prayers. Moreover, all the traditions concur on this point that he had excluded *suras* 113 and 114 from his Qur'an. But Nawawi (in *Sharh Tahdhib*) and Ibn Hazm both deny this as a false attribution to Ibn Mas'ud.[39]

The order of *suras* arranged by Ibn Mas'ud is different from the present Qur'an, though it is not chronological.

Ibn Mas'ud was called back from Kufa to Medina by Caliph 'Uthman. The people of Kufa wanted to restrain him from going to Medina, and were ready to help him against any oppression. But he replied that he had to obey the orders of the Caliphate and did not want to create differences and discord.[32]

However, he had the satisfaction of preaching his method of reading and pronunciation for more than twenty years. The result is that every Qur'an contains his readings also, in the form of footnotes.

His differences with Zaid were, as we shall see later on, based purely on the principles of phonetics. According to Ibn al-Nadim, all the copies of the Qur'an of Ibn Mas'ud differ from each other in the order of the *suras*.[40]

(iv) *Ubai b. Ka'b*. He is one of the four persons mentioned in a tradition of Bukhari who learnt the whole of the Qur'an by heart.[41] The Apostle had ordered Muslims to learn the Qur'an from him. He was a native of Medina and an Ansar.[41] He was present at the time of the second compilation in the days of Abu Bakr. He had also corroborated the evidence of Abu Khudhaima about the two verses of the Qur'an being a part of *sura* No. IX.[26] According to Ibn al-Nadim he had compiled his copy of the Qur'an at a village, which was at a distance of two *farsang* from Basra. This village was called Qaryat al-Ansar. His order of the different *suras* is also given by him.[42]

All this goes to prove that he was present at the time of the second collection during the Caliphate of Abu Bakr, and no order of *suras* was published at that time. Had they agreed to some order of the *suras*, Ubai would not have arranged his Qur'an on the basis of a different order.

(v) *'A'isha.* She was the widow of Muhammad. It was her house in which the Apostle died, and lies buried. Perhaps it was from this very room that the first written fragments of the Qur'an were collected and arranged by Zaid. She lived constantly with him during the last years of his life in Medina. She very often gave legal advice and religious decisions, basing her arguments on the Qur'an and the *sunna*. She had her own copy of the Qur'an. It is related by Bukhari that a man from Iraq come to her and asked her to lend him her copy, so that he might arrange the *suras* according to it. He said that the people read the Qur'an without any special order. She replied that there was no harm if a *sura* was read before another *sura.* Then she described the details of the method of Divine revelation. "In the beginning," she said, "small *suras* were revealed, in which heaven and hell were mentioned. When the number of Muslims increased, the teaching of lawful and unlawful began. If it was ordered all of a sudden to leave drinking wine or adultery, the people would have never left wine, and they would have persisted in adultery". Thus a real system of revolution by means of evolution was followed by the Apostle. The secret of the chronology of the Qur'an is also the secret of the Apostle's success. "Then 'A'isha gave her Qur'an to the 'Iraqi, who corrected his copy according to it."

It is clear that 'A'isha had a copy of the Qur'an which had some arrangement of the *suras*. Perhaps it was also a collection of loose sheets as was the original copy of Zaid's compilation. She also thought that no sequence of *suras* was necessary for reading the Qur'an, but if a man wanted to study the development of the Qur'an he had to follow the above rule laid down by her.

She is not reported to have differed from the official compilation for publication done by 'Uthman. If there was any departure from the original method adopted by her father, Abu Bakr, she would certainly have raised a voice against any innovation in the days of 'Uthman, *viz.*, at the time of the final compilation.

Caliph 'Uthman gave the first official version of the complete Qur'an to the Muslims in A.H. 30. Till then people relied on their memories primarily, and on their notes is the second place. But numerous mistakes had crept in the text, as it usual with a people who have just begun reading and writing. Most of them combined military pursuits with literary accomplishments. But as it was the first mark of a Muslim to be able to say his prayers, every one had to know more or less of the Qur'an.

During his Caliphate, 'Umar had done a great deal for the spread of the text of the Qur'an. Many Muslim men and women had memorized the whole of the Qur'an by heart. He, therefore, appointed paid teachers of the Qur'an, and compulsory education of the village folk (Bedouins) was inaugurated. One Abu Sufyan was appointed an inspector of Arab students. He was authorized to punish those who did not know a passage of the Qur'an. Mu'adh b. Jabal, 'Ubaida b. Thabit, Ubai b. Ka'b and Abu Darda' were sent to Syria to teach the Qur'an. Ibn Jauzi and Ibn Sa'd have given details of this system. A great impetus was perhaps given to the study of the Qur'an by the system of stipends and annuities which were paid to the learners.[43]

The attention of 'Uthman was drawn to the fact that mistakes were slowly creeping in the text of the Qur'an. He, therefore, issued an official copy in A.H. 30, and caused all the other copies to be burnt. It is said that there is a saying of the Apostle that Qur'an was revealed in seven kinds of meanings (*ahruf*). *Ahruf* is also translated to mean reading, pronunciation, point of view (*wajh*) or object of speech. This tradition, which is reported by Bukhari and others, is the nucleus of controversy and argument about the different readings which had crept in the Qur'an. Many other traditions of similar nature are narrated to explain away the fact that people read the Qur'an with not only different pronunciations, but with obviously different texts.

'Uthman caused the Qur'an to be compared from the original loose sheets in A.H. 30. Thus, for a period of 19 years (A.H. 11 to A.H. 30) the people not only learnt the different readings by heart but multiplied its copies. If 'Uthman could burn away the spurious writings it could not have been possible for him to erase the wrong words or passages from their memories. Moreover, it is not possible for a man of a different race or nationality to speak a language with as much a phonetic accuracy as the man who is brought up with a certain language of his own.

The second collection was written down by Zaid, who was a Medinite. But he must have written it as he heard from the Apostle himself. Even then it was feared that some mistakes in writing might creep in, and therefore he was guided by three persons of Quraish when he re-wrote the Qur'an in the days of Caliph 'Uthman.

We are not concerned here with the mistakes or variations which other people had done during this period of 19 years when no official copy was issued to him. In fact, they were novices in the art of writing and they could write whatever they thought correct. These mistakes of those not purely Meccan Companions of the Apostle may be summed up under the following heads:

(i) *Phonetic digressions.* Owing to the numerous non-Arab conversions to Islamit was natural that they pronounced certain words differently than the natives of Mecca. Even non-Quraish tribes had different kinds of pronunciation, e.g. (12:35) *'atta for hatta* (Ibn Mas'ud), (1:4) *hiyaka* for *iyaka*, and *tabuh* for *tabut*.[44]

(ii) *Mistakes in writing.* Writing was in its early stages in Arabia when people embraced Islam. They were keen to learn the writing because of the Qur'an. They committed many mistakes in writing Qur'an, and those mistakes would have been perpetuated if an authorized version was not issued promptly. Some people still attributed their mistakes to such men as Ibn Mas'ud, Ubai, 'Ali, Ibn 'Abbas and other authorities on *qir'at*, and persisted in writing their unauthorized versions. But as the majority of the companions of the Apostle had pronounced their verdict that the 'Uthmanic version was the only true version, these variants died out soon. Yet some of these were noted down either in good faith or by ingenious grammarians and readers to show their art. Instances of such a false show of learning are found in the readings proposed by Ibn Shambudh and Ya'qub, who acknowledged their crime after a chastisement from the Caliph and his Vizier.[45]

Variants due to writing do not matter. This can be understood only by those who know the peculiarities of the Arabic script. Short vowels were marked with the consonant in earlier days. They were invented later on. Even nowadays few books are printed with vowel marks. No non-Arab can read an Arabic book or newspaper without a good knowledge of Arabic grammar. It is quite unlike the Latin or Sanskrit scripts which contain vowel sounds marked in between the words while writing. Such mistakes, if mistakes they can be called, were many. It may be said that it was a form of writing of early Arab Muslims. Perhaps owing to a sense of reverence or fear of change, no attempt has yet been made to made the Qur'anic script up to date. Much advance has been made in the ordinary Arabic script, yet the Qur'an remains as it was first written in the days of Abu Bakr. It is difficult to give instances of writing to those who do not know Arabic script, yet the following examples may convey an idea of the Qur'anic script. What is written as *dhakut* and *salut* is read as *zakat* and *salat*. Similarly, *daht, aqai taghi* is readad as *dahi aqsa* and *tagha*.

But sometimes, the careless scribes dropped or increased a letter while copying. A few such mistakes may be noted down here.

2:116 *qalu for wa qalu.*

2:132 *wa ausa for wa wassa*

18:36 *Khairam minhuma* for *Khairam minha.*

21:30 *a lam yara* for *a wa lam yara.*

25:25 *wa nunzila* for *wa nuzzila.*

26:217 *fa twakkal* for *wa twakkal.*

36:35 *'amilat* for *'Amilathu.*

40:2 *minkum* for *minhum.*

40:26 *na an* for *au an.*

46:15 *hasana* for *ihsana*

57:24 *ghani* for *huwa'l-Ghani*

91:15 *fala* for *wala.*[46]

(iii) *Insertion of Comments*[47]. Sometimes the owner of a copy of a Qur'an inserted a note explaining certain words. This was not meant to form of the original text of the Qur'an. But when it passed on to the hands of others, they copied the whole thing *in toto,* and thought that it was a part of the Qur'an. Examples are:

2:22 *bisatan* (Yazid b. Asma'i) and *mitradan* (Talha) for firashan.
27:36 *Qasibatan* (Ibn Mas'ud) for *qati'atan.*
16:39 *la hadiya* (Ibn Mas'ud) for *la yahdi.*
4:44 *namla* (Ibn Mas'ud) for *gharra.*
26:61 *tara'at-il fi'atan* (anonymous) for *tara al-jam'an.*
89:26 *almutmaina* (Ubai) for *al-Nafs,* or it may have been written above *al-mutma'inna* as a meaning of the word, and not for *al-Nafs.*[48]

(iv) *Reading translation only*. There were some people who read the translation of the Qur'an only, and did not care for the original text. It is not known definitely who those persons were. It was however well known to Muslims generally that there were some companions of the Apostle who allowed it. The denial of this fact by Suyuti in *Itqan* is the only proof that some idea of this kind existed there.

It might have been those persons who wanted to create disunity and heresy is Islam, or it might have been the ingenuity of later writers and scholastics. Suyuti says: "And the person who says that some of the companions of the Apostle allowed (made in lawful) to read the translation of the Qur'an only is surely a liar. This kind of reading is termed *mudraj*, meaning increased in writing.[47]

Instances of such reading are given above (No. iii). A few more are as follows:

| | |
|---|---|
| 26:3 | *lau shi'na l'anzalna, for in nasha'u nunazzilu.* |
| 26:166 | *aslaha* (Ibn-Mas'ud), for *Khalaqa.* |
| 5:42 | *faqta'u aimanahum* for *faqta'u aidiyahum.* |
| 3:5 | has three readings: |
| 1 | *in taviluhu illa' indallah* (Ibu Mas'ud). |
| 2 | *wa ma ya'lamu taviluha illa'llah, wa qal al-rasikhun* etc. (Ubai). |
| 3 | *wa ma ya'lamu taviluha illa'llh, wa'Irasikhuna fi'l'ilm yaquluna* etc. (authorized version). |
| 4:23 | *wa ummahatu nisa'ikum* is not given by Ali, Ibn 'Umar, Zaid b. 'Ali and Ibn al-Zubair. |
| 25:1 | Instead of *li'l 'alamin,* Ibn al Zubair has *li'ljinni wa'l-insi* (it is clearly an explanation of *li'l 'alamin*). |
| 101:4 | *al-suf* for *al-'Ihn.* (*Fath al-Bari*, vol. ix, p. 19). |

Qadiu Abu Bakr denies all these traditions about variations in readings in his book *al-Intisar*. He says that all these reports are *ahad*, i.e. non-corroborated traditions of single reporters. There being an overwhelming concurrence of reports about the authenticity of the texts of the Qur'an, these single reporters cannot be relied upon.[49]

Tabrasi, an important Shi'a commentator, quoting Sharif Murtuda says in his commentary *Majma'al-Bayan* that the Qur'an was completely arranged in the life-time of the Apostle as it is now.[50]

In the end, we may note that there are many words in Arabic which themselves have different readings, but these readings do not affect their meanings. For instance, *kabd* may be read *kabid: kataf* may be read *katif* or *kitf; ladun, ladni, ludni; lad, lud, ludu; malik, malik; anjaina, najjaina* etc.

We may note also that there is only one evidence about the readings of the Qur'an (ahad), not corroborated by several independent witnesses (*mutawatir*). Therefore they cannot stand comparison with the present Qur'an which is reported by numberless authorities to be the same which was given by Apostle Muhammad.

## NOTES AND REFERENCES

1. Religious systems of the world. London, 1891, p. 292.
2. Margoliouth, Mohammad. London, 1905, p. xxviii.
3. Lanepole, Speeches and tabletalk of Mohammad, p. viii.
4. Ibn Hisham: sira (see Badr)
5. Ibn Hazm, Kitab al-Nasikh w`al Mansukh.
6. Abu Nuaim Isfahani, Dala` il-Nubuwa, vol 1, p. 79.
7. Quran 46: 78
8. Ibn Hazm, p. 213.
9. Ibid., pp. 213-14.
10. Ibn Abd al-Barr of Cordova, Kitab al-Istiab fi marifat al-ashab, Hyderabad, 1336 A H., vol I, p. 27
11. Ibid., p. 188.
12. Shibli Numani, Sirat al-Nabi, vol. II, p. 65.
13. Ibn Abd al-Barr, op cit., vol. I, p. 189.

14. Ibid., p. 188.
15. Ibid., vol. II, p. 435.
16. Ameer Ali, A short History of the Saracens, pp. 22-23.
17. Ibn al-Athir, al-Kamil, vol. II, p. 152.
18. Jarret, History of the Caliphs, Calcutta, 1887. p. 76.
19. Ibid., p. 77
20. Ibid., p. 78.
21. al-Suyuti, al-Itqan fil ulum il-Quran, Calcutta, 1854, p. 57.
22. al-Hakim Nishapuri, al-Mutadrik ala l-Sahihain, Hyderabad, 1334 AH, vol. II, p. 229.
23. al-Suyuthi, op cit., p. 58.
24. Ibid., p. 59.
25. Ibid., p. 52.
26. Ibid., p. 61.
27. Ibid., p. 60
28. Ibid., p. 55.
29. Syed Ali Naqi, Tahrif-i-Quran ki Haqiqat, Lucknow, 1933, p. 64.
30. Ibid., p. 168.
31. Ibn Abd al-Barr, Kitab al Istilab, p. 359; see also al-Burhanpuri, Kanz al-Ummal fi Sunan al-aqwal wal afal.
32. Ibid., p. 361.
33. Jarret, History of the Caliphs, p. 70.
34. al-Suyuti, al-Itqan, p. 57-8.
35. Syed Ali Naqi, Tahrif -i- Quran... p. 168.
36. Ibid., p. 106.
37. Aslam Jairajpuri, Tarikh al-Quran, Aligarh, 1341 AH.
38. Ameer Ali, p. 47.
39. al-Suyuti, p. 75.
40. Ibn al-Nadim, Fihrist, p. 26.
41. al-Suyuti, p. 70

42. Ibn al-Nadim, p. 28
43. Shibli Numani, Maqala -i- Madhabi, Azamgarh, 1930, pp. 20-21.
44. Aslam Jairajpuri, p. 56.
45. Ibid., p. 72.
46. Noldeke, Geschichte der Qorans, pp. 240-1.
47. al-Suyuti, p. 77.
48. Noldeke, p. 271.
49. al-Suyuti, p. 26.
50. Aslam Jairajpuri, p. 63.

---

**(Revised and edited; originally published in Studies in Islam, vol. 1, 1964).**

# 7

# Abraham in the Qur'an

**FRIDAY M. MBON**

Discusses the comparative references on Abraham, as seen in Quran and the Bible, with a special emphasis on his ideal as Hanif, the true monotheist, described in the Quran.

Abraham was not a Jew, nor yet a Christian, but he was a *Hanif* resigned, not of the idolaters. Verily, the people most worthy of Abraham are those who follow him and his prophets, and those who believe... Say, 'God speaks the truth, then follow the faith of Abraham, a *hanif*, who was not of the idolaters. (Qur'an : 60,89)[1].

Say: 'As for me, my Lord has guided me to a straight path, a right religion, the creed of Abraham a man of pure faith; he was no idolater.' (Qur'an 6:162)

November 21, 1979, was another milestone in Islamic history, as it marked the fourteenth centennial of the founding of Islam. It is appropriate, therefore, that, as the memory of this historic event is yet fresh in our minds, we reflect on the man whom the Qur'an recognizes as the spiritual founder of this religion. This essay is an attempt to reconstruct from the Qur'an what seems to be the manifold role of Abraham in the foundation and development of a religion which has influenced the lives of millions throughout the ages, this in spite of its name in world politics.[2]

This importance of the person of Abraham in Islamic religious history and thought cannot be over-emphasized. So significant is this ancient patriarch that reference is made to him in many *surahs* of the Qur'an.[3] Apart from Moses, Abraham is the only prophet mentioned so frequently in the Qur'an.

Just as there are many, often conflicting *hadiths* about the person of the Prophet Muhammad, so with the patriarch Abraham.[4] The present essay, however, does not go into all the Islamic legends about Abraham; it simply concentrates on the Quranic conception of the patriarch's role in the formation of Islam. At such, the Qur'an, since most orthodox Muslim consider it to be the primary and unimpeachable source of Muslim beliefs, is almost the sole source of the information presented herein.

**I. Abraham as the Physical Ancestor of Arab Muslims**

It will be obvious from later sections of the discussion that the Qur'an considers Abraham to be the spiritual ancestor of all Muslims since his time. But Abraham is more than just a spiritual ancestor of Muslim; he is also considered to be the physical ancestor of Arab Muslims through his son Ishmael. All three of the great monotheistic religions—Judaism, Christianity and Islam—attribute to Ishmael and ancestry of the Arabs.[5] It is significant that Ishmael, as well shall see, is also connected with the spiritual foundation of the Muslim world in general, and of the Arabs in particular, in that the Qur'an associates him and his father abraham with the founding of the Ka'ba in Mecca. Thus the Arabs are the physical members of the family of Abraham through Ishmael, and upon this family God has bestowed a special book of wisdom (4:54). Abraham is anxious that this incipient family of Allah and its progeny would remain loyal to the way and requirements of Allah, hence his prayer for them:

> My Lord,
> make this land secure, and turn me
> and my sons away from serving idols;
> my Lord, they have led astray many men,
> Then who so follows me belongs to me;
> and whose rebels against me, surely Thou

> art All-forgiving, All-compassionate.
> Our Lord, I have made some of my seed to
> dwell in a valley where is no sown land
> by Thy Holy House; Our Lord, let them
> perform the power, and make hearts of
> men yearn towards them, and provide them
> with fruits; haply they will be thankful.[6]

With its characteristic Arabic cultural distrust of ethnic or tribal "chosenness" or superiority, the Qur'an does not, however, subscribe to the Judeo-Christian tradition which views Abraham as the founder of a hereditary community of a chosen people. Rather, it sees in Abraham a courageous prototype and pattern of the Prophet Muhammad, the founder of a non-hereditary or non-familial community. In the Qur'an, Abraham is said to be the guide or leader (*imam*) of a non-hereditary community of God's people:

> And when his Lord tested Abraham
> with certain words, and he fulfilled them.
> He said, 'Behold, I make you a leader
> for the people.' Said he, 'And of my seed?'
> He said 'My covenant shall not reach
> the evildoers.[7]

This passage, obviously, is reminiscent of Genesis 14 and 22, where the biblical abraham also plays the role of the leader of God's people. The difference between the biblical and the Quranic concepts of God's people under Abraham lies, however, in the fact that in the latter concept emphasis is placed not on hereditary but on individual piety. Hence, the Qur'an does away with the idea of Isaac's rightful hereditary relationship to Abraham, and elevates Ishmael to a position of close association with Abraham in the all-important task of erecting the Meccan Ka'ba, thus making the entire undertaking completely Arabic (since Ishmael represents the Arabs, and Abraham a fore-runner of the Meccan Prophet). The community (*millah*) of Quranic Abraham is made up not of people of the same family or hereditary roots, but of people of any religious affiliation and commitment who have come to worship and be committed to the one true God, Allah. As Rev. E.F.F. Bishop is reported to have said. "it is only as children that relationship with Abraham becomes worth-while, and friends of God are brought into being pulsating with the warmth of close human relationships."[8] The stories of how Abraham and later, the Prophet Muhammad forsook their kin, in order to submit to the will of God, speak eloquently to support the fact that the religion of Abraham is not based on the family tree principle. In fact, the Prophet Muhammad is reported to have said on entering Mecca: "God has put an end to the pride in noble ancestry, you are all descended from Adam and Adam from dust, the noblest among you is the man who is most pious."[9] Thus, at the advent of Islam tribal or kin relations gave way to the brotherhood of all who process Islam.

Abraham's *millah* becomes a type of Islamic community under the Prophet Muhammad, comprising not only the Arabs, but peoples of other races and nations who come to embrace the new faith. Indeed, the emergence of Islam was to help eliminate kin relations by continuing in the tradition of Abraham, making Mecca the sole centre of monotheistic worship, which mode of worship served as an element of unity and solidarity among the different tribes of Mecca. The Prophet Muhammad naturally turned this element of monotheism to his best advantages in his political activities both in Mecca and Medina. Under Islam, all men are to be clients of God, the only patron, and, consequently, of His last of Seal of the prophets. Says the Qur'an:

> And warn therewith those who feat they shall be mustered to their Lord; they have, apart from God, no protector and no intercessor; haply they will be godfearing.[10]

Indeed, that the Muslim religion is not a religion based on blood relationships may be stressed further by reference to this traditional saying: "There are no genealogies in Islam."[11]

A second major difference between the Abraham in Genesis and Quranic Abraham lies in this; in Genesis, Abraham is commanded to leave an idolatrous people, emigrate to a strange land, and establish a new, God-fearing community. In the Qur'an, on the other hand, Abraham is not commanded to emigrate; instead, he is urged to denunciate idolatry where he is. We shall come back to this point in connection with the patriarch's struggle against the idolatry of his father and his tribesmen.

**II. Abraham as Prophet**

Abraham is also given a prophetic role in the Qur'an: "And mention in the Book Abraham; surely he was a true man, a Prophet" (19:42). Like other prophets before and after him, he has the prophetic and apostolic responsibility of admonishing and warning his people against the inevitable sad consequences of wilful disobedience to the will of God.[12] It is not quite clear from the Qur'an, however, whether Abraham's prophethood is that of a *rasul*—the prophet who brings divine message or information through a book—as opposed to a *nabi*—a prophet who brings divine information to his people orally.[13] Nevertheless, it does appear from 53:38 and 83:18-19 that Abraham may have left behind a written revelation. In the former passage reference is made to "... The scrolls of Moses and Abraham." But to prove the point either way probably requires another essay.

In *Surah* 14, which is dedicated to and almost exclusively deals with him, Abraham is portrayed as a prophet with a Book which has been sent down (*tanzil*), by which Book he is commanded to "bring forth mankind from the shadows to light by the leave of their Lord, to the path of the All-mighty, the All-laudable, God, to whom belongs all that is in the heavens and all that is in the earth" (14:1). Also, in this *surah* the message Abraham is to give to all mankind is unequivocally spelled out:

> This is a Message to be delivered to mankind
> that they may be warned by it,
> and that they may know that He
> is One God,

and that all possessed of minds may remember.[14]

This message is the unique characteristic and foundation of the religion of Abraham and, subsequently, of the Prophet Muhammad.

**III. Abraham as Founder of Monotheism**

The Qur'an specifically calls attention to Abraham's role as the founder of monotheism.[15] He is credited with attacking and destroying idol worship or the association of "partner gods" with Allah. To Abraham, and later to the Prophet Muhammad, this association of "partner gods' with Allah is polytheism or better, syntheism (Arabic *shirk*). *Surah* 37 gives this trenchand account of the patriarch's struggle against the idolatry of his father and his countrymen:

Of his party was also Abraham;
when he came unto his Lord with
a pure heart,
when he said to his father and his folk,
'What do you serve?
Is it a calumny, gods apart from God.
that you desire?
What think you then of the Lord
of all Being?" And he cast a glance at the stars,
and he said, 'Surely I am sick.'
But they went away from him,
turning their backs.
Then he turned to their gods and said,
'What do you eat?
What ails you, that you speak not?'
And he turned upon them smiting them
with his right hand.
Then came the others to him hastening.
He said, 'Do you serve what you hew,
and God created you and what you make'?

> They said, 'Build him a building, and cast him into the furnace!'[16]

Compare this passage with 19:41-50:

> And mention in the Book Abraham;
> surely he was a true man, a Prophet.
> When he said to his father, 'Father,
> why worshippest thou that which neither
> hears not sees, nor avails thee anything?
> Father, there has come to me knowledge
> such as came not to thee; so follow me,
> and I will guide thee on a level path.
> Father, serve not Satan; surely Satan
> is a rebel against the All-merciful.
> Father, I fear that some chastisement
> from the All-merciful will smite thee,
> so that thou becomest a friend to Satan.'
> Said he, 'What, art thou shrinking
> from my gods, Abraham? Surely, if thou
> givest not over, I shall stone thee;
> so forsake me now for some while.'
> He said, 'Peace be upon thee!
> I will ask my Lord to forgive thee;
> surely He is even gracious to me.
> Now I will go apart from you
> and that you call upon, apart from
> God; I will call upon my Lord,
> and haply I shall not be, in calling
> upon my Lord, unprosperous.'
> So, when he went apart from them
> and that they were serving, apart
> from God, We gave him Isaac and

Jacob, and each We made a Prophet;
and We gave them of Our mercy,
and We appointed unto them
a tongue of truthfulness, sublime.[17]

Thus, Abraham forever breaks away from the traditional way of worship of his father and his compatriots, and establishes, once and for all time, the true (monotheistic) way of worship.

In connection with the founding of monotheism, Abraham, assisted by his son Ishmael, erects in Mecca and Ka'ba, the "House of God" (*Bait-Allah*), as the centre of pilgrimage (*hajj*) and makes it into a place of complete monotheistic belief.[18] It is significant that it is Ishmael, not Isaac, whom the Qur'an associates with the building of the Ka`ba. The significance of this association lies in the fact that in recognizing Ishmael as the co-builder of the place for pure (that is, monotheistic) worship, the Qur'an departs, as we have remarked, from the Judeo-Christian tradition which makes Isaac the hereditary successor of Abraham, thus rejecting the entire hereditary principal.[19] In the Quranic preference of Ishmael over Isaac lies the whole Judeo-Christian-Muslim religio-political and historical controversy.

As monotheism is the most outstanding distinguishing mark of Islam, the non-confession of which is the one unforgivable sin in Muslim thought, it is understandable why this religion has come to be referred to simply as the party or community or the religion of Abraham *(millat Ibrahim)*, and Abraham himself given the epithet *hanif* (one who follows the original and true—monotheistic—religion) to which is often added that he was not an idolater.[20] In 4:124, in addition to his being referred to as *hanif*,[21] he is honorifically described also as the friend of God (*Khalil Allah*),[22] an appellation which is reminiscent of Isaiah 41:8, 2 Chron. 20:7, and James 2:23, where also Abraham is referred to as the friend of God. Hence, Abraham becomes the friend of God just as Moses is called the Spokesman of God (*Kalim Allah*)[23] and Jesus the Word of God (*Kalimat Allah*).[24] In his role as the *hanif*, Abraham, then, represents what a true worshipper ought to be, not only in the Arabic or Muslim community but universally. He becomes, therefore, the founder of true universal religious faith, his religion being the model for universal religion.

When the pagans ("polytheists" is probably a better word here) in Mecca oppose and attack the Prophet Muhammad for introducing monotheism, and accuse him of ignoring the traditional polytheistic belief of his forebears, the Prophet, in answer to this accusation, appeals to the religion of Abraham, pointing out to his opponents that he, in fact, is no innovator, but that he is following the true tradition—the tradition of the monotheistic religion of Abraham and of those prophets before him, such as Adam and Noah, to whom God has also revealed Himself. The Prophet further points out to his antagonists that is the only true tradition to which all true worshippers must adhere, be they Arabs, Jews, or Christians. This point is particularly significant in view of the Quranic claim that before Jews and Christians, Abraham was[25]. Abraham, says the Qur'an, is the guide of all the peoples of the world in matters of true religion (2:118).

Also, when the Prophet's prophetic office is called into question by the Jews and Christians of Medina, Qur'an (then scattered and not in the form in which we have it today) is appealed to, to meet the intellectual criticism and skepticism of the Jews and Christians. By developing the conception of the religion of Abraham in which the patriarch is said to be the *hanif*, the founder and follower of the true religion and a true prophet, the Qur'an affirms that Prophet Muhammad is a follower of this religion and, therefore, a true prophet, and that he is restoring the pure monotheism of Abraham which has been corrupted by Jews and christians.[26]

## IV. Abraham as Proto type of the Prophet Muhammad

Muhammad refers to Abraham as the first Muslim[27] and regards him as "the champion of a pure monotheistic faith,"[28] maintaining that Abraham, together with Ishmael, the ancestor of the Arabs, builds the Ka'ba and introduces the ceremonies of the Pilgrimage.

It is thus that Abraham becomes "the most important forerunner of the Arabian Prophet."[29] According to interpretation of the Qur'an, Abraham is believed to have actually lived in Mecca at which time he and Ishmael are said to have founded the Ka'ba and spread the pure monotheistic faith.[30] Non-Muslims, however, regard this view as nothing other than one of the unprovable *hadiths* of Islamic faith, and even go as far as to reject any mention of Abraham in the so-called Meccan *surahs*.[31] Alfred Guillaume, a typical exponent of this view, states:

> It is interesting to observe that, though the Meccan *suras* contain numerous references to Abraham, they do not assign him that position of paramount importance he obtained as the result of the more accurate information Muhammad acquired when the mixed daily with the flourishing community of Jews in Medina.[32]

Others (mostly Muslims), on the other hand, believe that in Medina the Prophet was "merely expanding and adapting to present circumstances an idea with which he had been familiar in his Meccan days."[33] For instance, A.J. Wensinck has commented on Muhammad's thought concerning Abraham thus: "In the earlier Surahs[34] he (Abraham) is an Apostle of God, fills the usual apostolic role of warner to his people, but does not yet appear as the founder of the Ka'bah or the first Muslim. In the Medinan Surahs, on the other hand, he is called *Hanif*, Muslim and founder of the Ka'bah."[35] Wensinck's explanation of the Prophet's seemingly changing view of Abraham's role in both Mecca and Medina, is that in Mecca the Prophet had appealed to the Jews, but in Medina where they turned against him, the Prophet was forced to find new support for the validity of his prophethood, hence his appealing to the tradition of the religion of Abraham, and his referring to the patriarch and the first Muslim and the precursor of Islam.[36] Richard Bell, on the other hand, is inclined to place 6: 74, 80-82 in the Meccan period, and only verses 75-79, 83 of *Surah* Six (which Wensinck places in the Meccan period) in the Medinan period, classifying this entire passage dealing with Abraham's dispute with his idol worshipping compatriots, as "Meccan scraps, revised in Medina."[37]

This matter belongs, obviously, to the larger and more complex question of the chronology of the Qur'an, and therefore needs another essay or even a thesis. But suffice it to say here that, since no one is *altogether sure* what *surahs* of the Qur'an belong to the so-called Meccan and Medinan periods respectively, and since the history of the chronology of the Quranic material seems to indicate that there is the possibility that revelations of the Meccan period may have been repeated during the Medinan period, and since the Medinan *surahs* make mention of events known to have occurred in Mecca, it seems to refrain from any dogmatic, categorical pronouncements as to which "Abrahamic" passages belong to the Meccan period and which to the Medinan. Historically speaking, it seems logical to argue, as does Guthrie, that

> it is after Muhammad has settled in Medina that we get the most significant references to Abraham. The Jews have referred to accept him and his utterances about the Patriarch undergo a marked transformation. There now comes the definite adoption of the 'religion of Abraham;' his association with Ka'bah. and the change of Qiblah as his answer to the Medinan Jews.[38]

The important point, however, is that Abraham in the Qur'an is a symbol or prototype of the Prophet Muhammad. Abraham's struggle against the paganistic worship among his people, the consequent opposition and persecution incurred by him from his fellow tribesmen (including his own father), are symbolic anticipations of the Prophet Muhammad against the idol worship and polytheism in Mecca and Medina, and of the resultant opposition which he suffers at the hands of the people.

A legend (obviously based on *Surah* 21:52ff. and 37:81ff.) states that one day Abraham's tribesmen left the town to offer sacrifices to their gods. Abraham, under the pretence of sickness, remains in the town. Armed with an axe he goes to the temple of the gods where tables are laid with food. He says to the idols: "Why do ye not eat," and strikes off the hand of one, the foot of another and the head of a third. He puts the axe into the hand of the largest god, and places various dishes before him. When the people of the town see this on their return, they accuse Abraham of the deed. He answers: "Verily, the biggest of them, had done this, ask them, if they can speak." The people tell him: "You surely know that they cannot speak." Thus Abraham subtly brings to their awareness the foolishness of worshipping that which can neither speak, help not harm them: "Will ye then serve, beside God, what cannot profit you at all, nor harm you? fie upon you, and what ye serve besides God! have ye no sense?" (21:66). The people get the point. But Abraham is said to have been thrown into a limekiln as a punishment; he leaves the limekiln unharmed, having been protected by the angels of Allah, after being there for about a week.[39] The point of this Quranic-legendary account of the victory of Abraham (which victory anticipates the victory of the Prophet later), is to underscore the superiority of Abraham's God over the heathen gods.

There is sense in which it can be said that the Qur'an presents Abraham as the lighthouse or director or pointer to the presence of God:

> The first House established by the people
> was that at Bekka (Mecca), a place holy,
> and a guidance to all things.
> Therein are clear signs—the station of Abraham,
> and whosoever enters it is in security.
> It is the duty of all men towards God to come
> to the House a pilgrim, if he is able to
> make his way there.[40]

One of the "signs" referred to here might possibly be the so-called "footprints" of Abraham. Muslim tradition has it that there were still visible footprints of Abraham in the Ka'ba at the time of the Prophet.[41] The reference to "the station of Abraham" (*maqam Ibrahim*) goes back to 2:119, where by it is meant the enclosure within the Ka'ba, where the patriarch is supposed to have prayed daily.[42] Thus is Abraham portrayed as an example of the praying

Muslim—an example not only to the Arabian Prophet, but also to all Muslims everywhere in succeeding generations. But "the station of Abraham" may also be a figurative way of referring to the standing ("station") which all devoted doers of God's will, shall have with God. (We have already referred to Abraham's prayer that his natural as well as his spiritual posterity—his household of faith—might continue in their loyalty and faithfulness to Allah.)[43]

The role of Abraham in the development of Muhammad's prophetic task and office as the guide of the Muslim community, may further be deduced from the following address of Allah to the Prophet:

> And they say, 'Be Jews or Christians and
> you shall be guided' Say thou: 'Nay, rather
> the creed of Abraham, a man of pure faith;
> he was no idolater.' Say you: 'We believe in God, and
> in that which has been sent down on us
> and sent down on Abraham, Ishmael,
> Isaac and Jacob, and the Tribes,
> and that which was given to Moses and Jesus
> and the Prophets, of their Lord; we
> make no division between any of them, and
> to Him we surrender.'
> And if they believe in the like of that you
> believe in, then they are truly guided; but if
> they turn away, then they are clearly in schism.[44]

Furthermore, in the Qur'an as the Prophet himself say:

> Say: As for me, my Lord has guided me
> to a straight path, a right religion,
> the creed of Abraham, a man of pure faith;
> he was no idolater.[45]

Thus, it is the creed or way of Abraham, not that either of the

Jews of the Christians (which, according to the Qur'an, has been distorted), that is to be the foundation or norm of the Prophet's religious and societal activities. For the Prophet, Jewish religion is too exclusive and the Christian religion in its trinitarian doctrine seems too polytheistic, to be true religions. Instead, he sees in the religion of Abraham not only a true, monotheistic faith but also a religion that is universally inclusive.[46]

The Abrahamic creed about which we have been speaking is, in fact, the same one followed by patriarchs and prophets before Muhammad. The implication here, then, is that if the Jews and the Christians would follow the way of Abraham, they would not go wrong, otherwise it is they, not the followers of Abraham, who "are clearly in schism." Hence, Abraham as the bearer of God's special message belongs neither to the Jews not to the Christians but to the Muslims, since it is only the Muslims who follow in the steps of Abraham.

Furthermore, as a prophet, founder and leader of a community, Abraham becomes a fore-runner of the Prophet Muhammad who also is to become a prophet, founder and leader of the Islamic community. Indeed, we might say that Abraham in the Qur'an is to the Prophet Muhammad what John the Baptist in the Christian tradition was to Jesus Christ. In the Christian tradition, Jesus (the one who is fore-run) is held in a more important position than the fore-runner. In Muslim tradition likewise, Prophet Muhammad (the one who is fore-run) is held in a more elevated position than Abraham the fore-runner, because the Prophet is said to be the Seal or the last of the Prophet, and therefore occupies a more privileged position than that of any of the other prophets, since no other prophet succeeds him.

The single most important contribution of Abraham to Muslim cultic life, as we have seen, is no doubt his founding, with Ishmael, of the Ka'ba in Mecca. Abraham's descendants are to come in pilgrimage to the Ka'ba, observing all that God has commanded them. But they are to come as *hanifs*, a community of worshippers of the true God. It is from this community that God has raised "a

Messenger, one of them, who shall recite to them Thy signs, and teach them the Book and the Wisdom, and purify them" (2:123).

This is the beginning of the true descendants of Abraham, the true people of God, for to be a true follower of Abraham or a Muslim, one must be submissive to only one God, Allah (2:127). For Islam means submission, signifying that the professors of this faith are submissive followers of God's commands (*amr*). In fact, Charles Torrey has remarked that when Muhammad named his religion '*Islam,* he was thinking of "the supreme test" to which the two ancestors of the Arab people had been subjected—this is, their "self-surrender" to the will of God.[47] Descent from Abraham, then, is a necessary condition to belonging to the people of God and, therefore, a necessary condition for salvation.

God demands that Abraham "become a Muslim" (2:125) and Abraham in turn charges his sons to follow his example (2:126). Jacob's sons promise their father that they would serve the God of their forefathers—that is, the God of Abraham, Ishmael and Isaac:

> And Abraham charged his sons with this
> and Jacob likewise: 'My sons, God has chosen
> for you the religion; see that you die not
> save in surrender.'
> Why, were you witnesses, when death came to
> Jacob? When he said to his sons,
> 'What will you serve after me?' They said,
> 'We will serve thy God and the God of thy fathers
> Abraham, Ishmael and Isaac, one God;
> to Him we surrender.'[48]

Although the immediate spiritual family of Abraham has passed away (2:128), God has raised another family after the pattern and in the tradition of that early Abrahamic community. The members of this new spiritual family are called Muslims, as were also members of Abraham's original spiritual family, to show that this new family is a continuity of the original. But this new family is no longer limited to the Arabic community; rather, it embraces all who follow the religion of Abraham anywhere in the world.

Abraham is also presented as a great man faith or as a symbol of the faithful. Commanded by God to sacrifice his only son,[49] he unquestioningly obeys the divine command and, consequently, is rewarded not only with another son but also with the fatherhood of all true believers (37:101ff). This story of Abraham's unreserved surrender to the will of God is a sublime example of the very essence of Islam or submission, resignation or self-surrender. In fact, the story is so significant in Islamic history that it is celebrated even today in the annual Feast of Sacrifice, "the *great* festival of the Muslim Year."[50] It is thus from this early expression of faith (*imam*) and submission to God's will (*islam*), that faith and submission become the two foundation principles of the religion of Prophet Muhammad, "for it is inconceivable that a man should have joined Muhammad and his religion without being ready to sacrifice his life in battle (and also his property) for God and His Prophet."[51]

**V. Conclusion**

It is clear that, in spite of everything else—political, cultural, or ideological influences—the most important of the multifarious roles of Abraham as portrayed in the Qur'an, is religious or spiritual, in so far as it is the basis for the existence of Islam as a religious community. Hence, in our discussion emphasis had been placed appropriately in the religious or spiritual significance of the patriarch. We are aware, nevertheless, of the possible politico-cultural or ideological parallels that may be drawn between Abraham and the Prophet Muhammad, but it seems to us that such parallels could best be reconstructed not so much from Quranic as from historical and mythical sources. Indeed, the political, cultural, intellectual or ideological flavour of this "religion of Abraham," may be regarded only as a by-product of the religious potency, conviction and commitment of Islam.

We have attempted to show here that Quranic Abraham is simultaneously the physical ancestor of the Arab Muslims and the spiritual progenitor of Muslims all over the world. Furthermore, the

Qur'an presents the patriarch as the first great iconoclast (idol breaker), prophet, and fore-runner of Prophet Muhammad, functioning as a model of courage and heroism for the Prophet, whose most important battle and contribution in the history and establishment of Islam, as in Abraham's case, were the destruction of the ancestral paganism of pre-Islamic Arabia, and the authentication of the unity of oneness of Allah.

Furthermore, as the father of Ishmael, the ancestor of Arabs, Abraham provides a firm historical basis for Islam—a historical basis to which the Prophet constantly pointed when accused of introducing a novel religious innovation into the Arabian community. Moreover, on the basis of the historical authenticity, Islam now declares publicly its autonomous status, refusing any dependence on the two monotheistic religions before it. It is now in the position to appeal to and claim the allegiance of men in its own right, not only in Arabia and its environs, but all over the world, for Abraham, its spiritual ancestor, is a universal symbol of the true worshipper (*hanif*),[52] a man of pure faith, and his religion a universal religion. But Abraham has to be an Arabian prophet (14:4) before he can be a universal Messenger for Allah, proclaiming the oneness of God to all the world, which task is continued and completed by the last successor, Prophet Muhammad, the Seal of the prophets. And Abraham and Ishmael being Arabs, as the Qur'an consistently insists, may explain why God has chosen them, and not Adam or Noah (Jews) who precede them. However, this point does not contradict the Quranic claim that "the religion of Abraham" is an inclusive one, calling upon non-Arabs to become spiritual heirs of the patriarch and hence spiritual Arabs, just as, in the Christian tradition, non-Israelites are invited to become spiritual Israelites.

## NOTES AND REFERENCES

1. Cf 2:129-34.

2. In 1979, see Mowahid H Shah, "Followers of Islam number (ed), about 800 million worldwide, "Islam and Justice", The Christian Century, December 5, 1979, p. 1202.

3. See surahs, for Abraham in Quran, 2:116ff, 3:58ff, 4:124, 6:74ff, etc.

4. See the accounts of William Muir, The Life of Mohammad (Edinburgh, John Grant, 1912).

5. Ismael's connection with Arabia is in the Bible, for Kedar (son of Ishmael, Gen. 25:13) (Ps. 120:5; Isaiah 42:11; 60:7)

6. 14:39-40; cf 2:120.

7. 2: 117-18.

8. In A Guthrie, "The significance of Abraham" The Muslim World, 45 (1955) p. 119, cf. Paul in Gal. 3:7ff.;

9. Al-Wakidi, Muhammad in Medina, trans. and abbreviated by Wallhausen (berlin, reimer, 1882), p. 338.

10. 6:51; cf. 2:258

11. In R Levy, An introduction to the sociology of Islam, vol. 2, (London, Williams and Norgate, 1933), p. 79.

12. See 6:74ff, 9:71, 15:5ff, 19:24ff., etc.

13. However, the distinction is arbitrary - not found in Quran. see John Wansbrough, Quranic Studies: Sources of methods of scriptural interpretation. Oxford Univ. Press, 1977. pp. 54-55.

14. 14:51; cf 37:34.

15. See 6:74-84; 19:41-50; 21:51-73, etc.

16. 37:81-95.

17. Cf. 6:74ff, 12:106, etc.

18. Cf. 2:214ff, 3:65-8, 95; etc.

19. See Kenneth Cragg, The privilege of man: A theme in Judiasm, Islam and Christianity. London, Athlone Press, 1968. p. 61-68.

20. See 2:129, 3:60, 89, 95; 4:124; etc

21. Hanif, in later Muslim thought, came to be used apologetically, see Arberry; W Montgomery Watt, `Hanif', in Ency. of Islam, new ed., vol 3, 1971, pp. 165-66; Cf John B Christopher, The Islamic tradition(New Yor, Harper, 1972)pp. 15, 17, 30.

22. Khalil, probably led to the burial place name of Abraham, Hebron is later called al-Khalil.

23. 19:53; 20:11-50.

24. 3:40.

25. See 2:129f; 3:60, 89.

26 For a Chinese Muslim tradition, in which God said to Abraham, see Liu Chai-Lien, The Arabian Prophet: A life of Mohammad from Chinese and Arabic sources, Shanghai, China, Commercial Press, 1921, p. 15.

27. 3:64ff.; 6:14.

28. R Paret, `Ibrahim', in Ency. of Islam, new ed., p. 981.

29. Ibid.

30. See a Guthrie, op cit., p. 114.

31. Ibid., pp. 116-17, op cit., p. 980.

32. "The influence of Judaism on Islam", in The legacy of Israel, eds. Edwyn R Bevan and Charles Singer (1927; rpt., Osford, Clarendon, 1969), p. 132.

33. Guthrie, op cit., p. 116.

34. 51:24; 15:5ff; 37:81ff; 6:74ff; etc.

35. "Ibrahim", in Ency. of Islam, vol. 2, 1927, p. 432.

36. Paret, op cit., p. 980.

37. The Quran: Translated with a critical re-arrangement of the Surahs, vol. 1 (Edinburgh, T.T.Clark, 1939), p. 122.

38. Guthrie, op cit., p. 117.

39. J Eisenberg, "Ibrahim", in Ency. of Islam, vol. 2, pp.431-32.

40. 3:90-91

41. See Liu Chai-Lien, op cit., pp. 45ff.

42. See Abdullah Yusuf Ali on verse 2:125; cf John Walker, Bible characters in the Koran (Paisley, London: Alexander Gardner, 1931) p. 26.

43. See 2:117-18; 14:39-43.

44. 2:129-31.

45. 6:162.

46. See Guthrie, op cit., p. 114.

47. See Charles C Torrey, The Jewish foundation of Islam (New York, Jewish Institute of Religion Press, 1933), pp. 102-104. Cf W C Smith, Islam in modern history (Princeton, Princeton Univ. Press, 1957), pp. 16, 17, note 11; and W C Smith "Some similarities and differences between Christianity and Islam: An essay in comparative religion," in The world of Islam: Studies in honour of Philip K Hitti, (London, Macmillan, 1959), pp. 50-51.

48. 2:126-27; cf. Gen. 18:19.

49. See 37:100-12.

50. Christopher, op cit., p. 48.

51. M M Bravmann, "On the spiritual background of early Islam and the history of its principal concepts," Le Museon, 64 (1951) p. 325.

52. Cragg op cit., p. 74.

---

(Revised and edited; originally published in Islam and the Modern Age, Vol. XI: no. 2.)

# 8

# The Function of the Occasion of Revelation Material

A RIPPIN

Covers a less considered topic in Quranic studies, i.e., the occasion of the revelation of the Quran, or sabab - purpose of revelation. Highlights the limitations of available literature on the same; al-Zarkashi and al-Suyuti have a distinct stand and hence this survey.

Extensive discussions on the role on *asbab al-nuzul* material in Qur'anic exegesis are far more infrequent in medieval Muslim literature than one may have hoped or perhaps even have expected. Likely places for such considerations would be introductions to actual exegetical works or within the genre of literature which has become known as *'ulum al-Qur'an*. Within the most famous books of that type, al-Suyuti (d. 911/1505), *al-Itqan fi 'Ulum al-Qur'an,* and al-Zarkashi (d. 794/1391), *al-Burhan fi 'Ulum al-Qur'an,* chapters are indeed found on the topic; their late date of composition and the ahistorical approach employed by both authors in their treatment of the subject has led, one suspects, to a blurring of any possible historical development in the conception of the topic and a glossing of contentious points by dogmatic assertion. Thus, to arrive at a comprehensive understanding of the role of the *sabab* in exegesis through a study of theoretical considerations of the topic in Arabic exegetical texts, a series of significant works from various centuries would be the most promising source. Unfortunately, a survey of earlier likely texts reveals that very little consideration of the topic of the *sabab* took place at all in form; other than discussion; within the context of limited discussions of the role of the *sabab* in the exegesis of a specific verse.

Probably the earliest work which gathers together any theoretical considerations about the Qur'an is Abu 'Ubayd (d. 224/838)[1]. *Fada'il al-Qur'an.* Despite its title, the work deals with much more than the merits of recitation of various portions of the Qur'an, the topic often understood by the rubric *fada'il.* While the first half of the text does treat *fada'il* topics[3], the rest of the work deals with such topics as variant readings, collection of the Qur'an and the language of the Qur'an. To some extent, this pattern is duplicated in latter *fada'il* works, such as al-Bukhari (d. 256/869), *Kitab Fada'il al-Qur'an[3],* and the commentary on that work by Ibn al-Kathir (d. 774/1372)[4], entitled *Fada'il al-Qur'an[5].* Folios 51a to 52b of the Berlin manuscript of Abu 'Ubayd's work are entitled "Chapter on the revelation of the Qur'an in Mecca and Medina and the description of the first and the last (to be revealed)"; dealt with here are all sorts of matters dealing with respective ordering of the passages of the Qur'an—the first and the last verses to be revealed, the order of Meccan and Medinan *surahs* including statements on how one determines that (for example, by the presence of *ayyuha al-ladhina amanu* in Medinan *surahs*) and also on the actual process of revelation over a period of some twenty years, but nowhere is the idea of the relevance of an individual *sabab* for a verse broached.

The next similar and promising text would appear to be the introduction to the *tafsir* by al-Tabari (d. 310/922) which is comprised of over one hundred pages of text in the Shakir edition. Al-Tabari even appears to have named the section separately: *Risalat al-Tafsir[6].* Al-Tabari's concerns in the introduction are, however, far from *asbab al-nuzul*; most of the space is devoted to a discussion of the language of the Qur'an, especially the meaning of the seven *ahruf,* the collection of the Qur'an and the distinction between *tafsir* and *ta'wil*, ending finally with an explication of "the names of the Qur'an, its *surahs* and its verses." That similar topics are covered in the introduction to the work by al-Tabari's near contemporary, al-Anbari (d. 328/939)[7], *Kitab Idah al-Waqf wa'l-Ibtida' fi Kitab Allah,*[8] would indicate that these were the topics of controversy during that era and that perhaps *asbab al-nuzul* was not of great concern.[9]

In 1954 Arthur Jeffery published two independent works under the title *Muqaddimatan fi 'ulum al-Qur'an.* The first work in the book, and the most extensive, is the introduction to the anonymous *Kitab al-Mabani li-Nazm al-Ma'ani.*[10] The author devotes considerable space to a listing of the chronological order of *surahs* and then to a consideration of the arrangement (*tartib, nazm*) of the Qur'an. Here the process of revelation comes in the documentation, the author stating that the Qur'an was revealed according to the needs of the situation (*'ala hasab al-hajah*) but that the arrangement of the Qur'an as it stands today mirrors in the *lawh mahfuz.*[11] The further implications of the "revelation by need" are not explored in any way other than by its naked assertion. The second text in the book, the *muqaddimah* to the *tafsir* by Ibn 'Atiyah (d. 541/1146)[12], *al-Jami al-Muharrar*[13], is similar in its treatment of topics to al-Tabari's *tafsir*, covering the merits (*fada'il*) of the Qur'an, the seven *ahruf* and the *i'jaz* of the Qur'an only.

The earliest discussion of the role of the *sabab* which appears to exist today is found in Ibn Taymiyah (d. 728/1327)[14], *Muqaddimah fi Usul al-Tafsir*[15]. This title, it is to be noted, is that given to the work by the editor. The actual title page of the manuscript calls the work *Qa'idah 'Azimat al-Qadr Sharifah fi Tabyin ma Yu'inu 'ala Fahm al-Qur'an*[16], while the introduction to the actual text of the work implies the title to be *Qawa'id Kulliyah Tu'inu 'ala Fahm al-Qur'an*[17]; it is thus probably identical to the only work al-Suyuti lists in his bibliographic introduction to *al-Itqan* by Ibn Taymiyah: *Qawa'id fi al-Tafsir*[18]. Regardless the actual title, the work is definitely a source for al-Suyuti's discussion and is quoted extensively in *al-Itqan*. Ibn Taymiyah's concern with the *sabab* is brought about by the presence of so much contradictory material within the collection; to explain how the apparent disagreement, *ikhtilaf*, arose among the "pious ancestors" (*salaf*) is the point of the chapter in which discussion of the *sabab* arises.[19]

The earliest extensive discussion of the role of *asbab al-nuzul*, as suggested above, would appear to be found in al-Zarkashi, *al-Burhan*. This work is the model after which al-Suyuti patterned his whole treatise and certainly after which he patterned most of his discussion on the *asbab al-nuzul*.[20] This, in fact, al-Suyuti himself makes clear in his introduction to *al-Itqan*: he had first written a book *al-Tahbir fi 'Ulum al-Tafsir*[21] but then he discovered *al-Burhan* and wrote, as a result, *al-Itqan*.

Prior to discovering the work of al-Zarkashi, al-Suyuti had known only two reasonably comprehensive but unsatisfactory *'ulum al-Qur'an* works[22]: one was by Muhyi al-Din al-Kafiyaji, (d. 879/1474)[23], the other by Jalal al-Din al-Bulqini, (d. 824/142'), entitled *Mawaqi' al-'Ulum min Mawaqi' al-Nujum*.[24] The fact that both of these authors are relatively late and that these two works are the only ones al-Suyuti brothers to mention as being similar to his work confirms what has been suggested above that al-Zarkashi's and al-Suyuti's works are the most significant works extant on *'ulum al-Qur'an*.

The sources quoted by al-Suyuti within his specific chapter on *ma'rifat sabab al-nuzul* likewise prove to be little help in finding other statements on the role of the *sabab*. Among those mentioned are, obviously enough, al-Wahidi (d. 468/1075) and al-Ja'bari (d. 732/1331), both of whom are connected with actual books on *asbab*.[25] Another person mentioned in Ibn Daqiq al-'Id (d. 702/1302), although it may be significant that al-Zarkashi attributes a quotation, credited by al-Suyuti[26] to Ibn Daqiq, to a certain unidentified Abu al-Fath al-Qushayri.[27] Finally, a work by Ibn Habib al-Nisaburi (d. 406/1015)[28], *al-Tanbih 'ala Fadl 'Ulum al-Qur'an*, is quoted by both al-Zarkashi and al-Suyuti, but it is used very infrequently;[29] one feels justified in presuming that the work was considered by none of them to be of great significance, despite its promising title, and that, therefore, not too much is being lost by its absence.[30]

Thus the only important, detailed texts are those by al-Suyuti and al-Zarkashi. Al-Suyuti's work, effectively being an edition and expansion of al-Zarkashi, does serve as a useful basis for the discussion of the role of the *sabab* by bringing together what few sources there were available to him as well as his own opinion on the matter, although the ahistorical nature of his approach, as mentioned above, does leave something to be desired.

Al-Suyuti's chapter on *ma'rifat sabab al-nuzul* takes a prominent position on his treatment of the Qur'anic sciences. The section is ninth, out of a total of eighty chapters, and follows on chapters devoted to other considerations of the process of revelation, for example, the time and physical place of revelation.[31] The discussion in the chapter itself is composed of answers to a series of five questions, which follows after a brief bibliographic introduction and a quote from al-Ja'bari to the effect that the Qur'an was revealed in two ways, "spontaneously" (*ibtida'*) or "as a result of a particular event (in Prophet's life) or a query (put to him)."[32] This, of course, is the theoretical basis of the entire concept of the *sabab*, that the revelation responded, at times, to the needs in the life of Muhammad, and that those situations and the Qur'anic response to them are recorded in the *asbab al-nuzul* material. The rest of al-Suyuti's chapter is then structured in the following way, dealing approximately with these topics:

Question 1 : Of what use is the *sabab* to exegesis? To this question, six points are delineated in response.[33]

Question 2 : Is a law derived from the generality of the expression (of the verse) or according to the particularity of the *sabab*?[34]

Question 3 : How does the *sabab* act in considerations of context?[35]

Question 4: What criteria make a *sabab* report valid?[36]

Question 5: Can one verse have more than one *sabab*?[37]

In attempting to discern the theoretical position on the function of the *sabab*, al-Suyuti's answers to the first three of these questions are of vital importance, the fourth and fifth questions being only marginally related.

The reply to Question 1 comes as a response to a statement of objection to the entire topic: the *sabab* is of no value, it is claimed, because "it is analogous to history." Such an objection may simply be implying that some exegetes felt that they could leave the *sabab* out of consideration because it was of no use in exegesis, since it was "only" history and thus a separate discipline; on the other hand, a more serious objection is perhaps being raised, that the Qur'an cannot be treated as historically conditioned in any sense (as the *sabab* may imply), for it is an uncreated work, written on the celestial tablet (*lawh makfaz*). It can hardly be claimed that what follows in al-Suyuti constitutes a really effective response to the first interpretation of the objection suggested above, even less so to the second; one may well doubt that the objection was really being taken seriously in al-Suyuti's time (or al-Zarkashi's where the exact same phrasing is found), the statement acting more as a convenient point of departure for the following discourse rather than as the basis of serious discussion.

Be that as it may, al-Suyuti then lists as part of his response to this, the first question, a series of six points comprising the functions the *sabab* fulfils in relationship to the proper understanding of the Qur'an, thus demonstrating its functional value. As the first point[38] al-Suyuti states that the *sabab* reveals "knowledge of the aspect of divine wisdom which provoked the promulgation of the ruling (contained in the verse)"; that is, the *sabab* reveals God's concern with His creation through His action in providing mankind with laws to guide its life. *Sabab* here is clearly the metaphorical "tent rope" connecting heaven and earth[39]. It might also be suggested that this too is the main emphasis, theologically, of Question 5, where the possibility of multiple revelation of a Qur'anic passage is endorsed. From a critical standpoint there can be little doubt that al-Suyuti is driven to this point because of the existence of vast quantities of contradictory material; that he, however, saw great merit in this feature, because of its emphasis on God's close involvement with His creation, can hardly be doubted.

The second point[40] in response to Question 1 consists of the idea that the *sabab* can reveal "the specification of the ruling by (the *sabab*), according to (the opinion of) those who hold that the precept is connected to the particularity of the *sabab*." A law in the Qur'an, according to this idea, can be understood as having either a specific relevance to the inhabitants of Arabia in the 7th century (CE) only or as being limited in its scope of application in later times by the circumstances of history at the time of its revelation. The important *proviso* here, however, is that is true (for the most part) only according to those who hold that opinion, for it is quite clear that al-Suyuti does not agree with this point the view. Indeed, al-Suyuti gives no examples of exactly what is meant by this statement, and it is only when one comes to Question 2 in his discussion that the full extent of the implications of the statement becomes clear.

Question 2 deals with the problem of interpreting the Qur'an : are legal rulings to be derived according to the generality of the wording of the verse or according to a particular situation implied by the *sabab*? Al-Suyuti clearly states that the former proposition is the soundest one. Many famous verses with widespread legal ramifications, he points out, were revealed concerning specific people (that is, with a specific *sabab*). For example, *ayat al-zihar* (Q. LVIII : 1) was revealed about Salamah ibn Sakhr[41], *ayat al-li'an* (Q XXIV : 6) about Hilal ibn Umayyah[42], and Q. XXIV: 11-12 about 'A'ishah specifically[43]. To interpret these verses not by the generality of their wording would imply that the ruling was limited to the specific situation given in the *sabab*. Quoted in this connection is al-Zamakh-shari's rejection of that position: "It is possible that the *sabab* is specific while the threat (*wa'id*) is general, for all who rejoice in that evil deed are included (*yatanawalu*) and that (threat) will certainly follow the same course as intimated." It is on this occasion that al-Suyuti quotes Ibn Taymiyah also,[45] the latter putting forth forcefully the point of view that one could not be considered a Muslim if one held that the ruling of a verse was to be limited to the person identified in the *sabab*; this is, of course, the generally accepted notion in Islam and the basis of the elaboration of *fiqh* and not something unique to Ibn Taymiyah's particular polemic. As he states it, a verse is not limited to a person specified by the *sabab*, but it includes (*mutanawil*) that person along with everyone else in the same situation (*bi-manzilatihi*).[46]

In certain cases, however, al-Suyuti acknowledges that specification by the *sabab* does, indeed, take place. His third point in dealing with Question 1 on the value of the *sabab* suggests that "perhaps the wording ( of the verse) is general but there exists evidence of specification (of the wording). If the *sabab* is known, then the specification is limited to what is required by the form (of the *sabab*). The inclusion of the *sabab* (in the derivation of the law) is the determining factor (*qat'i*) and exclusion (of the sense of the *sabab*) by *ijtihad* is prohibited."[47] Thus it seems clear that, on certain occasions, verses are made specific, but the key would appear to lie in the notion of the "evidence to specification (of the wording) (*al-dalil `ala takhsisihi*)." The full implications of this statement arise once more in Question 2, specifically in the *tanbih* ("additional note") at the end.[48] There, as Wansbrough has already pointed out, al-Suyuti embarks on "a discussion of the elative *al-atqa* in Q. XCII : 17, `He who is (the) most pious shall be spared.' Desire to restrict that reference to Abu Bakr provoked some very dogmatic observations on the grammatical function on the definite article."[49] The reason is, for al-Suyuti at least, that, in theory, a *sabab* does not make a verse specific in and by itself; it can only confirm a specification known by some other means, as in the case above, by the qualities of the definite article. In other instances, it would seem to be the prior existence of a law which then needs Qur'anic support that acts as the "other means" of specification. But, as point three of Question 1 certainly does indicate, the *sabab* at least in theory overrides *Ijtihad* (and *Ijama*' in al-Zarkashi it is to be noted)[50] within the discussions of specification. This is not really very surprising in a sense because of the *sabab* is generally considered a part of the Prophetic *sunnah*, abiding by its rules and regulations, and thus within the hierarchy of the *usul* to be rated second only to the Qur'an. Question 4 in al-Suyuti's discussion delves into this topic, prefaced by al-Wahidi's only statement of his criterion of *asbab* reports, that they be valid *hadith* reports.[51] For al-Suyuti, it is to be noted, this is one method of separating the wheat from the chaff in the voluminous assortment of *asbab* material; his actual work on the *asbab* often quotes the judgement of the *isnad* by *hadith* criteria for the individual reports.[52]

A further aspect of the problem of specification is brought up by al-Suyuti in his Question 3, where the possibility of a verse which has a specific intent but which has been put within a context of general intent due to the dictates of *nazm/tartib* is broached.[53] It is important to note at this time that all the discussions of "generality of the wording" or "specification of the wording" are based on an unenunciated theory of the "plain meaning" of the Qur'an. The "plain meaning" intended by al-Suyuti in these instances is, of course, simply the meaning that he feels to be "authoritative" at that point.[54] There is not, and many would argue that there cannot be, any universally accepted "plain meaning" of any given text; any interpretation varies according to one's own presuppositions and intellectual background. Thus, it may be fairly argued that al-Suyuti's problem of a specific verse versus the general context is one that arises only through approaching the Qur'an with presuppositions and expectations of desired result. The desire is to use a given Qur'anic passage to support already existing law; the result is a possible rapture of the context of the Qur'anic passage in question. Al-Suyuti cites only one Qur'anic example of this phenomenon in action at this point of his discussion, Q. IV : 58, the legal intent of which is separate from the context created by Q. IV : 51 and following. Verse 51 begins "Have you not seen those who were given a portion of the Book...?," referring, by general consensus in interpretation, to the Jews of 7th century (CE) Arabia and their conspiracy to hide the description of Muhammad in the Torah; this description of Muhammad, al-Suyuti explains, was their "covenantal obligation" or "trust" (*amanah*). Verse 58 then goes on to state, "God orders you to give the trusts (*amanat*) to their owners." If one were governed in interpretation by the specific *sabab*, verse 58 would refer to the Jews also; but, in fact, al-Suyuti argues, verse 58 is general, in reference to everything given in trust by anyone. Thus, a specific verse (Q. IV : 51) has been joined to a general context (Q. IV : 58).[55]

The whole topic of the "joining together" of verses and the

subsequent problems is treated more extensively in a separate chapter in *al-Itqan* and especially in *al-Burhan* where al-Zarkashi devotes the very next chapter after *ma'rifat asbab al-nuzul* to *ma'rifat munasabat al-ayat.*[56] It is also to be noted that the relationship between this genre and that of *al-waqf wa'l-ibtida'* is quite close also; although the latter is often thought to be connected only to *tajwid*, it is exegetical in intent and probably in origin.[57]

While it requires leaving the order of points as discussed by al-Suyuti, it seems sensible to deal with point five in answer to Question I now, for it too deals with the problem of specification and the *sabab* but from the other way around than the previous point. A verse may appear in its "plain meaning" to be specific or limited in its application but, in fact, when the *sabab* is taken into account, the true intent of the verse is revealed; thus, the *sabab* acts to "reject the illusion of limitation."[58] The prime example of this proposition is a quote from al-Shafi'i found in both al-Suyuti and al-Zarkashi but not *in extenso* in any other text consulted.[59] The problem here revolves around Q.VI: 145, "Say: I do not find in what is revealed to me anything forbidden to one who eats it, except dead animals, blood poured out, pork—it is an abomination—or impure (meat) hallowed by (a name) other than God's." The difficulty here clearly is that, in fact, foods other than those mentioned in this list are known to be forbidden to people.[60] Abrogation of the verse is a logical answer but apparently not a popular one, although it does find minority mention in the exegetical tradition.[61] Al-Shafi`i's answer, however, was to say that the verse was revealed specifically about the unbelievers who "forbade what God permitted and permitted what God forbade"; the specific items listed in this verse were those things the unbelievers permitted of what God had forbidden. The verse listed only the relevant items and "did not intend to permit other things beside them. The intention was to assert the forbidding, not assert the permitting."[62] Thus, while the verse would appear to limit the actual number of things forbidden, that limitation is rejected due to the *sabab* which acts to establish the context of the verse in question.

It is evident that in the above example the *sabab* serves primarily an exegetical function by taking the Qur'anic phraseology and elaborating it through narrative embellishment in order to remove the apparent intra-Qur'anic conflict, and that the *sabab* does not simply act as an external verificant of time and place of revelation. This trend is actually developed by al-Suyuti's point four in answer to Question I where the explanation is given that the *sabab* serves to "explicate the meaning and eliminate ambiguity." Several quotes preface the actual examples of this aspect of the *sabab* function, all of which witness the importance of the *sabab* in explication of the meaning of a verse.[63] The Qur'anic examples which al-Suyuti gives reveal, once again, that it is the "plain meaning" which seems to contradict the generally accepted legal derivation connected with the verse and thus the *sabab* plays a role only slightly different from point five treated above.

An example given by al-Suyuti in dealing with this point is what he calls "the most difficult" example, in the case of Q.III: 188: "Think not that those who rejoice in what they have brought...that they are in a place of security from the punishment."

> Marwan ibn al-Hakam used to say: "If everyone who rejoices in what he has brought and likes to be praised for what he has not done will be punished, then all of us will be punished," until Ibn 'Abbas explained that the verse was revealed about the *ahl al-Kitab* when the Prophet asked them about something and they concealed (the answer) from him and told him something else. It appeared that they had told him what he had asked them and they asked to be praised for that.[64]

Once again, the *sabab* acts to correct misinterpretation, not by extensive historical detail of time and place of revelation but by exegetical explanation through specification of a narrative context.

Finally, point six in answer to Question I indicates another function of the *sabab*, "knowledge about whom the verse was revealed and identification of the ambiguous in it."[65] It is the haggadic function of the *sabab* which is alluded to here, the exegetical aspect that fills in the details especially in narrative passages. Only one example is given by al-Suyuti, that Marwan thought Q.XLVI: 17 was revealed about 'Abd al-Rahman ibn Abi Bakr until 'A'ishah corrected him on that score and told him of itscorrect *sabab;* thus; 'A'ishah is pictured as stating that the *sabab* is the key to identification.[66] The methodological principle established, al-Suyuti does not even brother to state the correct identification; he does, however, deal with the topic more extensively in a later chapter of *al-itqan*.[67]

Considering al-Suyuti's presentation as a whole, it should be evident that he sees the halakic or legal function of the *sabab* as primary; specific and general aspects of wording are to be verified through the *sabab*. The *sabab* does, however, have other functions. Exegetical examples have been noted although they seem often to be close to the halakic specification role; the haggadic function of the *sabab* seems minor according to al-Suyuti's summary, although it is certainly manifested. Finally, the significance of point one in answer to Question I cannot be overlooked; the *sabab* acts in a historical-theological way, acting as the guarantor of the veracity of God's revelation to man and His concern for His creation; there is a polemical and theological value to the *sabab* over and above its exegetical role.

## NOTESANDREFERENCES

1. SeeCarl Brockelmann, Geschichtedes Arabischen Litteratur [hereafter = GAL], (Leiden, 1937-1949), voli, pp. 105-107, Suppl [=S], vol. i, 166-67; Fuat Sezgin, Geschichte des Arabischen schrifttums[=GAS] (Leiden, 1967), vol. i, p. 48.

2. Berlin, Stattsbibliothek Preussischer Kulturbesitz, Orientabteilung, Petermann, 499.

3. Al-Sahih (Cairo, 1978), vol. vi, pp. 473-522.

4. See GAL, vol. ii, p. 49; S, vol. ii, pp. 48-49.

5. See pp. 1-58, vol. iv, his Tafsir al-Quran al-Azim (n.d.)

6. Jami al-Bayan an Tawil al Quran (Cairo, AH 1374-1388), vol i, pp. 8-113.

7. See GAL, vol. i, p. 119; S vol.i, pp. 182-83; GAS vol i. p. 18.
8. Idah al-Waqf wal ibtida (Damacus, 1971), vol. i, pp.4-148.
9. Tabari deals only within a limited context on the value of *sabab*.
10. See pp. 5-250 of Jeffrey's text (2nd ed., Cairo, 1972),
11. See passim, al-fasl al-thalith, esp. p.40.
12. See GAL, vol.i, p.412; S,vol.i,p.732.
13. See pp. 252 93 of Jeffreyy's text Muqaddimah, Cairo, 1974., vol.1.
14. See GAL, vol.ii,pp.100-105; S, vol.ii,pp.119-26.
15. Beirut, 1972; see pp.44-49.
16. See Muqaddimah, p. [27],
17. Muqaddimah, p. 13.
18. Al-Itqan fil ulum al-Quran (Cairo, 1967), vol.i, p.19(lines 5-6)
19. See Ibn Taiymiyah's ideas on asbab in al-Suyuti's discussion.
20. See K E Nolin, "The Itqan and its sources", Ph.D. Thesis, Hartford Seminary, 1968, esp. pp.2-31; see also Mana al-Qattan, Mabahith fi ulum al-Quran (Beirut, 1978).
21. Al-Itqan,vol.i,pp6-10; al-Tabir is in Chester Beatty 4655and 5112.
22. Al-Itqan, vol.i,p.4.
23. See GAL vol.ii, pp.114-15;S, vol.ii, pp.140-41.(see also GAL and Princeton Yahuda 4515=Mach 118)
24. See GAL, vol.ii, pp.112-13; S, vol.ii, p. 139.(British Library OR 1553-1557).
25. See my article "The exegetical genre asbab al-nuzul: Abibliographical and terminological survey," BSOAS, XLVIII (1985).
26. See ibid.,
27. Al-Itqan, vol.i, p.83; al-Zarkashi, alBurhan fil ulum al-Quran (Cairo, 1957), vol.i, p.22. (See also Nolin, pp. 80-84).
28. See my article "The exegetical genre asbab al-nuzul"; althogh this work is not in GAS, vol.i, p.47.
29. See the index to al-Itqan, vol.iv,p. 280; al-Burhan, vol.iv, p.502.
30. See Abu Bakr al-Udhfawi's al-Istighna fi ulum al-Quran (se Ibn al-Jazari, Ghayat al-Nihayah [Cairo, 1932], entry no. 3240).

31. Cf. Zarkashi's arrangement of al-Burhan, Marifat asbab al-nuzul, naw 1; marifat al-Makki wal Madani, naw 9- out of atotal of 47 chapters..

32. Al-Itqan, vol.i, p. 82; see also John Wansbrough, Quranic studies: Sources and methods of scriptural interpretations. [=QS] (Oxford, 1977), p.178.

33. Al-Itqan, vol.i, pp.82-85; cf. al-Burhan, vol.i, pp.22-29.

34. Al-Itqan, vol.i, pp.85-87.

35. Ibid., pp. 87-88; cf. al- Burhan, vol.i, p.32.

36. Al-Itqan, vol.i, pp. 89-91.

37. Ibid., pp. 91-98; cf. al-Burhan, vol.i, pp. 29-32.

38. Al-Itqan, vol.i, p. 83; also al-Burhan,voli,p.22 first point.

39. For the term asbab see"The exegetical Genre asbab al-nuzul",.

40. Al-Itqan, vol.i,p. 82; also al-Burhan, vol.i, p. 22, second point.

41. See Ibn Taymiyah, Muqaddimah, p.44 and al-Burhan, vol.i, pp. 24-25.; cf. al-Wahidi, Asbab nuzul al-quran (cairo, 1969), pp.433-34, and al-Suyuti, Lubab al-nuqul fi asbab al-nuzul (Cairo, AH 1382).

42. See al-Wahidi, Asbabpp. 328-30; al-Suyuti, Lubab, p. 124.

43. See al-Wahidi, Asbab, pp. 330-55; al-Suyuti, Lubab, pp. 125-26.

44. Al-Itqan, vol.i, p.85; also al-Burhan, vol.i, p.32. See al-Zamakshari, al-Kashshaf an haqaiq al-Tanzil (Calcuta, 1856), vol.ii, p. 1631 (ad. Q. CIV:1).

45. AlItqan, voli, pp. 86-87; ibn Taymiyah, Muqaddimah, pp. 44-47.

46. See D. Daube, "Rabbanic methods of interpretation and Hellenistic rhetoric," HUCA XXII (1949), pp. 239-64, esp. pp. 251-52 and J Bowker, The targums and Rabbanic literature (Cambridge, 1969), pp. 315-18. also QS, pp. 166-70.

47. Al-Itqan, vol. i, p. 82; cf. al-Burhan, vol. i, p. 22-23.

48. Al-Itqan, vol.i, p. 87.

49. Qs. p. 178.

50. Al-Burhan, vol.i, p. 23; al-Itqan, vol. i. p.85.

51. See al-Wahidi, Asbab, p.4; QS, p. 179.

52. See al-Suyuti, Lubab, e.g. p. 16.

53. See also al-Burhan, vol.i, pp. 25-26.

54. Raphael Loewe, "The plain meaning of scripture in early Jewish

exegesis" Papers of the Institute of Jewish Studies London, vol.i, (1964), pp. 140-85.

55. See also Ibn al-Arabi, Ahkam al-Quran (Cairo, 1959), vol.i, pp. 449-50, esp. question three.

56. Al-Burhan, vol.i, pp. 35-52; al_Itqan, vol.iii, p. 323-38, naw`62.

57. See al-Anbari, Kitab idah al-waqf wal-ibtida, vol.ii, p. 778 )ad. Q. XXI:95) and cf. my article "Quran 21:95," JSS, XXIV (1979)pp 43-53.

58. Al-Itqan, vol.i, p. 84; al-Burhan, vol.i, pp. 23-26, fifth point.

59. Al-Jassas, Ahkam al-Quran (Istanbul), AH 1335), vol. ii, pp.16-17; al-Qurtubi, al-Jami li-ahkam al-Quran (Cairo, 1935-36), vol. ii, p. 116.

60. Makki al Qaysi, al-Idah li-Nasikh al-Quran wa-mansukhihi (Riyad, 1976), pp. 249-50.; ibn al-Arabi, vol. ii, p. 756.

61. Makky al-Qaysi, pp. 249-50; see John Burton, The collection of the Quran (Cambridge, 1977), esp. pp. 50-59.

62. Al-Qurtubi, al-Jami, vol.vii, pp. 115-19; Ibn al-Arabi, vol.ii, pp. 755-59; al-Jassas, vol. ii, pp. 16-23.

63. Al-Itqan, vol.i, pp. 82-84; al-Burhan, vol. i, p. 22 and 27-29; al-Zarkashi's third point and sixth combine to form point four in Suyuti. See Muqaddimah, p. 47.

64. Al-Itqan, vol.i, p. 83; al-Burhan vol. i, p.27 (also al-Bukhari, vol. iv, pp.73-74; Muslim (Cairo, AH 1390), vol. v, pp. 648-49, report 7; al-Musnad (Cairo, AH 1313), vol i, p. 298, bottom.

65. Al-Itqan, vol.i, pp.84-85.

66. See also al-Suyuti, Lubab, p. 194.

67. Al-Itqan, vol.iv, pp. 58-101 (na' 69-71); also al-Burhan, vol.i, pp. 155-63 (naw' 6).

---

(Revised and edited; originally published in Islamic Culture, July 1985).

# 9

# Qur'anic Studies: An Overview

MUNAWAR AHMAD ANEES & ALIA NASREEN ATHAR

Presents an overview of al-Quran's (i.e, Umm al-Kitab, the mother of Books) history of revelation, its collection, exegetical devepments, etc.

## Introduction

The Word *Qur'an* is derived from the Arabic root *qura*, meaning 'he read. Al-Qur'an thus signifies the 'reading' or that which should be read. Qur'an, also has different names, like, *Al-Furqan* (A Discrimination), *Tanzil* (Descended from Heaven), *Kitab Allah* (The Book of Allah), *Mushaf* (The Supreme Code), *Al-Mubin* (The Enlightener), *Umm al-Kitab* (The Mother of all Books), *Al-Bayan* (The Explanation), and *Al-Haqq* (The Truth). As Kwaw-Swanzy (1979 : 16) notes: '.. *in the Book itself, the Qur'an is called by 54 other names of titles.'*

## What is the significance of these names or appellations?

*'In these appellations one finds the profound significance of this Book of Islam..It is.. a Furqan or discrimination in that it is the instrument by which man can come to discriminate between Truth and falsehood, to discern between the Real and the unreal, the Absolute and the relative, the Good and the evil, the Beautiful and ugly... as the 'Mother of Books', the Qur'an is the prototype of all 'Books,' that is, of all knowledge. From the Islamic point of view all knowledge is contained in essence in the Qur'an, the knowledge of all orders of reality.'*(Nasr, 1972: 49-50).

And here is the Qur'anic self-annunciation (*Sura* 5:17-18):

There hath come to you
From God a (new) light
And a perspicuous Book,—

Wherewith God guideth all
Who seek His good pleasure
To ways of peace and safety,
And leadeth them out
Of darkness, by His Will,
Unto the light,—guideth them
To a Path that is Straight.

Al-Qur'an is the sacred book of Islam. Every work in Al-Qur'an is the Word of Allah, revealed in clear Arabic speech, to the last of Allah's Messengers, Muhammad Rasul Allah (peace be upon him) through the agency of *Ruh al-Amin Jibra'il* (Gabriel). He received the first Qur'anic *wahi* (revelation) at the age of forty during the month of *Ramadan* in the year 610 C.E., while he was in the cave at the foot of *Jabal al-Nur* (Mount *Hira*), 2-3 miles north of Makkah. The revelation started with the following five *Ayat (Sura 96 : 1-5):*

Proclaim! (or Read!)
In the name
Of the Lord and Cherisher,
Who created—
Created man, out of
A (mere) clot
Of congealed blood:
Proclaim! And thy Lord
Is Most Bountiful,—

He Who taught
(The use of ) the Pen,—

Taught man that
Which he knew not.

and continued 'at intervals' for the next twenty-two years and five months, ending shortly before his death in the year 632 C.E., with the following *Ayat* (*Sura* 5:4):

This day have I
Perfected your religion
For you, completed
My favour upon you,
And have chosen for you
Islam as your religion.

Al-Qur'an contains 114 *Suwar* (plural of *Sura*) with a total of 6,236 *Ayat*. There are 321,265 letters forming a total of 86,430 Qur'anic words. The textual arrangement of *Suwar* and *Ayat*, which does not coincide with the sequence of *wahi* (revelation), was communicated to Muhammad Rasul Allah by *Jibra'il* and is, therefore, the arrangement prescribed by Allah.

Muhammad Rasul Allah has been called *al-Nabi al-Ummi* since he himself could not read or write. It was, therefore, his practice to dictate the wahi as soon as he received it, to one of his *Ashab* (the Companions, may Allah be pleased with them all) who could write. At least forty *Kuttab al-Wahi* (scribers of the revelation) from among the *Ashab* are known to have recorded the *wahi* at one or other time. The most prominent among them were Abu Bakr Siddiq, 'Umar ibn al-Khattab, 'Uthman Ghani, 'Ali ibn Talib, Zayd ibn Thabit, 'Abd-Allah ibn Mas'ud, 'Abdallah ibn Sa'd, and Zubair ibn Awwam.

One of the unique aspects of the collection and the preservation of Al-Qur'an was the practice of the *Ashab* of Rasul Allah to memorise the *wahi*. There is evidence that seven of the male *Ashab* memorised the whole of Al-Qur'an. They were 'Uthman Ghani, 'Ali ibn Talib, 'Ali ibn Ka'ab, Zayd ibn Thabit, 'Abdallah ibn

Mas'ud, Abu Darda, and Abu Musa al-Ash'ari. Four of the female *Ashab* who memorised were 'Aisha bint Abu Bakr, Umm Salma, Hafsa bint 'Umar, and Umm Warqa ibn Nawfal (May Allah be pleased with them all).

Efforts for the compilation of Al-Qur'an in a single unified text started shortly after the death of Rasul Allah in the year 632 C.E., (Draz, 1969). Abu Bakr Siddiq, the first *Khalifah* (Caliph) is reported to have instructed Zayd ibn Thabit, the principal scriber of the Qur'an, to collect all the written fragments of Al-Qur'an. The completed text remained in the custody of Abu Bakr Siddiq (d. 634 C.E.), and after his death, was passed onto 'Umar ibn al-Khattab, the second of the four *Khulafa' al-Rashidun* (the rightly-guided Caliphs) who entrusted it to his daughter Hafsa (one of the wives of Rasul Allah). After the death of 'Umar ibn al-Khattab (may Allah be pleased with him) in the year 644 C.E. 'Uthman, the third *Khalifah*, with the help of a committee of *Ashab*, including Zayd ibn Thabit, prepared the final standard version of Al-Qur'an. Upon completion, copies were sent to Makkah, al-Fustat, al-Kufa, al-Jazira, San'a, al-Basrah, and al-Bahrain. One copy of Al-Qur'an was retained in Madina. All other versions were put to flames. The historical evidence thus upholds the Qur'anic claim of its genuineness and of its being totally free of human interpolation. Al-Qur'an proclaims (*Sura* 15:9):

> We have, without doubt,
> Sent down the Message;
> And We will assuredly
> Guard it (from corruption).

Fourteen hundred years of the history of Al-Qur'an are a vivid testimony of the absolute integrity of its contents. Works by Draz (1969), al-Said (1975) and Burton (1977) provide an insight into the history of the collection of Al-Qur'an. Abbott (1939) has given an account of some of the earliest manuscripts of Al-Qur'an preserved at the Oriental Institute of the University of Chicago; Nadvi (1968) has discussed the geographical and historical background of Al-Qur'an; the compilation by Arberry (1967) reproduces some of the rare works of the Qur'anic calligraphy: and the works by Penrice (1873) and Shah (1906) are important aids in the study of the language of Al-Qur'an. A monumental work by Sezgin (1967), for which he was awarded the King Faisal International Prize last year, lists the rare manuscripts of Al-Qur'an preserved worldwide.

**Tafsir al-Qur'an (The Qur'anic Exegesis)**

The need for explanation of the Qur'anic *Ayat* arose during the lifetime of Rasul Allah when *Ashab* asked him a multitude of questions in response to the *wahi*. Tradition records that Rasul Allah always offered them a satisfactory interpretation and satisfied them on matters big or small ranging from the meaning of a word to the spiritual and moral commands contained in Al-Qur'an. The devotion and fervour of *Ashab* led them to memorise each and every utterance of Rasul Allah. Later, they preserved it all in writing— the record which became a part of the *Hadith* literature.

For quite sometime after the death of Rasul Allah, the *Tafsir* existed as a part of *Hadith* literature. However, it developed into an independent branch by the end of the second century of *Hijra* when the Muslim scholars had started pursuing it very actively. Some of the pioneering works of *Tafsir* may be mentioned here: *Jami' al-Bayan 'an Tawil al-Qur'an* by Abu Ja'far Muhammad ibn Jarir al-Tabari (d. 310 *Hijra*); *Al-Kashshaf 'an Haqa' iqat al-Tanzil* by Abu Qasim Mahmud al-Zamakhshari (d. 38 *Hijra*); *Anwar at-Tanzil wa Asrar at-Tawil* by Qadi Nasir al-Din Abu Sa'id al-Baydawi (d. 685 *Hijra*); *Tafsir Kabir* by Fakhr al-Din Muhammad al-Razi (d. 606 *Hijra*); and *Itqan fi 'Ulum al-Qur'an* by Jalal al-Din al-Suyuti (d. 911 *Hijra*).

These and numerous other *Mufassirun* (Exegetes) have devoted a great deal of time in mastering Arabic lexicography, phonology, phonetics and grammar, in their zeal to illuminate the message of Al-Qur'an. Just how meticulously these scholars worked toward the development of *Tafsir* literature becomes evident by knowing merely the fact that they dealt with at least over a dozen discrete branches of *Tafsir*:

> *The authors of Qur'anic sciences dealt with numerous branches of Tafsir in their respective works. For example,* 'Ilm al-qira'a ( *reading Qur'an*); Ilm al-asbab al-nuzul (*the causes of revelation*); Ilm al-naisikh wa al-mansukh ( *abrogating and abrogated passages of the Qur'an*); Ilm al-muhkam wa al-mutashabih (*precise and obscure passages of the Qur'an*); Ilm i'jaz al-Qur'an (*inimitability of the Qur'an*); ilm ahkam al-Qur'an (*laws of the Qur'an*) 'Ilm i'rab al-Qur'an (*grammatical analysis of the Qur'an*); Ilm ghara'ib al-Qur'an (*extraordinary points of the Qur'an*); 'Ilm fada'il al-Qur'an (*excellent qualities of the Qur'an*); Ilm mushkil al-Qur'an (*language of the Qur'an*); Ilm mushkil al-Qur'an (*difficult passages of the Qur'an*); Ilm amthal al-Qur'an (*examples of the Qur'an*); 'Ilm mufradat al-Qur'an (*words of the Qur'an*); Ilm badai' al-Qur'an (*metaphor and good styles of the Qur'an*); 'Ilm al-wujuh wa al-naza'ir fi al-Qur'an or briefly Wujuh al-Qur'an (*the "meaning' of the Qur'an*), *and so forth* (Abdus Sattar, 1978: 137)

The extraordinary scholarly tradition of writing the *Tafsir* has continued in our times, albeit with less intensity. Among the modern scholars of *Tafsir* are included: Sayyid Ahmad Khan (1817-1898 CE), Sheikh Muhammad Abduh (1849-1905 C.E.) Abu al-Kalam Azad (1888-1958) and Abul Ala Mawdudi (1903-1979). The history of modern *Tafsir* literature during the period 1880-1960 has been worked out by Baljon (1961). Many of the interpretations by Baljon are, however, of doubtful integrity. Birkelland (1955) provides us with an insight into the older literature dealing with the subject. The works of Abdul Aleem (1933), Ahmad (1968), Ali (1969), Smith (1975), Abdul (1976) and Abdus Sattar (1978) may be pursued for further study of the history and principles of *Tafsir al-Qur'an.*

One of the modern trends in *Tafsir* literature is to seek interpretation of the Qur'anic vocabulary in the light of advances in scientific and technical knowledge. Opinions differ on this issue whether the scientific 'empiricism' be injected into the time-honoured tradition of *Tafsir*. However, a recent study of the Bible and Al-

Qur'an by a French scholar, Maurice Bucaille deserves attention. His work is not a *Tafsir* but a comparative textual criticism of the degree of 'compatibility' between the texts of the Holy Scriptures and the advanced scientific knowledge. Of the Old Testament and the Gospels, he wrote:

> *'I did not even have to go beyond the first book, Genesis, to find statements totally out of keeping with the cast-iron facts of modern science.* (Bucaille, 1978: vii)

and concluded the study with these words:

> *'In view of the level of knowledge in Muhammad's day, it is inconceivable that many of the statements in the Qur'an which are connected with science could have been the work of a man. It is, moreover, perfectly legitimate not only to regard the Qur'an as the expression of a revelation, but also to award it a very special place, on account of the guarantee of authenticity it provides and the presence in it of scientific statements which, when studied today, appear as a challenge to explanation in human terms.* (Bucaille, 1978: 251-252)

Finally, a few remarks may be made here about the Qur'anic letters, the explanation of which has been attempted for centuries but with little success. Out of the 114 *Suwar* of Al-Qur'an, 29 are preceded by one to five letters of Arabic alphabet. Various explanations on the presence of these Qur'anic initials have been sought by exegetes and commentators of Al-Qur'an (Ali, 1962; Cachia, 1968) but a plausible one has never been offered. It has been commented by some exegetes that only Allah knows the meanings and the significance of these letters. Nevertheless, Khalifa (1973) carried out a computer-assisted study of the mathematical properties and the distribution of the 14 of these Qur'anic initials with the conclusion that it would take 626,000,000,000,000,000,000,000,000, 'combinations of alpha betic letters in order to produce the mathematical distribution of the Qur'an's alphabets. This study has come under sharp criticism by Ahmad (1978), who argues that the authenticity of Al-Qur'an is not in need of such 'ultimate proofs'

Attention is drawn here to a more recent suggestion for the creation of a computerized data base for storage and retrieval of Al-Qur'an (Misbahul Islam and Masood Hussain, 1979).

**Translations of Al-Qur'an**

The expansion of Islam outside the confines of Arabia brought many non-Arabic speaking people into its fold and the question arose whether Al-Qur'an can be translated into other languages. The early ideas of the Muslim scholars (upto the fifth century *Hijra*) have been recounted in an illuminating article by Tibawi (1962). It is an account of the opinions held by Muslim jurists and commentators on the subject of translation of Al-Qur'an. However, Shakir, an Egyptian scholar, writing as late as 1926 voiced his opinion against the translation of Al-Qur'an into other languages (q.v., Shakir, 1926). Of course, there can be little doubt that any translation of Al-Qur'an is no more than an approximation of the Qur'anic meanings. Therefore, it is legitimate to state that translations of Al-Qur'an, no matter how 'perfect' those may be, can never replace Al-Qur'an per se. Muslims all over the world, whether Arabic-speaking or otherwise, are obliged to recite it in its original language—the Arabic. How the language of Al-Qur'an has worked for the Muslim spirit is evident from Tibawi's statement:

> *'Not only is Islam superior to any other religion, but the Arabic language is peerless. The union between two objects of pride and love is achieved in the Qur'an which is thus venerated alike as a sacred book and as a unique literary classic, so much so that non-Arab Muslims who rose to become authorities in exegesis, tradition, jurisprudence, and philosophy, did not contribute less, rather more than the native Arabs in shaping Muslim opinion on the double role of the Qur'an.* (Tibawi, 1962: 11)

The first-ever translation of Al-Qur'an in the European languages appeared first in Latin, made under the direction of Peter the Venerable, head of the Benedictine Abbey of Cluny in 1141 C.E. It was published in 1543 C.E. by Theodore Bibliander from Basle, Switzerland. The first English-language translation of Al-Qur'an, by Alexander Ross, was published by Randal and Taylor, London, in the year 1649 C.E. Its title, quoted here in full, is reflective of the knowledge of Islam possessed by the Europeans during the seventeenth century:

> *'The Alcoran of Mahomet, translated out of the Arabic into French by the Sieur du Ryer, Lord of Malezair, and resident of the French King at Alexandria, and newly established for the satisfaction of all that desire to look into the Turkish vanities, to which is prefixed the life of Mahomet, the prophet of the Turks, and author of the Alcoran, with a needful caveat, or admonition, for those who desire to know what use may be made of, or if there be danger in reading, the Alcoran.'*

These and later translation of Al-Qur'an by the Occidental writers are no more than cynical attempts to give a Judaeo-Christological interpretation of Al-Qur'an, which in turn are indicative of their poverty in knowledge about Al-Qur'an and Islam. Perhaps, Jeffery (1952) has reasserted Ross's convictions!

The first English-language translation of Al-Qur'an by a Muslim scholar was that of Dr. Muhammad abdul Hakim Khan, published from Patiala, India, in 1905. This was followed by a number of other translations of which those by Muhammad Marmaduke Pickthall and Allama Abdallah Yusuf Ali have been given a greater credibility. Ali (1961) has carried out a highly useful study of the modern resource literature of Qur'anic studies. It is unfortunate that it has remained unpublished.

The translations of Al-Qur'an in languages such as Czech, Dutch, English, French, German, Greek, Hebrew, Hindi, Hungarian, Italian, Latin, Persian, Polish, Russian, Spanish, Swedish, Turkish and Urdu, which appeared over half a century ago, have been cited by Woolworth Jr., (1927). The work on translation of Al-Qur'an has continued since then and translations abound in many other languages of the world. This reminds us of an urgent need for an up-to-date bibliography of these translations.

**I'jaz al-Qur'an (Inimitability of Al-Qur'an)**

Al-Qur'an is inimitable. We find in it an open challenge for the whole of mankind, (*Sura* 2:23):

> And if ye are in doubt
> As to what We have revealed
> From time to time of Our servant,
> Then produce a Sura
> Like thereunto;
> And call your witnesses or helpers
> (If there are any) besides God,
> If your (doubts) are true.

No wonder that the non-believers, in spite of their attempts, have always failed to anwer the challenge of producing even one *Sura* equal in eloquence and style to that of Al-Qur'an. And, of course, no one will ever be able to surpass or even match the inimitability of Al-Qur'an, (*Sura* 17:*88*):

> Say: "If the whole
> Of mankind the Jinns
> Were to gather together
> To produce the like
> Of this Qur'an, they
> Could not produce
> The like thereof, even if
> They backed up each other
> With help and support.

It is indeed astonishing to note a whole line of the Orientalists bent upon wasteful scholarship. It is vehemently argued by these writers that Al-Qur'an was the product of borrowings from the Judaeo-Christian sources Jeffery (1952) is at pains to 'prove' that 'the Qur'an is Muhammad's book.' More recently, the Reverent W. Montgomery Watt has called for putting up a rather more reconciliatory attitude towards Al-Qur'an, although in a highly deceptive tone:

> *'Courtesy and an eirenic outlook certainly now demand that we should not speak of the Qur'an as the product of Muhammad's conscious mind; but I hold that the same demand is also made by sound scholarship.'* (Watt, 1970: vi)

Clearly, the fallacies perpetrated under the garb of 'courtesy' are not acceptable means of the so-called sound scholarship. Thus, the works by these self-styled Oriental experts demand our close scrutiny and refutation of the utterly false notions, mischievously spread to discredit Islam, Al-Qur'an and Rasul Allah (peace be upon him). These 'experts,' the claimants of knowledge of Islam and the Arabic language—have they ever been able to answer the eternal challenge of the inimitability of Al-Qur'an? An answer to this question has been provided by Al-Qur'an itself, (*Sura* 2:24):

> But if ye cannot—
> And of a surety ye cannot—
> Then fear the Fire
> Whose fuel is Men and Stones,
> Which is prepared for those
> Who reject faith.

**Al-Qur'an and the Muslims**

What does Al-Qur'an mean to a Muslim? What is its significance in the life of a Muslim? How is the message of Al-Qur'an perceived by Muslim? As-Said (1975) had provided us with a lucid answer:

> *'As a Word from God, the Qur'an is the foundation of the Muslim's life. It provides for him the way to fulfilment in the world beyond and to happiness in the present one. There is for him no situation imaginable for which it does not afford guidance, no problem for which it does not have a solution. It is the ultimate source of all truth, the final vindication of all right, the primary criterion of all value, and the original basis of the authority. Both public and private affairs, religious and secular, fall under its jurisdiction. Its domination is universal. All nations, great and small, past and present,*

*stand accountable before it; all are summoned to heed its warnings and to learn from its tales of judgement meted out to ancient peoples. It is a miracle of miracles both in content and form, the proof of its Prophet, the sum and substance of all previous revelations. Of the several Heavenly Books given to man it alone has stood the test of time; it alone has been preserved intact in the hearts of a people, sheltered from all corruption and change.'* (As-Said, 1975: 11-12)

Verily this Qur'an
Doth guide to that
Which is most right (or stable)
And giveth the glad tidings
To the Believers who work
Deeds of righteousness,
That they shall have
A magnificent reward (*Sura* 17:9).

## REFERENCES

Abbott, Nabia (1939) The rise of the North Arabic script and its Quranic development - with a description of the Quranic manuscripts in the Oriental Institute, University of Chicago, Oriental Inst. Pub., vol. L, Chicago, xxxi + 103 pp. plus 33 plates.

Studies in Arabic literary papyri, II. Quranic commentary and tradition, The Univ. of Chicago, Oriental Inst. Pub., vol. LXXVI, Chicago, xvi+293 pp. plus 27 plates 1967.

Abdul M.O.A (1976) "The historical development of Tafsir", Islamic Culture, 50 (3), 141-153.

Abdul Aleem (1933) "Ijaz al-Quran", Islamic Culture 7:64-82 and 7:215-233.

Abdul Lateef, Said, (1952) The mind al-Quran builds. Lahore, Accurate Printers, xi+114 pp.

Abdul Sattar, Muhammad, (1978), "Wujuh al-Quran: A branch of Tafsir literature", Islamic Studies, 17 (2): 137-152.

Ahmad, Anis (1978) "The miracle called Quran at the mercy of charlatans", Al-Ittihad 15(2) : 45-62.

Ahmad, Rasheed (1968) "Quranic exegesis and the classical Tafsir," Islamic Quar. 12 (1-2) 71-119.

Ali, Abdallah Yusuf, (1969) Principles of Tafsir and some works of Tafsir" Al-Ittihad, 6 (2) : 28-30.

Ali, Hashim Amir (1962), "The mysterious letters of the Quran: A plausible solution to a thirteen hundered years old problem", Islamic Culture, 36 (1): iii-iv.

Ali, Muzaffar (1961) A reference manual for Quranic studies, Master of Library Science Thesis, Mc Gill Univ., Montreal, (unpublished), vi+251 pp.

Arberry, Arthur J. (1967) The Quran illuminated, A handlist of the Qurans in the Chester Beatty Lib., Dublin: Hodges, Figgis and Co. ltd. xxvvii+83 pp. 70 plates.

Baljon, J.M.S. (1961) Modern Muslim Quran interpretation (1880-1960), Leiden, E J Brill, ix, +135pp.

Birkeland, Harris (1955) Old Muslim opposition against interpretation of the Quran, UppasalaAlmsquist and Wiksells, 42pp.

Bucaille, Maurice (1978) The Bible, The Quran and science: The holy scriptures examined in the light of modern knowledge. Indianapolis, North American Trust Pub., ix, 253 pp.

Burton, John (1977) The collection of the Quran, Cambridge, Univ. Press, vii, 273 pp.

Draz, M A (1969) "initiatioin into the Holy Quran: how the revealed text of the Quran was composed", Al-Ittihad, 6(1): 6-13.

Jeffery, Arthur (1952) The Quran as scripture, New York, Russell F Moore co. 103 pp.

Kwaw-Swanzy, Bashir (1979) "1400th anniversary of the revelation of the Quran," J. Rabit al-Alam al-Islami 6(12): 16-21.

Misbahul Islam and Masood Hussain (1979)" Database of the Holy Quran," J Rabit al-Alam al-Islami &:1:17-20.

Nadvi, S. Muzaffar ud-din (1968) A geographical history of the Quran, 2nd ed. Lahore, Sh. Muh. Ashraf, xi+143pp.

Nasr, S. Hossein (1972) Ideals and realities of Islam, Boston, Beacon Press, xv+184pp.

Penrice, John (1873) Dictionary and glossary of the Quran...rep 1971, New York, Praeger Pub., vii+166pp.

---

(Revised and edited; orginally in *Islamic Culture,* October 1980.)

# 10

## Haman in the Quran: A Historical Assessment

SHER MOHAMMAD SYED

Deals with the historical controversy of Haman who, according to the Quran, was associated with the Court of Pharaoh to whom Moses was deputed as a prophet by Allah. Marraccio, George Sale, Rev. E.M. Wherry and the Encyclopaedia of Islam are some of the noteworthy references which have raised critical questions on this issue. Examines various aspects of the controversy in the light of recent historical researches and archaeological discoveries.

### Haman in the Quran

He has been mentioned at six places in the Quran. Below is Pickthall's translation of the verses containing reference to Haman:

(a) Lo! Pharaoh exalted himself in the earth and made its people castes. A tribe among them he oppressed, killing their sons and sparing their women. Lo! He was of those who worked corruption. And we desired to show favour upto those who were oppressed in the earth, and to make them examples and to make them the inheritors. And to establish them in the earth, and to show Pharaoh and Haman and their hosts that which they feared from them.(28: 4-6)

(b) And the family of Pharaoh took him up, that he might become for them an enemy and a sorrow. Lo! Pharaoh and Haman and their hosts were ever sinning. (28: 8)

(c) And Pharaoh said: O Chiefs. I know not that ye that a god other than me, so kindle for me (a fire), O Haman, to bake the mud; and set up for me a lofty tower in order that I may survey the God of Moses; and Lo! I deem him of the liars.(28: 38)

(d) And Korah, Pharaoh, and Haman! Moses come unto them with clear proofs (of Allah's Sovereignty), but they were boastful in the land. And they were not winners (in the race).(29: 39)

(e) And verily We sent Moses with Our revelations and a clear warrant Unto Pharaoh and Haman and Korah, but they said: A lying sorcerer! And when he brought them the Truth from Our Presence, they said: Slay the sons of those who believe with him, and spare their women. But the plot of the disbelievers is in naught but error. (40: 23-25)

(f) And Pharaoh said: O Haman! Build for me a tower that haply I may reach the roads, the roads of the heavens, and may look upon the God of Moses, though verily I think him a liar. Thus was the evil that he did make fair seeming unto Pharaoh, and he was debarred from the (right) way. The plot of Pharaoh ended but in ruin.(40: 36-37)

**Criticism of Western Scholars**

Some prominent orientalists have not been able to identify correctly the Haman of the Quran and hence their criticism about his historicity. The first critic to enter the lists in this behalf was Marraccio, confessor to Pope Innocent XI. Criticism of other orientalists in by and large based on his critical note. We reproduce here their critical observations:

(a) The English rendering of critical Note I on para 526 on Marraccio's Latin Translation of the Quran is:—"Mahumet has mixed up Sacred Stories. He took Haman as an adviser of Pharaoh whereas in reality he was adviser of Ahaseures, King of Persia. He also thought that the Pharaoh ordered construction for him of a lofty tower from the top of which he could see the God of Moses which if true would be inferior to him. There is no doubt that he borrowed the story of the Tower from the story of the Tower of Babel. It is certain that in the Sacred Scriptures there is no such story of the Pharaoh. Be that as it may, he (Mahumet) has related a most incredible story".[1]

(b) George Sale and Wherry have stated:
"Haman! This name is given to Pharaoh's Chief Minister, from which it is generally inferred that Muhammad has here made Haman the favourite of Ahasuerus, King of Persia, and who indisputably lived many ages after Moses, to be that Prophet's (Moses') contemporary. But how-probable-so-ever this mistake may be seen by us, it will be very hard, if not impossible, to convince a Muhammadan of it."[2]

(c) There are a few more critics: e.g. (i) Prof. Torrey who has indulged in criticism to the effect that the Prophet Mohammad drew upon the Rabbinic legend of Esther and even adapted the story of the Tower of Babel[3]; and (ii) Prof. Lammens who has mentioned "the most glaring anachronism" and "the confusion between Haman, minister of King Ahasuerus and the minister of Moses' Pharaoh"[4]. Even the Encyclopaedia Britannica (1929 and 1960 editions) alleged that the confusion existed in the Quran.[5]

(d) (1) The Encyclopaedia of Islam, 1927 edition quotes: "Haman, the Persian Minister hostile to the Jews in the Book of Esther, according to the Koran (XL 25 i.e. e of II' above) acted with Karun (Korah) on Firaun's council and filled the office of grand-vizier. These two learned of the approaching birth of Musa and advised that the boys should be slain and the girls allowed to live. When Musa appeared as a Prophet of God, they called him a liar. Firaun said, "O Haman, build me a tower, on which I shall reach the paths, the paths to heaven, and ascend to the God of Musa (Sura XL 38 et Seq i.e. "f of II' above). That Muhammad placed Haman in this period betrays his confused knowledge of history."[6]

(2) The Encyclopaedia of Islam, 1971 edition states."Hamán, name of a person whom the Kuran associates with Pharaoh (Firaun) because of a still unexplained confusion with the minister of Ahasuerus in the Biblical Book of Esther."[7]

Before proceeding further, we would like to emphasis that the information given by Encyclopaedia of Islam as reproduced at (1) above is replete with grave blunders which are misleading. In the first place, the Quran does *not* at all describe Haman as "Grand Vizier" or "Chief Minister" of Pharaoh. Moreover, it has nowhere stated that Karun (Korah) was his 'minister'. What is worst is: Verse No. 25 of Surah No. XL does *not* at all relate to the period preceding the birth of Musa as erroneously presumed. On the contrary, it relates to the period following Musa's presentation of his credentials as prophet to Pharaoh, Haman, and Korah whereupon the three rejected his commission, dubbing him a lying sorcerer. Not only that, they plotted also to kill the sons of his followers, sparing their daughters. What immediately follows in verse No. 26 of the quoted Surah is obviously the considered proposal of Pharaoh to kill Musa himself. It is moreover, significant that the Quran does not support the statement to the effect that these two (namely, Haman & Kuran) learned of the approaching birth of Musa and advised that the boys should be slain and the girls allowed to live. Obviously realizing the utter untenability of these statements made in the 1927 edition of the Encyclopaedia of Islam, its editors deleted them in the subsequent edition. The unfounded allegation regarding confusion relating to Haman still persists which we shall deal with hereafter.

**Identification of Haman**

We give hereunder extracts from recent works of historians of world repute and of eminent archaeologists to establish the identity of Haman, contemporaneous with the Pharaoh as mentioned in the Quran:

(a) "The dispersion of the worship of Amen is noted above as pointing to its coming through the Oases; and there seems no reason to question that the primitive Oasis worship of Ammon or Hammon, was the origin on the one hand of the Egyptian Aman of Amun, and on the other of the Carthaginian Baal Haman."[8]

(b) Impersonation or incarnation of the god Amon (which is the same as Haman as is clear from 'a' above) is also a well-established fact. That the high priest of Amon used to personate the god Amon is clear from the following quotation:
"Possibly the combination arose from priests wearing the heads of animals when personating the god, as the high priest wore the ram's skin when personating Amon."[9]

By way of elaboration, it may be added that according to the creed of ancient Egyptians, it was customary for the priests and priestesses to personify or personate their gods and goddesses, as will be clear from the following quotations:

(a) "This chapter may be fittingly ended by a few extracts from the Songs of Isis and Nephthys which were sung in the temple of Amen-Ra at Thebes by two priestesses who personified the two goddesses."[10]

(b) "After the end of the Old Kingdom a vast wave of democratization passed through Egyptian religious and funerary ideas and conceptions, and all those privileges which had formerly been the prerogative of the King were now transferred to other mortals, every dead person was now identified with Osiris, and his son or any officiant performing the rites in his stead was regarded as Horus."[11]

(c) It should be borne in mind that just as Pharaoh was the generic name of the kings of ancient Egypt but not the proper name of any particular king, so Amon or Haman was the generic title of the high priests when personating the god Amon.

We may add for the information of our readers that Amon is variously spelt as Aman, Amen, Aman , Amon, Amun, Haman, Hammon etc.

**Sacerdotal and Political Status of Haman (Amon)**

The identity of Haman having been established, it is but appropriate to examine what independent and impartial authorities have stated as to his status, titles, and functions which substantiates his description in Quran. That Amon (or Haman) was a very powerful and influential god whose high priest, personating him as indicated above, wielded great power will be clear from a perusal of the following extracts from the works of world famous historians and archaeologists:

(a) "He was regarded by the people as their great protector and no higher praise could be preferred to Amon when addressed by a worshipper than to call him 'the Poor man's vizier' who does not accept the bribe of the guilty."

(b) "The High Priest (of Amon) appears as "Viceroy of Kush" Already... Amon had gained possession of the Nubian gold-country; the High Priest has now gone a step further and seized the whole of the great province of the Upper Nile. The same inscription calls him also 'Overseer of the double granary', who.. was the most important fiscal officer in the State, next the chief treasurer himself. There is now nothing left in the way of authority and power for the High Priest to absorb; he is commander of all the armies, viceroy of Kush, holds the treasury in his hands, and executes the buildings of the gods."[12]

(c) "Thus the 'first Prophet' of the high priest of Amon, was at the same time the 'Great Superintendent of Works' and in this capacity was required to take under his charge the extensive building operations connected with the temple, and 'to provide splendour in his sanctuary'. As 'General of the Troops of the God' he commanded the military forces of the temple, like a mediaevel archbishop and as `Prefect of the Treasury' had under his control the by no means simple administration of finance. Nor did his authority extend only over the Amon temple and its priesthood. He was also "Prefect of the Prophets of the Gods of Thebes' and 'Prefect of the Prophets of all Gods of the South and the North'." This can mean nothing else than that all the priests of the country were subordinate to him and that he was the supreme spiritual authority of the realm. Of this power he knew how to make good use; and it not infrequently happens that the offices of high priest in other temples, for example, that of the sun-god of Heliopolis, together with his special subordinate members of the college of Amon, were filled in accordance with his choice. In this manner not only was great political power concentrated in the hands of the Theban priesthood, but great material advantages accrued to it as well, since the rich revenues of the old temple lands flowed unto the chest of a single body of priests".[13]

(d) "The priesthood of Amen received a seventh of the cultivated land of Egypt, a fiftieth of the population as foreign slaves, and half a million of cattle. This was in addition to all that previous kings had bestowed. As all this property was free of taxes the strain on the rest of the country must have been very heavy. It is no wonder that the high priests seized the office as an hereditary possession, and that they ruled upper Egypt. There was practically no independent king after Ramessu-III the rest of the family were increasingly in the hands of a dominant hereditary priesthood, which was the wealthiest in the land."[14]

**Creed of the Ladder to the Sky**

Let us now proceed to examine the significance of the command of the Pharaoh to Haman to burn the (mud) bricks and to erect therewith a sky-high tower with stairway. The question arises: was the suggestion to ascent thereby to the sky (to survey if there really existed this Allah of Moses) made by way of sarcasm or did it conform to the prevailing Egyptian religious notions of that hoary past?

(a) The idea of the Pharaoh going up the ladder to reach the sky to see the God of Moses, is in consonance with the mythology of ancient Egypt. "The ladder leading to the sky was originally an element of the Solar faith."[15]

(b) "The desire to ascend to the gods in the sky" was an article of ancient Egyptian religion.[16]

A critical reader would naturally ask the questions: Were mud bricks made and burnt in Egypt in those remote times? It is a well-known fact, borne out by archaeological research, that mud bricks and baked bricks were manufactured in those remote ages in Egypt and Babylon.

(a) When Moses accompanied by Aaron (Harun) confronted the Pharaoh with the divine message, he (the Pharaoh) dismissed them with the sharp phrase — "Get you unto your burdens" implying thereby that "they ought to be at work at the kilns or in the brick fields.'[17]

(b) "Burned bricks, no doubt, had already been produced by containing a fire with mud bricks. In Ur potters discovered the principle of the closed kiln, in which heat could be controlled." That there existed inter-communication between Ur and Ancient Egypt is borne out by the travels of Abraham and his tribesmen to and back from Egypt much earlier than the times of Moses.

(c) "The elements which Egypt borrowed from her eastern neighbour (Mesopotamia) are quite clear... There was monumental architecture, using bricks in a decorative panelling, a technique which can be traced to its origins in Mesopotamia but which appeared fully developed in Egypt at this final pre-dynastic period."[19]

(d) "Several most unusual occurrences of burnt bricks in buildings of the 19th and 20th dynasty" were discovered

> at Nabeshah and Defenneh by Sir Flinders Petrie. It is thus in the very nature of things of the Pharaoh to have commanded Haman, i.e., the High Priest of Amen, who inter alia was the "Great Superintendent of Works" to prepare mud bricks and then to bake them so as to build a sky-high tower with a ladder in order to go up into the sky to see the God of Moses, though in his heart of hearts he (the Pharaoh) believed that Moses was a lying sorcerer.[20]

**Confrontation between the Pharaoh and Moses**

The next question that arises is: Why did the Pharaoh and Haman reject the divine message of Moses?

(a) "It is an indisputable fact of history that by the long usage of the country, the Pharaoh was looked upon as a 'god upon earth'—*neter nefer*, 'the good god', and *netar aa* 'the great god'—'son of the Sun', 'the living Horus,' who inherited from his father the idea that he was actually on a par with the greatest of the recognized divinities, with Re and Tum, with Phthah, and Ammon and Horus... No pure monotheism (as preached by Moses) would for a moment have been compatible with such an intense exaltation"[21] and with "the number of gods and goddesses included into the pantheon running over two thousands."[22]

(b) The high priest of Amon (i.e. Haman) himself personated the most influential good (Amon) and often deputised for the Pharaoh (who was in fact the chief priest) on ceremonial occasions. The divine message of Moses from the one and only Allah, the Sole Creator and Sustainer of the whole universe, therefore, constituted a grave challenge to the old established faith and the authority of the two who marshalled all their stratagem and stupendous resources to defeat it.

**Critical Examination of the Controversy Raised by Orientalists**

We hope we have adduced impartial corroborative evidence to

establish the historicity of Haman as mentioned in the Quran. Let us now proceed to examine the historicity of the sources of information of our worthy orientalists with a view to assess the validity of their criticism which draws its inspiration only from the book of Esther as incorporated in the Old Testament. We cite below the comments of well-known Jewish of Christian Authorities on its historicity:

(a) "The majority of scholars, however, regard the book as a romance reflecting the customs of later times and given an ancient setting to avoid giving offence. They point out that the 127 provinces mentioned are in strange contrast to the historical twenty Persian Satrapies; that it is astonishing that while Mordecai is known to be a Jew, his ward and cousin, Esther, can conceal the fact that she is a Jewess—that the known queen of Xerxes, Amestris, can be identified with neither Vashti nor Esther; that it would have been impossible for a non-Persian person to be appointed prime minister or for a queen to be selected except from the seven highest noble families; that Mordecai's ready access to the palaces is not in consonance with the strictness with which the Persian harems were guarded; that the laws of the Medes and Persians were never irrevocable; and that the state of affairs in the book, amounting practically in civil war, could not have passed unnoticed by historians if this had actually occurred. The very tone of the book itself, its literary craftsmanship and the patness of its situations, point rather to a romantic story than a historical chronicle." "Some Scholars even trace it to a non-Jewish origin entirely; it is, in their opinion, either a reworking of a triumph of the Babylonian god Marduk (Mordecai) and Isthar (Esther) over the Elamite god Hamman (Haman) and Mashti (Vashti) or of the suppression of the Magians by Darius or even of the resistance of the Babylonians to the decree of Artaxerxes II. According to this view, Purim is a Babylonian feast which was taken over by the Jews, and the story of which was given a Jewish colouring... The book of Esther did not get into the Bible canon without a struggle."[23]

(b) comparatively few modern scholars of note consider the narrative of Esther to rest on an historical foundation... The vast majority of modern expositors have reached the conclusion that the book is a piece of pure fiction, although some writers qualify their criticism by an attempt to treat it as a historical romance. Most of the proper names in Esther which are given as Persian appear to be rather of Semitic than of Iranian Origin... In view of all the evidence the authority of the Book of Esther an an historical record must be definitely rejected."[24]

(c) Various historical and chronological inaccuracies and improbabilities lead to the conclusion that the book is something less than dependable history... Significant is also the fact that as yet no fragment of the book has been found among the Dead Sea Scrolls, produced by the Qumran Community and existed *circa* 150 B.C.—A.D. 70, nor is there any allusion to it in the N.T."

(d) "Neither Jews not Christians, however, have been happy with the presence of the book in the canon of the holy scripture. Its status was hotly debated by the rabbies all through the first two centuries A.D., and they obviously accepted it only because of the demand of the masses. Among Christians also there was question about its status. Martin Luther declared that he wished it did not exist. It must be admitted that without the popularity of the festival of Purim the book would have had little to recommend it for a place in the canon."[25]

(e) "the story as such has not been confirmed by any Persian record, and it is often supposed that it cannot be fitted into what is known of Persian History."[26]

(f) Above all, the story of the Book of Esther has been adjudged as "a tissue of improbabilities and

> impossibilities..." "Further, notwithstanding the dates which he gives us, the author had in reality no notion of chronology.... That the Book of Esther cannot be regarded as a genuine historical work is avowed even by many ecclesiastical traditionalists... The most essential parts of the story.. are together unhistorical and we are forced to the conclusion that the whole narrative is fictitious."[27]

From the foregoing quotations it is quite clear that no historian can place any reliance on the fable of the Book of Esther and no scholar can say that the characters therein and particularly Haman of the Esther, had any historical existence. The scene of the romantic fable of Esther was laid in the region of the so-called king named Ahasuerus. There is wide divergence of opinion among the authorities as to correct identity even of this allegedly Persian King. Some authorities opine that he was Artaxerxes, others say that he was Artaxerxes I, while still others would have us believe that he was Artaxerxes II, Artaxerxes III, Cambyses, or even Darius I. We cannot help quoting from the same authority the following significant statement: "Hoshiander has made elaborate argument in favour of Artaxerxes II (404-309 B.C.E.) suggesting that the other name was used because the Jews did not went to offend the Greeks whom Artaxerxes had assisted."[28]

Webster's Biographical Dictionary (1958 edition) contains the following notes on Ahasuerus: "Name, as used in the Bible, of two unidentified kings of Persia: (i) the great king whose capital was at Shuhan, modern Susa, sometimes identified with Xerxes the Great, but chronological and other data conflict; (ii) the father of Darius the Mede."[29]

**Conclusion**

In the light of recent historical researches and archaeological discoveries made by authorities quoted above, we hope we have convincingly established the historicity of the Haman of the Quran who enjoyed an eminent position in the court of the Pharaoh who was confronted by Moses (Peace be upon him). The veracity of the statements made in the Quran as far as fourteen centuries back is thus quite unassailable.

## NOTES AND REFERENCES


1. Note on p. 526 of the Latin trans. of the Quran with critical notes by Pope Innocent XI. Padua, Italy, 1968.
2. George Sale, trans. Quran, footnote `h' on p. 239 vol. II, London, 1825; first appeared in 1734 ed.; Wheerry reproduced it as not no. 5, p. 154, vol. III in "Comprehensive commentary on the Quran", London, Keagen Paul, 1896.
3. Jewish foundation of Islam, by Prof. Torry, New York, 1933. pp. 117 & 119.
4. Islam beliefs & institutions, by Prof. Lammens, trans. from French by E Denison Ross. London, Metheun, 1929. p. 39.
5. Ency. Britannica, vol. 13, 1929. ed. p. 483, and 1960 ed. p. 479.
6. Ency. of Islam, vol. II, 1927 ed., U.K, pp. 244-245.
7. Ency. of Islam, vol. III, 1971 ed., U.K., p.110.
8. Religious life in ancient Egypt, by Flinders Petrice. London, Constable & co., 1924.,p. 21 .
9. The Religion of ancient Egypt, by W M Flinders Petrice. London, Archibald Constable & Co., 1908. p. 30.
10. Egyptian religion, by Wallis Budge, New York, Bell, 1959, pp. 105-106.
11. Ancient Egyptian religion, by Jaroslav Cerny, London, Hutchinson's Univ. Library, pp. 100-???.
12. A history of Egypt, by Prof. Breasted, New York, Scribners, 1950, p. 244.
13. Religion of ancient Egyptians, by Prof. Stendorff, New York, Putnam, 1905, p. 96-97.
14. Religious life in ancient Egypt, by Flinders Petrice, London, Constable, 1924, p.54-55.
15. Development of religion and thought in ancient Egypt, Prof. Breasted, London, Hodder & Stroughton, 1912, p.153,
16. Religious life in ancient Egypt, pp. 84 & 208-209.

17. Moses: His life and times, by George Rawlinson, New Yor, Flemming H Revell, 1887, p. 90.

18. Ency. Britannica, vol II, 1974 ed., p. 163.

19. The burden of Egypt, by John A Wilson, Univ. of Chicago Press, 1951. p.37.

20. Egyptian materials and Industries, by A Lucas, London, Edward Arnold, 1948. pp. 63-64.

21. Moses., p. 88.

22. Ancient Egypt, by Manchip White, London, George Allen & Unwin, 1970.

23. Universal Jewish Ency., vol. IV., New York, 1948, p. 170.

24. Jewish Ency., vol. V., London, Funk and Wagnalls, 1903, p. 235-236.

25. "Interpreters" One Volume Commentary on the Bible, London, William Collins, 1972, p. 232-233..

26. The new Bible dictionary, Leicester, England, Inter-varsity Press, 1977, p. 393.

27. Ency. Biblica, vol. II, London, Adam & Charles Black, 1901, columns 1400-1407.

28. Universal Jewish Ency., vol. I, p. 137.

29. Webster's Biographical dictionary, Springfield, G & C Merriam & Co., p. 17.

---

(Revised & edited; originally in *Islamic Quarterly*.)

# 11

# The Qur'an and the Orientalists:

## A Note on the Authenticity of the Satanic Verses

M M AHSAN

Satanic verses, refer to, the alleged historic reference stating that the Prophet Muhammad under Satanic inspiration added two verses to Sura al-Najm. Let alone the non-Muslim allegation, Muslim historians like Tabari, Ibn Sa`d, etc. have also recorded this story, but the scholars in Islam have not accepted it, and insists that this is a fabrication. Analyses the Orientalists' allegations about the incorporation of the Satanic verses in the Qur'an—a theme discussed with relish by almost all Western writers on the life of the Prophet.

Number of Orientalists have specialised in the Qur'an and its exegesis and some have translated it into European languages. But their attitude has been unsympathetic and sometimes hostile. There are some who still regard the Qur'an as the writing of the Prophet and not, as the revealed word of God. Many allege that it is all borrowing from Judaeo-Christian sources. Such erroneous assertions have taken on a formulaic significance and echoes often even after their own research has shown otherwise.

A reader of secondary writings on Islam becomes puzzled when he finds two diametrically opposed conclusions reached by Orientalists and Muslim writers using the same sources and materials. It seems that Muslims are not too far wrong when they allege that the Orientalists build their edifice on the foundations of so-called objectivity, using the tolls of analytical research and critical examination which lead to interpretations not necessarily based on facts but pure speculation, hypothetical assumption and sometimes deliberate distortion. Evidently a deliberate attempt has been made by many Orientalists to cast doubt on the teachings of Islam by challenging the authenticity of the Qur'an and the *Sunnah*. Christian, Marxist and Jewish Orientalists have often tried to prove, directly or indirectly, that at least some portions of the Qur'an and Hadith are fabricated or inconsistent and are therefore unreliable sources for the Islamic way of life. However, they base their attack on the flimsiest of intellectual grounds.

Let us look at the story of the Satanic verses which Orientalists like William Muir, Theodor Noldeke, among earlier writers, and Montgomery Watt among contemporary 'biographers' of the Prophet narrate with their usually 'masterly' comments. These writers apparently base it on sources which on first sight seem quite weighty but on investigation fail to satisfy criteria of historical criticism. Muslim writers in the past such as Ibn Ishaq, Ibn Hisham, Suhayli (the commentator of Ibn Hisham), Ibn Kathir, Bayhaqi, Qadi Iyad, Ibn Khuzayma, Razi, Qurtubi, 'Ayni, Shawkani, etc., as well as contemporary writers like Mawdudi, Sayyid Qutb, Haykal, etc., have all rejected the story as preposterous and without foundation.

Tabari, Ibn Sa'd and some other Muslim writers have mentioned (though they vary considerable in matters of detail) that the Prophet under Satanic inspiration added two verses to the *Sura al-Najm* (53), which are as follows:

These are the high-soaring ones, whose intercession is to be hoped for!

The Prophet, it is claimed, recited these along with other verses of *Sura al-Najm* in the prayer. The idolaters of Makka who were present in the Ka'ba joined him in the prayer because he praised their deities and thus won their hearts. The story afterwards reached Abyssinia and many Muslim migrants returned to Makka under the impression that the disbelievers no longer opposed the Islamic movement. The story also indicates that the Angel Gabriel came to the Prophet the same evening and told him about the mistake he had committed by reciting verses never revealed to him. This naturally made the Prophet worried and apprehensive. Then, 'admonishing' the Prophet, God revealed the following verse of *Sura* 17, which read:

> "They were constantly trying to tempt you away from that which We have revealed to you, so that you may substitute in its place something of your own, in which case they would have actively taken you as friend. And if We had not made you firm, you might have indeed inclined to them a little.
>
> Then We would have made you taste a double punishment in this life and a double punishment after death and then you would not have found any helper against Us."

This made the Prophet feel guilty and ashamed until God revealed the following consoling verse from *Sura al-Hajj* 22:52:

> Whenever We sent a messenger or a Prophet before you and he framed a desire, Satan put obstacles in it. Then Allah removes the obstacles placed by Satan and He firmly establishes His signs.

This is the gist of the story mentioned by Tabari and some other sources which has been used by Orientalists to reinforce their view of the Qur'an. The story would, among other things, imply that the Prophet and his companions took the Satanic verses as a true revelation from God. Let us examine now the story and its contents in the light of internal and external evidence and evaluate it on the criteria of historical criticism. In doing so, first of all one has to find out the chronological sequence in the story and establish whether or not all its details relate to one period and are interconnected. Special attention should also be devoted to determining the periods of revelation of the three verses mentioned in the report which will validate or falsify the episode.

It can easily be gleaned from the story that the alleged incident of reciting the Satanic verses and the consequent prostration of disbelievers in the Ka'ba happened after the batch of Muslims migrated to Abyssinia. This emigration, according to all historical sources, occurred in the 5th year of the Prophetic call or about 8 years before the *Hijra* to Madina. Therefore, the incident must have happened close to this date and not long after the migration to Abyssinia.

The verses of *Sura Bani Isra'il* which were revealed, according to the story, to 'admonish' the Prophet for allegedly reciting the 'Satanic verses' in fact were not revealed until after the *Mi'raj*. The *Mi'raj* or the Ascent of the Prophet, according to historical records, occurred in the 10th or 11th year of the Prophetic call, i.e., about 2 or 3 years before the *Hijra* to Madina. If this is so, then it implies that God did not detect the Satanic verses or for some reason He kept quiet about the alleged interpolation of the verses for five or six years and only afterwards admonished the Prophet for the misdeed.

The verse of *Sura al-Hajj* according to the commentators on the Qur'an was revealed in the first year of *Hijra*. i.e., about 8 to 9 years after the incident and about two and a half years after the admonition of the Prophet by God. Could anybody who knows about the Qur'an, its history and revelation, understand and explain how the incident of interpolation was tolerated by God for six years and on top of that why He did not abrogate them until after nine years? Watt's theory that 'the earliest versions do not specify how long afterwards this (abrogation) happened; the probability is that it was weeks or even months is nothing but conjecture. Had he cared to investigate the chronology of the three revelations relative to the story, he could not possibly have missed the facts we have gathered.

Let us now turn to some internal evidence. It has been said in the story that the Satanic interpolation occurred in *Sura al-Najm* (53:18f), that it delighted the idolaters present at the Ka'ba and that as a gesture of friendship, they all bowed down with the Prophet. In order to comment on the story it would seem necessary to read the verses of Qur'an adding the two alleged Satanic verses and find out what God wants to convey here. It would read as follows:

> "Have you considered al-Lat and Al-Uzza and Manat, the third, the other! *These are the high-soaring ones, whose intercession is to be hoped for!* Are the males for you and for Him (God) the females. This indeed is an unjust division. They are but names which you have named, you and your fathers, for which God has revealed no authority. They follow but conjecture and what (their) soul desire. And now the guidance has come to them from their Lord."

If one reads the underlined words of the alleged Satanic verses, one fails to understand how God on the one hand is praising the deities and at the same time discrediting them by the subsequent phrases quotes above. It is also difficult to see how the Quraysh leaders drew the conclusion from this chapter that Muhammad was making a conciliatory move and was adopting the policy of give and take.

Drawing conclusions from various reports connected with the story, Watt suggests that 'at one time Muhammad must have publicly recited the Satanic verses as part of Qur'an; it is unthinkable that the story could have been invented later by Muslims or foisted upon them by non-Muslims. Secondly, at some later time Muhammad announced that these verses were not really part of the Qur'an and should be replaced by others of a vastly different import'. Watt's suggestion that Muhammad replaced the Satanic verses with some others of a vastly different import is nothing but speculation. If one takes the Satanic verses to be true, it would imply that the verses to be found in Sura 53 (19f) were not revealed in the same period. Watt's suggestion also implies that Muhammad and his followers read the Satanic verses in place of or in addition to the verses found in the Qur'an for 'weeks and even months' and that when Muhammad later realised that these verses could not be correct, then the true continuation of the passage was revealed to him. This supposition is again pure speculation and not based on any historical data. The story which we have summarised in the beginning suggests that Muhammad did not realise his fault until God admonished him six years later and that the matter was rectified perhaps another two and a half years after.

It is obvious that Watt and other Orientalists accept part of the story and reject other parts apparently because they are unable to find any link or sequence. Had there been any element of truth in the story, it could have caused a scandal against Islam and the Prophet and every detail must have found its place in the *Hadith* literature. Why is the authentic *Hadith* collections (namely the *Sihah as-Sitta*) conspicuously silent about the scandalous part of the story? Does it not lead to the conclusion, contrary to established fact, that *Hadith* literature itself is very defective as it failed to record such an important event which led the Prophet and his companions to read the Satanic verses for weeks, months or perhaps years without realising their error. In fact, Bukhari, Muslim, Abu Dawud, Nasa'i and Ahmad b. Hanbal do all record the story, but only to extent that was true. They all mention that the Prophet recited *Sura al-Najm* (53) and at the end, when he prostrated, the idolators present became so impressed or overawed that they also joined him in prostration. These leading *Muhaddithun* do not mention the blasphemous story which other sources have recorded. The fact that idolators became overawed and joined Muhammad in prostration is not difficult to believe as they all knew the magical effect of the Qur'an on the listener, which was one of the reasons why they called the Qur'an "a magic" and the Prophet "a magician." There is much historical data to substantiate the validity of this statement. It will suffice to mention the story of the acceptance of Islam by 'Umar and the listening to the Qur'an by jinns (cf. *Sura al-Jinn*). It is quite likely that after their prostration of Quraysh became ashamed and tried to convince others by inventing the story that they heard Muhammad praising their deities which made them join him in prostration. The news of the idolators and Muslims prostrating together spread quickly and it even reached Abyssinia with the additional rumour that Muhammad had reconciled with the Quraysh and hostility no longer existed

Apart from the absurd nature of the story and the external and internal criticism which cannot stand, there is another criterion of evaluation which one should not lose sight of. Muslim traditionalists quite often evaluate *hadith* on the basis of *riwaya* (the statement or the news based on the chain of narrators and the text of the *hadith*) as well as *diraya* (credibility of the statement). It means that if something has been attributed to the Prophet or Islam through apparently sound *Hadith*, it will not automatically be accepted if it goes against the Qur'an and other established traditions and cannot be justified by intellect. It is here that even if one regards the story of the 'Satanic verses' as sound on the grounds that it was narrated by a number of Muslim scholars or because it conforms to the requirements of a true narration (which it does not), no Muslim traditionist will accept this story because it stands in clear contradiction to the established belief of Muslim. The first few verses of *Sura al-Najm* itself very clearly says:

> "By the star when it sets; your companion errs not, nor does he deviate; nor does he speak out of desire. It is noting but revelation that is revealed — one Mighty in power has taught him."

> In *Sura al-Jinn* god further declares:"He reveals not His secrets to any, except to him whom He chooses as a Messenger; for surely He makes a guard to march before him and after him, so that He may know that they have truly delivered the message of their Lord."

These and other verses make it clear that it is not possible for the Prophet to accept anything in Qur'an from any external source. If this is so, then how can one take seriously, let alone believe in, the so-called story of 'Satanic revelation'? This is why the leading traditionists and exegists in Islam have regarded the story as malicious and without foundation. The fact that Tabari, Ibn Sa'd and some other historians and scholars recorded this story in their books does not prove that the story itself is true. Modern researchers know that there are a number of reports and events which have been proved incorrect in the light of historical criticism and other available facts. One may refer, for instance, to the article *'Abbasa* in the new *Encyclopaedia of Islam*, where Tabari reports that Harum's sister Abbasa was secretly in love with Harun's Vizier, has been proved incorrect and misleading.

## NOTES AND REFERENCES

1. There is very less in European languages, more so in English about Orientalists' views on Islam. A L Tibawi, Maryam Jameelah, etc are a few significant voices.
2. In Muslim sources the whole saga is known as hadith al-Gharaniq or the tradition of Gharaniq, the high soaring ones. Muir is perhaps the first to call it Satanic verses, and it is explained as one of the most striking instances of abrogation and substitution by a Jewish researcher, Ise Lichtenstader, "A Note on the Gharaniq and related Quranic problems," Israel Oriental Studies, 5 (1975), pp. 54-61.
3. W.M.Watt, Muhammad at Mecca, Oxford, 1960, pp. 101-109; and Watt, What is Islam, Longman, 1968; see also his teacher's work Richard Bell, The introduction to the Quran, revised by Watt, 1970, pp. 55-56.
4. Mawdudi, Tafhim al-Quran (Urdu), Lahorre, 1972, vol. III, pp. 238-245; see also Sayyid Qutb, Fi zilal al-Quran, (Arabic) Beirut, 1974, vol. IV. pp. 2431-33 and Zakaria Bashier, The Meccan crucible, London, 1978, pp. 180-186.
5. Watt, Muhammad at Mecca, p. 103.
6. Ibid.
7. Cf. Mawdudi, vol. III. p. 337, chapter 38: note 38.
8. Cf. Encyclopaedia. of Islam (2), S.V. 'Abbasa (J. Horrovitz).

---

Revised & edited; originally published in Islamic Quarterly.

# 12

# The 'Month' in the Qur'an

HASHIMAMIRALI

Shahr, meaning 'month', acquires different meanings according to the context in Meccan & Medinan Surahs. In view of the importance of this word, and the little attention on it, this paper focuses on different forms and connotations for more expert analysis

## I. Recurrence and Derivatives

Derivates of the root *shahr* occur 21 times in the Qur'an as shown in the accompanying tabular statement—4 times in the Meccan Suras, which together constitute two-thirds of the Qur'anic text, and 17 times in the remaining one-third text covering the 24 Medinan Suras. Arithmetically speaking, one could conclude that 'months' were 8 times more worthy of notice in the Medinan period than in the earlier Meccan years.

## II. In the Meccan Suras

In all the four Meccan verses *shahr* occurs only in the singular form although in two it stands for one month and in the other two verses it obviously refers to more than one month. Likewise, in all four cases it signifies an unspecified and approximate duration of 30 days irrespective of the seasons. These four cases are dealt with below:

1. In Sura 97:3, one of the earliest revelations, the singular form of *shahr* is used for a glaring plural—almost as an opening challenge to later lexicographers:

2. In Sura 46:15, the same singular form is used for thirty 'months:'

3 & 4. The twice occurring *shahr* in 34 : 12,

Provides an example of how, it has confused translators and commentators. The verse refers to Solomon's cargo ships that sailed east and west with the seasonal winds. The words *ghuduwwuha* and *rawahuha* are, obviously, ancient nautical terms for the eastern and western trade-winds. Naturally, these were unfamiliar words to the earlier landlocked commentators of the Qur'an. Their naive interpretations were piously repeated generation after generation until even in our own times. Muhammad Ali, the third Muslim to translate the Qur'an into English, renders the verse as follows:

> "12 And (We made) the wind (subservient) to Solomon, which made a month's journey in the morning and a month's journey in the evening..."

Interpreted logically, this would mean that the speed of the wind, at the command of Solomon, was sixty times that of ordinary sea-travel. Dissociated from pious belief, this would amount to gale which no sailing ship could survive month after month.

Sale and Sarwar render the passage as "it blew in the morning for a month and in the evening for a month" This too, naturally, borders on the fantastic. In my own translation I find I have rendered it as follows: "We made the winds subservient to Sulaiman; a month they blew towards the sunrise, a month to where it set..."

I hope this makes a little more sense; but obviously the word *shahr*, here too rendered as 'month' has a still wider meaning. Trade winds change and alter directions not by the months but by the seasons. Hence it would be logical to assume, and perhaps even render, the word here as 'season'. In short the word *shahr* like many other words, at least in the Suras of the Meccan period, has to be interpreted more liberally than lexicographers would have us do.

**III. In the Medinan Suras**

5. The very first two recurrences of *shahr* in the Medinan

Suras are found in 2: 185. In the first instance the word is specified as 'month of *Ramadan*' and is therefore, appropriately in the singular form. But here too a nuance in its meaning is generally overlooked. Since this Sura is accepted as having been revealed mostly in the earliest part of the Medinan period, the revelation of this verse too must have been about 8 years *before* the condemnation of the adjusting *Nasi*. Therefore the *Ramadan* mentioned therein must be taken as the luni-solar month oscillating between May and June of our present calendar. *Ramadan* here, therefore, does not signify a lunar month of our existing Muslim calendar which revolves round the seasons. This point needs to be particularly emphasized because it is rarely, if ever, pointed out by Qur'anic commentatory.

6. The second occurrence of this word as *al-shahr* in the same verse, 2: 185, deserves still more analysis:

It has divided the translators and commentators into two distinct camps. Among the complete English translations available to me at the moment, thirteen of them take the word *shahr* here also as meaning 'month;' only Rodwell (1861) and 'Abdul Latif (1971) support present-day orthodoxy by rendering the word as 'moon;' Abdul Fazl started with the former rendering in his 1910 edition, but changed to the latter meaning in his 1916 edition, adhering to it in the 1955 edition also. In his *Gharib-ul-Qur'an* (1947) he quotes the *Qamus* as authority for the world to mean both the 'moon' and the 'month' of *Ramadan*. But this *Qamaus*, I gather, is a relatively recent compilation being a lexicon prepared by Abu Tahir Muhammad of Firozabad in Iran and its date of compilation is about 729 A.H./1328 A.D. This compromise of attributing two different meanings to the word *shahr* leads to the controversy as to whether fasting is prescribed for the whole *month* and *Ramadan*, or only on seeing the *moon* of *Ramadan*. We need not go further in deliberating on the validity of one or the other meaning. All that we need to keep in mind in that in this verse the word *shahr* has been taken to mean 'the moon' also.

## IV. The Four Sacred Months

7. In verse 194 of the same Sura *Baqr*, occurs a passing reference to the Sacred Month:

Although the context emphasizes the 'equity of retaliation' rather than the sacredness attached to some months of the old Pagan calendar, the important role which four particular and sacred months enjoyed in the Arab life of those days necessitates a cursory survey of this cultural pattern before we proceed further in the analysis of the different connotations attached to the word *shahr* in the Medinan period.

The Four Sacred months, which we come across several times in the Suras of the medinan period were split in two different parts of the Pagan intercalated year—*Rajab* stood all by itself; the three others, *Dhu'l Qa'd, Dhu'l Hajja* and *Muharram* occurred consecutively, except when a *Nasi* intervened between the last two. We shall study these two periods below:

(a) *Rajab*, owing to the practice of intercalation which persisted until it was condemned in the last year of the Prophet's life, 632 A.D., oscillated over March-April of out present-day calendar. Long experience had made violence and tribal raids taboo in this month because it corresponded with the ripening of the dates which constituted an integral part of Arab existence; and it was in the season that people gathered in Mecca to exchange goods brought from the South in the course of the *Rihlat ash Shita* and to prepare for the carrying of goods to the North in the coming *Rihlat as Saif* that would take place in the coming summer. The equable climate of the season catered to the success of this assembly which came to be known as *Hajj al Asghar* and the inviolability attached to this one sacred month guaranteed peace and security.

(b) The other sacred period covering three months began with the waning of summer and extended into the autumn. Each of these months played a distinct role as shown below:

(i) The first of these three months, *Dhu'l Qa'd* corresponded with the July-August of out own times. Partial relief from the intensity of summer gave rise to an urge to spread into the open. Camels had multiplied and spelt prosperity for the pastoral culture of the region. The need to exchange goods and camels impelled people to assemble at their focal centre, the *Ka'ba* in Mecca.

(ii) The second of the three months of this period *Dhu'l Hajja*, was the month of the Major Pilgrimage, the *Hajj-al-Akbar* itself. It corresponded to August-September of our own times and represented the most prosperous season when spirits were high. Feasting, conspicuous waste, gambling and what not were marked features of the ten-day festival opening with the new moon and culminating with the Festive Night picturesquely described in Sura 79:1-5. Trade and exchange of goods was completed soon afterwards and before the clear autumn moon began to wane people began to pack their acquisitions and start back towards the towns and hamlets, oases and herdsmen's tents from which they had moved out. To provide security for men and animals and goods, the period preceding the great gathering, during the gathering itself, and for the safe return from this gathering, a longer period of non-violence was imperative.

(iii) That is why the taboos on violence extended into *Muharram,* the third of these three months and also the first month of the succeeding year. This month corresponded with September-October of our own times and commenced every year close to the autumn equinox, the 23rd of September.

The purpose of this somewhat elaborate mention of these Four Sacred Months is to emphasize that the *month* mentioned in 2:194 and in several other verses we shall mention below, were *seasonal months* running parallel to the moon-months of the Jews and the Hindus and not the revolving *Rajab, Dhu'l Qa'd,*

*Dhu'l Hajja* and *Muharram* of our current, post-Prophet, Muslim calendar.[1]

In the light of the above outline we shall now examine all the five references to these Four Sacred Months constituting two distinct periods—one covering the single spring months of *Rajab*, and the other covering the three summer-autumn months.

There is little new to learn from the last two of the above five instances; they represent the plural form of *shahr*; in No. 4 the qualification of 'sacred' is not specified but is clearly indicated in the context; in No. 5 both the sacredness and the plural are specified but the number is left to be understood by the context; each covers both the one sacred month as well as the three sacred months; hence there is no ambiguity in these last two instances.

On the contrary, the first three of the five instances above, referring as they do to 'the one sacred month' lend themselves to several questions. Do they apply to any one, or only to a particular one, of the sacred months?

For example, the name of the month of *Muharram*, being itself a form of the root *h r m*, embodies sacredness in its verbal composition; on the other hand, it is not distinguishably sacred compared to the two preceding sacred a months. Nor with *Dhu'l Hajja*, despite its being 'the month of Hajj,' more sacred than its preceding or following months as far as inviolability was concerned. The claim of *Rajab* to be 'the one sacred month' was stronger because it stood by itself and thereby enjoyed a distinctiveness in comparison with the other three which were contiguous.

## V. The Months of Hajj

Going back to an allied recurrence, we come to similar confusion in 2:197. As in examples 4 and 5 discussed in the preceding section we find here also the plural form *ashhurun* which would imply 'three or more' months.

But, as a general rule, applying to all but exceptional plurals, grammarians concede that plurals cover the dual from as well. That means that the form *ashhurun* in verse 2:197 need not necessarily imply only 'three or more' it can imply even 'two.' The question therefore arises: Can the word *ashhurun* in this verse mean "the two months Hajj (namely *Rajab* and *Dhu'l Hajja*) are well-known?"

Obviously, there is much difference between 'can mean' and 'does mean.' Let us therefore consider whether, and how far, we can be justified in interpreting this 'can mean' as 'does mean.'

Muslims, ever since the condemnation of the thirteenth adjusting month of *nasi*, during the Farewell Pilgrimage of 632 A.D., have only observed the one Hajj of *Dhu'l Hajja* which revolves around the seasons. Our religious 'year' no longer corresponds, even approximately, to the year observed by Nature, the rest of the human family, or even by ourselves in all but the religious aspects of our existence. Consequently, both early and recent commentators of the Qur'an have avoided—consciously or unconsciously—the possibility of the word *ashhurun* in this verse implying the two seasonal Hajj-months of the superseded Pagan calendar based on the adjusting *Nasi*.

The grammatical obstacle in interpreting *ashhurun* as a *singular* form, combined with their disinclination to accept it as a *dual* form, leaves only the *plural* for which has to cover at least *three* months. But even that does not solve the problem because for thirteen hundred years we Muslims have known of only *one* months of Hajj and that is the month of *Khu'l Hajja*. We cannot perform the Hajj in the preceding *Dhu'l Qa'd* nor in the following *Muharram*, not even after the 10th of *Dhu'l Ḥajja*! How then can the plural form *ashhurun* be used for that one month?

Hedged in between these limitations, our modern commentators, Muhammad 'Ali, Yusuf 'Ali and Abdul Majid Daryabadi, all quote their medieval predecessors, and safeguard their own position by asserting that, "the well-known period of Hajj extends over three months from the beginning of *Shawwal* to the 10th of *Dhu'l Hajj*."

To justify the plural (i.e., 'at least three') they are thus obliged to antedate "the well-known months" to include *Shawwal*, a month which was not protected by the taboo against violence; but even so "the well-known months" would not amount to three and so justify the plural. Besides, the months of Hajj" would defeat the very purpose of sacredness. Pilgrims embarking on Hajj in the month of *Shawwal* would not be safe from danger to person or property.

In brief then, the word *ashhurun* in this verse cannot be taken as singular, i.e., as 'one month'; nor can it be taken as plural, i.e., as 'three or more months.' Therefore, it can be interpreted only as the dual form and it is thus that 'can' is transformed into 'does': we can, with confidence, state that this clause. *al hajju ashhurun ma'lumat* does, in fact, mean:

"The two months of Hajj (*Rajab* and *Dhu'l Hajja*) are well- known."

To conclude: it is obvious that the seasonal significance of the Sacred Months, the Hajj and even the *Ramadan* have all been eclipsed by a single historical fact: All Qur'anic references to these annual events had been revealed years prior to the elimination of the adjusting *Nasi* in the Farewell Pilgrimage of 632 A.D.

The resulting unadjusted Hijrah 'year' of only twelve moon-months, together losing no less than 11 days in each seasonal year, has ruled the annual religious schedule of Islam ever since. Even by the time that commentaries began to be compiled— a century after that elimination—the old adjusted lunar calendar had been erased from Muslim memory.

It is the historical fact that makes us grope for guidance in the commentaries that invariably fail to shed light on these aspects of the Qur'an.

## VI. The Unspecified Months

The unspecified 'months', that is months without any seasonal or calendrical significance occur five times in the Medinan Suras:

| | | |
|---|---|---|
| 1. | 11 | 2:226 |
| 2. | 12 | 2:234 |
| 3. | 13 | 4:92 |
| 4. | 16 | 58:4 |
| 5. | 17 | 65:4 |

The first occurrence refers to conjugal relations; the second to the period a woman need wait after the loss of her husband before she may marry again; the third and fourth refer to the two consecutive months of fasting enjoined as expiation for those not capable of making amends for loss of life. The last recurrence refers to the period of waiting prescribed for a woman between divorce and remarriage. Consisting of legal regulations the dual and the plural forms are employed meticulously in all five instances. But even here the exact duration, whether a month should consist of 29,30 or 31 days, is left to the conscience of the person concerned.

## VII. Ithna 'Ashara Shahran: The Twelve Months

Finally, we come to the last and the most important of the recurrences of *shahr*, in 9:36.

Yusuf 'Ali, the currently most popular translator of the Qur'an, renders it as follows:

36. The number of months
In the sight of God
Is twelve (in a year)
So ordained be Him
The day He created
The heavens and the earth:

A more literal translation, to include the two recurrences of *shahr* in this one verse, would be as follows:

36. Verily, the number of the months (*al shuhur*) with Allah is (*ithna ashara shahran*) twelve months (embedded) in the law of Allah since He made the heavens and the earth.

Of course, minor differences of rendering will always be there according to individual preferences and inclinations; but, apparently, there is not much in dispute about the rendering of this verse into English in one way or the other. That is why it did not give rise to any controversy. And yet, ironically, this simple clause *ithna 'ashara shahran* can have not one but three different meanings:

1. It can mean the twelve months of the old luni-solar calendar which Pagans used to adjust with the seasons by the addition of a thirteenth month every two or three years. That calendar of 12 (+1) months still prevails, with less or more tenacity, in all the religions of the East, including Judaism, Hinduism and even Christianity. A 'month' in this sense would cover one lunation but would still be *approximately seasonal.*

2. It can mean the twelve months of the purely lunar religious reckoning which became current in Islam after the demise of the Prophet, and as a consequence of the condemnation of the intercalary *nasi* (9:37). A 'month' in this sense would also cover one lunation butt would have *no relation whatsoever with the seasons.*

3. It can mean the twelve months of the purely solar calendar based on the movement of the sun through the twelve constellations of the sky and entirely oblivious of the moon. A 'month' in this sense would extend over 29 to 31 days but would always correspond *exactly with the seasons*.

So, let us see which of these three categories of 'twelve months' qualifies best as a logical outcome of the definition in this important verse:

1. The first alternative meaning is ruled out because in it a thirteenth adjusting month recurs every two or three years, and

the perpetual recurrence of only twelve months, 'since the day He made the heavens and the earth,' disqualifies it altogether.

2. Then come the 'twelve months' of the purely lunar reckoning in which they revolve round the seasons: Can they meet the definition? Deep reflection and objective analysis cannot but lead us to the conclusion that they DO NOT. Have these twelve months, revolving round the seasons, ever in time, or anywhere in space, constituted the basis of the year EXCEPT during the 13 centuries of Islamic history? Have any other people, "since He made the heavens and the earth," or in any part of His earthly domain, based either their religious or secular life on a cycle of twelve moon-months the revolve round the seasons and which, therefore, *have no seasonal significance whatsoever*?

3. If the fullest endeavours to obtain objectively provable answers in favour to the above second alternative fail to bring our religious calendar of twelve revolving months under the Qur'anic definition, viz., "the twelve months prevailing since He made the heavens and the earth," we shall be left—at least in seems to me—with no alternative but to accept that the twelve months mentioned in the verse, can be understood to mean only the twelve solar months based on the movement of the sun through the twelve constellations, a movement which has been in existence "ever since He made the heavens and the earth." Would not the rejection of this third and logical alternative be a blasphemous challenge to Omniscience itself?

**VIII. Conclusion**

My qualification to the above thesis—'it seems to me'—needs here to be particularly noticed. I have worked on this thesis for more than thirty years;[2] still, I am a ḥuman being with many limitations of perception and understanding. The questions which this thesis raises are too important for any one man to deal with on his own responsibility. They reach far into the past, the present and the future of Islam. Is it not therefore the duty of all Muslim intellectuals, indeed, the duty of the intellectuals of all mankind, to give thought to these questions which directly affect one-seventh of the human race and, indirectly, the entire human family?

The semantics of the Arabic root shahr are, indeed, of human interest.

## NOTES AND REFERENCES

1. The HIjra calendar was adopted six years after the death of the Prophet, see M Hamidullah, "The Hijrah calendar," J. Pak. Hist. Soc., January 1968, pp. 1-2.

2. See my works: a) "Perceval's notes (1843)on the Arab Calendar before Islam," Islamic Culture, April 1947. b) "Fresh observations on Perceval's hundered years old notes", Islamic Culture, April 1948. c) " Facts and fancies - our four calendars",Islamic Culture, October 1948. d) "The crescent and the moon", J. Calendar Reform, June 1953. e) "The first decade in Islam", Muslim World, March 1954. f) "Must the Hajj rotate round the seasons?", Islamic Review, March 1956, g) "The genesis of the purely lunar calendar," Paper presented at the meeting of the Amer. Oriental Society, Philadelphia, March 1976.

---

(Revised and edited; originally published in *Islamic Culture,* January 1977.)

# 13

# The Qur'an and Interest in the Islamic Society

S M QADRI

The Qur'anic theories of interest will be explained in the context of Islamic social system. The Quranic term for interest is Riba, and there is a serious problem confronting all scholars and economists about the real meaning of the term.

If it is held unscientific to deal with the economic theories of capitalism in the context of communism, or to apply the principles and concepts of communism to the problems of capitalist system, then it is equally unscientific to study the Qur'anic concepts and theories in the context of either capitalism of communism.

"Riba" is a Qur'anic term, and as such, it should be studied in the context of Islamic social system as envisaged by the Qur'an and al-Sunna.

The Qur'an and Sunna form the main framework of the Islamic social system, and the early righteous Muslims lived upto them and had geared their entire economy on the principles laid down by these two original sources, and flourished for many centuries in their "Age of Glory."

Ever since the holy Prophet (peace be on him) trampled down the institution of "Riba" under his feet in the Hajjatal-Wida the institution of interest bearing loans remained prohibited in the Muslim domain.

Thus, both the theories and concepts of the holy sources and the historical records of the early Muslim people enable us to approach the Qur'anic economic problem with the deductive as well as inductive methods.

Along with these two scientific methods of enquiry and analysis, the angle of vision also is of basic importance in the study Islamic economics.

The modern economic science confines itself to the mundane life of the people and approaches our economic problems either with the micro or macro-economics.

But the Qur'an takes the human life in its entirety without disintegrating Ma'ash with Ma'ad. This integrity of human life cannot be bifurcated in Islamic studies, be it in "Khilafat-fi-al-Ard" or in `Khilafat-fi-al-Ma'ishat.'

This basic point, therefore, should not be lost sight of, that the Qur'anic economic system studies the human economic problems not only within micro and macro economics, but with an integral approach to the eternal life here and hereafter.

Thus, while stating the economic activities of the mundane life, the Qur'an links it up ultimately with the life hereafter:

In view of the fact that the Qur'an envisages a complete and perfect social system of its own, we will have to study the Qur'anic economic concepts, theories and principles in the very framework of Islam which lays down certain specific promises of its own.

The teachings of the holy Qur'an and the precepts and practice of the Apostle of God (peace be on him) relating to consumption, production, distribution, exchange and public finance lay down the broad premises of the economic system of Islam.

The Islamic social system consists of three distinct sectors, viz. (1) public (2) social, private or semi-govt. and (3) individual, i.e. exclusively private.

**The Broad Premises of the Islamic Social System:**

A decent standard of living is encouraged. Islam conceives of a standard of comfort not exceeding to the limits of luxurious life:

In the matter of expenditure one is directed to spend according to one's needs. Neither should one be niggardly nor a spendthrift.

For the criterion of one's real wages the Qur'an sets it to be equal to the worth of labour. The excess amount is the gift of God:

God, the sustainer, is the originator of wealth, which He besto ws on man. A man (or a labourer and entrepreneur) acts as his vicegerent, and is expected to behave as a trustee in his own wealth.

Man is encouraged and directed to explore for the wealth in the bounties of God. God promises to give not only the wages of labour, but something more as a free gift of nature.

The surplus income or superfluous wealth denotes the gift of nature, as an unearned increment, not due to the labour but mainly due to the grace of God. The owner in the trustee of this unearned income, and he is directed to distribute such wealth among his kith and kin, near relatives, needy persons, orphans and way-farers, etc.

From the near relatives to the remote friends and needy persons all are real claimants such a surplus. The needy persons have got a right to the wealth of the affluent persons.

Land is the main source of economic wealth. It belongs to the entire nation. Rich and poor, all have a right to its produce. The right channel for the flow of wealth is from the rich to the poor and needy.

No part of national wealth should stagnate in the hands of a few rich persons. The surplus and superfluous part of the wealth should again and again be distributed among the needy people of all categories.

Thus Islam stands for as equitable a distribution of national wealth as possible.

**Premises of the Islamic Economic System**

Along with the broad guidelines and directive principles of the Qur'an for the evolution of a complete and comprehensive social system, the Qur'an has ordained the Muslim people to form certain economic institutions. These institutions were established by the holy Prophet (peace be on him) during his own lifetime. Subsequently these organisations developed into full-fledged permanent economic institutions. These institutions have become a permanent feature of the Islamic social and economic order. Some important institutions which enjoy the sanctity of the Qur'an are mentioned below:

(1) "Zakat" and "Bait-al-mal"
(2) "Qarda-i-Hasna"
(3) Compulsory Sadaqat, Fitra, Kuffara, Nazar (Diyat), etc.
(4) Spoils of War-"Genima" and "Fai"
(5) Inheritance and "Wasaya"
(6) "Infaq fi-sabilillah" e.g. Waqf, Hiba gifts, etc.

This last institution is based on the directive principle of al-'Af or expenditure of surplus and superfluous wealth among the needy persons. This is the best instrument for equitable distribution of wealth.

The Qur'anic concept of "Al-'Af" is much wider in macro-economics than has hitherto been explained and expressed in its narrower sense of micro-economics.

**Recipients of the (Charitable) Wealth**

The Qur'an has mentioned certain categories of people who permanently remain in need of help in all societies. They are the genuine claimants of the surplus wealth of the rich and affluent persons and deserve all kinds of help. This is the residual claimant theory of the Qur'an which aims at the maximum welfare of the maximum number. According to the Qur'an, these claimant categories are:

(1) Parents and direct descendants, near relatives and close friends;
(2) Orphans;
(3) Paupers and needy persons;
(4) Invalid and old persons;
(5) Administrative machinery of the charitable funds;
(6) New converts to Islam—for their appeasement and temporary help till they get adjusted in the new society;
(7) Insolvents—for the redemption of the old debts;
(8) Charity in the name of God—Waqf;
(9) Wayfarers, and
(10) Slaves—Emancipation of slaves.

**Qur'anic Theories of Interest**

The Qur'anic verses relating to "Riba" are not more than five or six in number. From the very words and the context of the Qur'an we can deduce and derive some theories which are given below:

(1) The theory of unjust dealings.
(2) The theory of fraudulent tactics.
(3) The theory of reverse circulation of (capital) wealth.
(4) The theory of incidence of interest.
(5) The theory of negative rate of interest.
(6) "Usurious nature of simple interest" (interest is usury in disguise):

**The Theory of Incidence of Interest**

The productivity theory of the classical economists justifies interest on the plea, that money-capital commands capital goods, and capital goods are productive in the sense that they enhance production, and interest is nothing but a fractional part of this product which is paid to the money-lender as a reward for the services of his money-capital.

The micro-economic approach generally confines itself to the bilateral translation, and confuses the issue. The macro-economic approach would give a clear picture of the incidence of interest and how it affects the national economy.

An analytical study of the processes of production would help us in tracing the effects of the incidence of interest to their logical end.

Since consumption precedes in economic activities and production follows, every productive activity ends at consumption.

We will take an industry to illustrate our theory.

**Illustration of the Incidence Theory of Interest**

The consumption goods which are offered for sale in the markets pass through many processes before they change into finished goods.

An analytical study of an industry (say shoe-making) can give us a true picture of the widespread incidence of interest, both on production and consumption.

| *Source of Money capital Banks* | | *Processes of Production* | *Cost of Production* |
|---|---|---|---|
| (A) | 1. | Pasture lands | Costs+Interest |
| (B) | 2. | Sheep-rearing industry | " " |
| (C) | 3. | Wolesalers of sheep | " " |
| (D) | 4. | Slaughter-houses | " " |
| (E) | 5. | Wolesalers of skins | " " |
| (F) | 6. | Tanning | " " |
| (G) | 7. | Wholesalers of hides | " " |
| (H) | 8. | Shoe-manufacturing industries | " " |
| (I) | 9. | Wholesalers of shoes | " " |
| (J) | 10. | Retailers | " " |

| | *Consumers* | *Supply price* |
|---|---|---|
| The interest paid by the consumers flows back to the banks. | bear the entire burden of the accumulated interest. | Total costs plus accumulated interest. |

## Inference from the Incidence Theory of Interest

We can infer from this illustration some important points of far-reaching economic importance which help us in understanding the true Qur'anic concept of Riba and its adverse effects on the national economy as a whole.

In the bilateral transactions the banks advance loans to producers at simple rate of interest. This simple interest changes into the cost of production and remains an integral part of costs at every stage of production and passes on from process to process at an accelarating compound rate of interest, enhancing the supply price stage by stage till the goods reach their final shape.

Thus the finished commodity's supply price consists not only of the costs of other factors of production, but also the accumulated amount of the roling compound interest.

It is evident from the illustration that the so-called simple interest on productive loans is technically a compound interest which waxes stage by stage at the rate of.

Besides the general concept of compound interest, this technical concept also conforms and interprets the Qur'anic verse. It is true to say that every rate of interest, however small, is usurious in its nature. Hence interest is usury in disguise.

The apologists among the economists of capitalism plead for the justification of the institution of *Riba* on the ground, that in the ancient and medieval periods, interest was taken on the consumption loans, which in their opinion was unjust, but modern interest, on the productive loans is quite just in their view, because it is paid from the excess amount of the produce. This simply means that on the consumption loans, interest is unjust in their opinion and on production loans it is just and reasonable, because it is finally exacted from the consumers.

But our theory of incidence and of cost of production proves that every hint of interest, including that of productive loans, in extracted finally from the consumers. Hence every kind of interest is unjust

The Qur'an prohibits emphatically the very genus of interest "al-Riba."

Hence interest in all its forms and shapes is prohibited, and it can never enjoy and legal support in the Islamic economic system. The Qur'an has distinguished between *Bai* and *Riba* permitting the one and prohibiting the other.

Without going into minute details, in comparing and contrasting the institution of *Bai* and *Riba* only one basic point can be stressed here to show the fundamental difference between the two institutions. Interest enters the cost of production and becomes a significant factor for determining the supply price of the commodities.

But in the market it is the cost of production of the marginal form or far which determines the value of a commodity. Profit or surplus returns accrue to such of the business units as enjoy a more advantageous economic position than the marginal units. The profits therefore do not form a part of the cost price, nor do they determine the market price. Unlike *Riba*, they are determined by the price. Thus the *Riba* is extracted on contractual basis from the consumers and borrowers, while the profits are given by God through the operations of natural economic forces in the free play of market. This economic phenomenon, therefore, in quite is conformity with the Qur'anic verse:

**The Theory of Reverse Circulation of Capital**

The illustration of the incidence theory reveals one more basic point of far-reaching economic importance. It is to be studied in macro-economics. As has been shown, the accumulated interest is finally paid by the poor consumers to the commercial concerns, and this interest goes back to the rich money-lenders or banks, who control the money-market. Thus the money flows back from the poorer strata of society to the rich people to the accumulated in their coffers for further exploitation. This fact runs counter to the directive principle of the Qur'an. "The wealth should not accumulate in few hands:" The institution of *Riba*, therefore, is an instrument of reverse circulation of capital. Such a behaviour of the alien rival institution of *Riba*, if permitted to operate freely and legally in the Islamic order of life, would wreck the structure and constitution of the Islamic system from within. Therefore, all such institutions as run counter to the mainstream of the Islamic system would be regarded to be in conflict with the main system of Islamic economics.

This technical interpretation of Qur'anic verse is quite consistent with the behaviour of the interest-hunting money-lenders who persistenly refute the Qur'anic injunction and thus wage a war against the divine system. Besides, the macro-economic angle of vision would reveal the fact that the reverse circulation of wealth not only accumulates the national wealth in the hands of the few wealthy people, but stagnates it in the vaults of the banks, which control the money-market and create artificial scarcity of money and consequently impede the circulation of capital and the velocity of money. Such a behaviour of *Riba* institution hampers the economic growth of the country and affects adversely the equitable distribution of national wealth. Hence we can infer from this phenomenon that the institution of *Riba* does not help in the growth of national wealth but indirectly impedes its increase: While condemning and prohibiting the institution of *Riba*, the Qur'an emphatically stresses the institution of "Zakat" and "Sadaqat" as the best and most natural instruments for the growth as well as for the equitable distribution of national wealth.

Both the institutions of Zakat and Sadaqat are institutions of expenditure and not of income, and obviously they cause a decrease in the wealth of the payer, but the Qur'an says that they are institutions which cause an increase in the national wealth:

Paradoxical though it may appear, the statement is quite true in its ultimate effects.

A macro-economic approach to the problem can give us the technical interpretation of the phenomenon. Zakat and Sadaqat are generally paid from the surplus income, which according to the Qur'an, is meant for expenditure on the poor and needy persons.

Such a flow of wealth from the rich to the poor, results in an increase of the purchasing power of the poorer strata of society and thereby in an expansion of the home-market for the industrial and agriculture output of the country, and in the creation of more and more avenues of employment for the coming generations.

Therefore Zakat and Sadaqat are the best instruments to keep the flow of the national wealth intact with the natural mainstream of the Islamic system, while *Riba* and other institutions of exploitation reverse the circuit of wealth and cause stagnation of wealth in the efforts to create artificial scarcity for interest-hunting activities. This is the technical and logical interpretation of the Qur'anic verse, which obviously appears to be quite contrary to the facts and realities of the micro-economics.

In such a progressive society as that of Islam there would be no dearth of money-capital, either for development projects or for consumption purposes. When the supply of money-capital outstrips the demand for loanable capital the money-lenders die their own death. Lord Maynard Keynes probably had such a type of society in view when he remarked that "In a progressive society, the rate of interest tends towards zero." The utopian vision of Lord Keynes is a practical proposition of the Islamic economic system which puts a ceiling on the zero rate of interest. In regard to the monetary loans, the trend of Islamic economics is more towards negative rate.

The Qur'anic doctrine of negative interest is also based on the same logic of Zakat and Sadaqat. The interest free loans, or qarda hasna, are generally advanced from the surplus wealth, which is actually meant from the satisfaction of the demands of the needy persons.

If a poor borrower finds it difficult to redeem his debt on the due date, the rich money lender is advised to allow the borrower enough time for the repayment of the debt. If in the mean while the borrower becomes insolvent, the lender is advised by the Qur'an either to scale down his debt or to forego the entire capital amount and forgive the poor debtor, who has sunk deep in the quagmire of pain economy. Says the Qur'an:

Thus the society envisaged by the Qur'an and established by the holy Prophet (peace be on him) and his disciples and true followers was actually far more progressive than the visionary society of Lord Keynes, which is yet to be born. The Qur'anic doctrine of negative interest can be expressed briefly as follows:

In the dynamic humanitarian society of Islam the rate of interest tends towards negative side but can never exceed the positive side of zero. The Qur'an lays stress on fair dealing in every walk of life and never tolerates any kind of undue exploitation. Man is greedy by nature, and he tries to gain as much benefit for himself as is possible for him. In the struggle of life he follows the line of least resistance and tries to gain his end at the expense of others by fair or by foul means. To stop exploitation the establishment of the entire Islamic system is necessary.

The complex economic structure of our modern life deems it necessary to codify a comprehensive system of Islamic economic law to guide and direct the activities of the Muslim people according to the norms laid down by the holy Qur'an and "sunna". Macro-economic problems fall within the purview of the government. The Islamic government is responsible not only for maintaining law and order, but also for administering justice in the political, social and economic life of the people. For the smooth functioning of the entire social system, the rights and responsibilities of all the three sectors of the Islamic social structure should be demarcated to be reorganised into horizontal and vertical combinations on co-operative basis.

The implementation of the Qur'anic laws and the operation of the economic institution of Islam would mould the conduct of the people on the right lines. Such an atmosphere, if created, would enable us to study a *posteriori* the economic behaviour of the Muslim people, which is the very basis of our modern science.

Unfortunately the economic science had not yet been evolved during the Islamic age of glory and the great savants of that age could not develop their thinking on these scientific lines. Today, when all the Muslim countries have gained their independence and life is throbbing everywhere, and the Muslim renaissance has set in, the time appears to be very opportune for the development of social sciences of Islamic grounds.

To evolve the Islamic system in the framework of the Qur'an and al-sunna, we need not discard the western economic institution in toto. Science and civilization are the heritage of the entire humanity. Without disturbing the structural set-up of the Islamic society, an earnest move towards re-orientation, renovation, reorganisation and reform on modern economic lines would pave the way for a dynamic Muslim society. What we need is the Islamization of the western economic institutions. For instances, by the elimination of the element of interest we can adopt the banking and co-operative systems in our life. Instead of paying interest, the depositors can be paid dividends as share-holders and dividends are the best alternative to interest. Qard-i-Hasna banks can be developed and organised on modern lines to advance loans for consumption and production purposes. Other Islamic institutions can also be organised on modern lines if the Muslim economists work out an economic plan in an international economic academy.

The failure of most of the Muslim countries to establish true Islamic states in their territories is mainly due to the fact that the Muslim people have not yet developed their Islamic political, social and economic systems on modern scientific lines. So long as this basic need remains unfulfilled we cannot dream of establishing Islamic states on the progressive patterns of the modern world.

We are living in an age of science and ideologies. Unless we equip ourselves with the modern weapons of ideology, science and technology, neither will we be able to answer the challenges of the modern world nor will we be able to save our Islamic life from the encroachments of the foreign ideologies and the inroads of alien system of life.

I, for one, am quite optimist, that the Muslims can contribute a perfect social system to the material western world which is completely devoid of spiritual elements of sublime life.

This task demands the establishment of an International Academy of Islamic Social Sciences[1] (with special emphasis on economic science) to be participated in by all the Muslim economists and sociologists of the world with earnest devotion and missionary zeal.

## REFERENCE

1. Note: Since that date of writing the article, there have been a few associations of Muslim Social Scientists, in India, USA, etc. (Editor).

---

Revised and edited; orignially published in *Islamic Culture* January 1981.

# 14

# A Millennium-Old Qur'anic Puzzle: The Matter on Polygyny

HASHIM AMIR ALI

Submits a disconcerting re-interpretation of a verse of the Qur'an. To acquire plausibility it has to be presented along with brief accounts of: (a) the background of the puzzle;(b) the sudden, mutational evolution of a possible solution;(c) corroborative evidence; (d) support from Sunnah; (e) hurdles in the way of its acceptance.

## A. Background

Verse 3 of Sura IV, *Nisa*, probably constitutes the only and the long accepted 'decree' allegedly permitting restricted polygyny in Islam. Professor A.J. Arberry is quoted here on the verse who (a) had the benefit of the interpretive legacy left by Sale, Rodwell, Palmer and a dozen later translators into English, and (b) whose translation, *The Koran Interpreted*, had been hailed as "the first really worthy translation of the Muslim scripture." "At last", wrote Prof. Guillaum in *The Muslim World,* "The Qur'an has found a worthy translator... a work which will be recognized as the authoritative English version of the Qur'an for generations to come." Here is the verbatim, line for line, rendering:

> "If you fear that you will not act justly
> towards the orphans, marry such women
> as seem good to you, two, three, four;
> but if you fear you will not be equitable
> then only one, or what your right hands own;
> so it is likelier you will not be partial."

I have prefaced the above rendering with its eulogy to lend it further authority but, no matter which of the several English translations you may refer to, or which of the hundreds of Qur'anic commentaries by Muslim scholars, in Arabic and other languages, you may scan, you will find little difference in general understanding of this verse.

And yet, if you examine these innumerable closely resembling translations objectively and without the mental receptivity conditioned by an absence of contradiction, you will find it difficult to make any clear sense of what has been enjoined. The verse, as seen above, opens with a conditional phrase, "If you are concerned about orphans...then,[1] marry such women as seem good to you, two, three, four.." Where is the logical connection between the two emphatically consecutive clauses? How is a concern for orphans to be remedied by a multiplication of wives? And then, as suddenly, "If you fear you will not be equitable, then only one." Once again another swift turn: "or what your right hands own; so it is likelier you will not be partial."

I plead guilty of having compulsively taken recourse to a similar disjointed and "recondite" interpretation in my own published translation of the Qur'an,[2] and, therefore, I sympathize with the above-quoted savant as well as the numerous others of his kind who preceded or followed him: such are the letters worn by all those who dare to interpret the text of a sublime document in a tribal language that had inflorescenced a millennium before their own times.

But this universally accepted understanding of the verse had for long rankled in my own mind. Claiming, however, to be a student rather than a scholar in the bastion of Qur'anic learning, I kept this inner dissatisfaction to myself and, having no alternative to offer, even my tentative commentary expressing my misgivings has not yet been shown to any other besides the two or three of the most curious among my close associated. In brief, like all others, I too had, at least formally, accepted this thrice-ambiguous rendering until a recent fortuitous circumstances opened up an unexpected solution to this tantalizing puzzle.

**B. Mutational Solution**

Here I must apologize for deliberate emphasis on the first person singular in the narration of this experience; but I cannot avoid it if what I have to say is to acquire plausibility and invite impersonal consideration.

In the beginning of this very month, April 1978, I found myself visiting the Aligarh Muslim University in connection with a bibliographical work which one of the Nizam's Religious Trusts in Hyderabad had sponsored. Seven of us sat at a light repast in the Guest House talking academic shop. Casually, one of the gathering, whose very name I was not aware of mentioned this verse 3 of sura *Nisa*. He was expressing his puzzlement and perplexity at its disjointed construction and was saying that, as far as he was concerned, he took it as a recommendation for the survivors among the *Ummah* to give marital protection to the widows of their comrades who had left several orphans. This half-heard remarks suddenly touched a chord in my conscious mind, for I did not then remember ever having heard this interpretation before. As it happened, there sat next to me Muslim divine whose Urdu translation of the Qur'an had been under publication by instalments for the couple of decades. I turned to him for comment. Unexpectedly, he affirmed that this alternative too had been suggested by some commentators. This supporting evidence seems to have carried the idea from the conscious to my incubatory sub-conscious.

Now, scores if not hundreds of fellow seekers, irrespective of their lines of research, have borne testimony that, in the early hours of dawn, one sometimes wakes up with a ready-made solution to a problem which had been teasing them over long periods. Call it what you will, explain it as you please, reject it as an illusion, but that is exactly what happened to me early next morning.

Suddenly, while still half awake, I found myself asking, "what is this *mathna wa thulatha, wa ruba'a*, this 'twos and threes and fours?' Instead of being unusual forms of mere numerals, can they possibly be pastoral epithets for females respectively with two, three or four offspring? And, a little later: *wahida...* does it apply to a female with one child only?

I remember finding myself breathing hard to keep pace with my racing thoughts.

It is generally accepted that when this verse was revealed the *Ummah* in Madina had just experienced the attack by the Meccan Quraish at the neighbouring place called Uhud.[3] The few hundreds of the faithful had lost three or four score of their comrades and left perhaps as many widows and orphans. The Prophet himself had been wounded. Did not this interpretation of verse 3 constitute a logical and ad hoc solution for attending to the human needs of these many stricken at Uhud? Would it not be a practical rider to verse IV : 127: "Men are the protectors of women..?"

There was no Red Cross, there were no orphanages or children's homes, no trusts or foundations to cater to the helpless. It was then essentially a primitive, pastoral, patriarchal society in which, as in all human societies, monogyny was the general rule, but, considering divergent circumstances, prohibition against polygyny did not constitute a fetish. How else was its divinely inspired patriarch to attend to the economic and psychological needs of the suddenly stricken families of the immigrant community and the survivors of those who had so generously befriended them in Madina? How was he to replenish life, confidence and feeling of oneness[4] to both the groups that looked to him for inspired guidance?

And would not such a sociological solution, if carried out in good faith, leave a legacy of benign practice to supplement the precepts of social solidarity for the generations of the faithful that would follow?

Rapidly, an alternative meaning of the verse evolved in my mind: "If you are concerned about the (newly-made) orphans, then take under matrimonial protection the matrons who suit you: (preferably) two-kidded, three-kidded, four-kidded; but if (considering your individual circumstances) you fear that you will be doing them injustice, then a one-kidded widow; or a widow of your protege; that is how you can absolve yourselves from your duty (to the stricken community)."

This, of course, was a tentative and initial effort; some day a litterature will certainly be able to render this new meaning in a form worthy of Qur'anic translation.

**C. Search for Corroborative Evidence**

Later that morning, I went and communicated this idea to the comparatively young co-worker who had done commendable work in revising an Arabic-Urdu bibliography for us and who had heard the remark which had initiated my line of thought the previous evening. I told him that, working in a University library, he was in a more favourable position to substantiate lexicographically and from *Sirah* and *Hadith* literature the plausibility, or far-fetchedness of my sudden and unexpected solution.

Next, I went to the savant who had lent support to the idea at the stage reached on the previous evening. It now appeared that in a footnote to his Urdu translation of this verse he had already committed himself to the idea that the term 'women' recommended for matrimony included the possibility of choosing from among the widowed mothers of the orphans. About my additional suggestion that the world *mathna wa thulatha wa ruba's* may refer to mothers of two or three or four orphans, he promised to examine the possibility and let me know his reaction when he visited Hyderabad the very next week.

Naturally, when I returned to my home town I searched out the 8-volume Arabic-English Lexicon by Edward Lane, justly qualified by oriental scholars as the most detailed lexicographical achievement on any language of the world. From this I extracted the following text:

"Mathanin or Thinyun = A she-camel that has brought forth twice (Sihah) or two (*Mohkam*) or a second

| | |
|---|---|
| | time (*Qamus*); in like manner it it applied to a woman (*Sihah, Mohkam*) metaphorically.[5] |
| *ardh mathniatun* = | Land or ground, turned over twice for sowing or cultivation (*Asas Taj*). |

But I also found under the same heading (Vol. I, p. 335, col. I) a warning:

> "One does not say *thulthu* (as meaning one that has brought forth thrice) nor use any similar epithet above this (*Sihah Taj*)."

Neither the variation between the forms of the words as mentioned in the Lexicon and in the Qur'an, nor the warning mentioned above, need be a rigid obstacle in the way of accepting this epithetical meaning to the word *mathna* in this verse. Such variations abound in the dialects of one Beduin tribe and another; it is the transcendentalism of the Qur'an, the *i'jaz al-Qur'an* as it is called, that picks up these nodules of a desert, and with its magic chisel, transforms them into literary jewels. In this case this fact is emphasized by a passage in the *Tafsir-i Kabir* by Fakhruddin Razi on this very word *mathna*. He says it is found nowhere else but in the Qur'an in this particular form. Nor will, I presume, the other words, *thultaha* and *ruba's* and *wahida* be found elsewhere in exactly the forms found in this verse. How then can the lexicographers of the Arabic language provide for such exceptions to be found only in the Qur'an? While on this subject, one cannot help mentioning Arthur Jeffery's *Foreign Vocabulary of the Qur'an*[6] which brings together hundreds of Qur'anic words which have direct or indirect relations with distant languages of remote peoples.

To accept plausible meanings dictated by thought, intelligence and research, or to refuse all but the traditional meanings however far- fetched they might be, can only be left to individuals with predilections of one kind or another. Religious controversy has often been based on such group preferences. Some find the word *Sinin* (95:1) as denoting a different place because it differs from the well-known *Tur Sina*; other interpret *Ilyasin* (37:130) as denoting some other entity apart from *Ilyas* in spite of the fact that it follows mention of the very Prophet's commendation (37:123). And yet such variations constitute one of the outstanding features of the Qur'an: it expresses sublime truths succinctly with just such departures from the norm in a dialect wherein the same word means both 'enjoined' (6:151) and 'forbidden' (16:115); a language pattern in which the *mudhari'*, the active form the verbs, might mean past, or present or future according to the context!

To my great surprise and delight I found a young scholar'[7] (who is said to have earned the *khil'at* of Mujthaid from the Seminary of Najaf) more receptive and broad-minded than I had dared to hope. He is so struck with the aptness of the newly suggested meaning of verse IV:3 and has so much access to Arabic and Muslim lore than I am beginning to hope that, even if I do not live long enough to see the wide discussion of this thesis, he might live to enjoy the satisfaction of having worked early towards finding a satisfactory solution of a Qur'anic puzzle that has been the bane of Islam and which has caught at least some devotees of this Scripture in a confusing situation over the centuries.

**D. Support from the Sunnah**

We Muslims believe that whatever the Qur'an enjoined by precept, the Prophet corroborated with his practice. When, therefore, (a) the verse under analysis, alleged to limit the number of wives to *four*, confronts (b) the claims of the *Sirah* that during the last years of his life the Prophet actually had *nine* wives, we meet a contradiction between precept and practice, that is, to say the least, embarrassing to us.

This fresh interpretation removes this embarrassing contradiction and patently absolves him from the charge of himself not observing a restriction imposed on his followers. On the contrary; in the light of this thesis his whole life shines forth as a lustrous example of his consideration for his flock and the conspicuous absence of lust in both adulthood and middle age.

At the age of twenty-five, when young men are prone to folly, he accepts the hand of a mature woman who has twice lost a husband, and who, at least according to one section of his *Ummah*, had come to come with three daughters by former husbands. For the next twenty-five years he is happy in this sedate, monogamous domesticity. At the age of fifty, when his devoted companion is no more, the pattern and habitat of his life change. Virtually driven away from his beloved city of Mecca, he is welcomed in Madina and becomes the leader of several disparate tribes, an arbitrator for dissenting communities, a custodian of peace and welfare. He has to protect the weak against the strong, the peace-loving from the compulsively aggressive. He has to do his best to unify and assimilate the Jews and the Christians and the Believers in the new dispensation. He has to care for the widows and the orphans.

The repeated aggressions of the Meccan Quraish as well as the police actions which he has to initiate for the survival of his flock cannot but involve some loss of life and property; the social cohesion which he aims at has to be achieved in spite of the obstacles engendered by these conflicts and reprisals. He has to offer sympathy to both friends and foes. To more then one widow of a companion who had fought for him, he offers protection through marriage to dry their tears. To the widow of a fallen rebel leader who had defied his authority he offers the land of a conqueror whose age precluded him from the charge of lust.

"We are parts of one or another", "men are the protectors of women, these are the messages he inculcates in every such action.

A friend of mine has asked a question on the margin of a preliminary draft of this paper: "Is there any historical evidence that this injunction to marry the widows for protection of the orphans was acted upon by any of the surviving Companions?"

The answer to this valid query is obvious: No Companion ever claimed to be an exemplar of Qur'anic teaching however much he might have acted in accordance with it. It is the Prophet himself who had always been the witness in this regard. Irrespective of his own personal convenience he obviously practised what he preached. In fact, no stronger evidence than this *sunnah* can be submitted in support of the plausibility and veracity of this fresh interpretation of the verse under scrutiny.

**E. Hurdles in the Way of Acceptance**

However much Lexicons and *Tafasir, Sunnah* and *Hadith* literature may support this re-interpretation; however much the *ulul albab* 'the men with opens hearts' may be inclined to look favourably on this rendering built upon reason and circumstantial evidence, there will always be the amiable diehards who find it not only difficult but impossible to accept anything new, just because it is new. They are bound to ask: "If this 'simple meaning' as you call it, is so obvious, how is it that it had escaped the perspicuity of Companions and scholars and commentators whose mother-tongue itself was the Arabic of the desert?"

"And, secondly, why were the generations upon generations of Muslim and other savants satisfied with an interpretation that is, to you, so disconnected, cumbersome, distorted and forced?"

Some may even indulge in personal recriminations: "How dare a person with your limitations, who at best can know only the rudiments of Arabic, suggest new meanings which have not been mentioned even as possible alternatives by great commentators who have left their stamp on Qur'anic commentary for all time?"

All three are valid questions and view-points. Let me deal with them one after the other to the best of my limited capacity.

(a) The answer to the first question lies in the very early history of Islam itself. Edward Lane, in his preface to his Lexicon, says that the Arabic language had begun to be transformed in the life-time of the Prophet himself. And, considering the moral and intellectual metamorphosis of Arab society which only twenty-three years of his mission had brought about—the period of what one writer calls "The advent of the Qur'an"—one need not wonder at the statement.

During the fifty years following the demise of the Prophet the cultural changes were even more cataclysmic for linguistic continuity. Within three months, thanks to the looseness of meaning which the word *shahr* (month) lent itself to, the *Nasi* passage (Sura 9:36-7), was tragically misunderstood, With incredible nonchalance the age-old calendrical device to adjust the moon-calendar with the solar cycle went unnoticed when intercalation became due in August 632. That tragically thoughtless abandonment suddenly upset the ecological basis of Meccan culture. The synchronization of trade and tribal actual with the seasons of the year—eulogized only a score of years earlier, in the sura *Quraish*—was ruptured without leaving a trace in the recorded history of the *Khilafat-e Rashida!*

Consequently the *ushr*—the age-old 'tithes'—began to be demanded in the Muharram which arrived a months before the harvest had been reaped, economic dissatisfaction led to near-revolt which was misunderstood as apostasy. The attempts at suppression led to the outbreak of violence. Trade and animal husbandry gave place to militancy and territorial expansion.

The seasonal amnesty provided by the Four Sacred Months lost all its sociological significance when those some four months began to revolve around all four seasons. Languages and dialects of distant peoples gradually overspread and overlapped the dialects of the region around the two citadels of culture—Mecca and Medina. These towns became subsidiary to Damascus and Baghdad.

"Even so early as the close of the first century of the Hijrah, the great Khalif, Walid ibn 'Abdul Malik (705-715), spoke so corrupt a dialect that he could not make himself understood by the Arabs of the desert."

"The unlettered Bedouin who came to Damascus with camels or horses from the desert was, for the use of words and their correct pronunciation, a greater authority than most learned grammarians."

Is it then a wonder that purely pastoral epithets like *mathna* and *thulatha* and *ruba'a* soon ceased to possess their pastoral as well as Qur'anic meaning? Is it not logical that only their surface meaning, as forms of numerals, came to be exclusively accepted even in that still nascent period?

(b) The answer to the second question involves as psychological explanation and has its roots in human likes and dislikes. Some wit has said that the 'truths' which survive are sometimes no more than the lies that please. We, human beings, by our very nature, are inclined to accept with alacrity that which is pleasant to us and to pass over unperceived that which is unpleasant. "Marry the women that please you by twos and threes and fours" is so delectable an offer to the polygynous masculinity in man that the process of thought is pleasurably submerged under the emotion of delight. But when the possible alternate meaning involves the taking over of social responsibility for widows and orphans, his mind is bound to be altogether insensitive to this other meaning. It is probably these positive and negative pulls, acting simultaneously, that have affaced one meaning and, with relish, ensconced the other in its place. (c) As regards my personal effrontery all I have to say is that the simple form of narration which I have purposely adopted is itself to affirm that I claim neither genius nor erudition as the basis of this fresh interpretation. An accidental sequence of circumstances led to an idea which seems to dovetail the obstinate clauses of an important Qur'anic verse and I have submitted it here for consideration in the form of a question to both the learned and the layman. If they are fair and magnanimous enough to concede that this question is thought-provoking and favour me with their reactions, favourable or otherwise, I shall be able to reconsider my thesis in the light of their comments. If they convince me of the invalidity of my proposition I shall record my withdrawing it.

What I will insist on, however, is for them not to entangle this semantic thesis about the meaning of the words, *mathna*, etc., into a controversy as to whether plurality of wives is prohibited or restricted, permitted or recommended in the Qur'an. I refuse to be drawn into such argument. All that I have said here is that verse, *Nisa*: 3 is concerned with widows having orphans and has nothing to do with polygyny or monogyny as matters of societal concern.

## NOTES AND REFERENCES

1. Arberry has omitted the rendering of this connecting line, the `fa' in the original. Nor has he expressed the numeral as "twos and threes and fours" as others has done.
2. The message of the Quran - Presented in perspective, Tuttle, Tokyo and Rultand, Vermont, 1974.
3. June 625. See Sura III, verse 138 onwards.
4. III:95; New Testament: Romans XII:5 and Eph. IV:25.
5. Verse 34:46, and 35:1; Verse IV:3; 34:46; 35:1; Fowler's Modern English usage (1957 ed.) p. 388.
6. Maharaj of Baroda Research Pub., 1938.
7. Not named to avoid the charge of heresy.

---

(Revised & edited; Originally in *Islamic Culture,* July 1978.)

# 15

# Why the Devil is Called "Iblis" in the Qur'an

ABDULAHAD DAVOUD

It is one of the characteristic features of the Qur'an that almost all the proper and common nouns contained in it possess a plain meaning, and that they are introduced into all the languages spoken by Muslims, in their original Arabic forms without the least change of pronunciation or orthography. The wisdom of such a course is obvious; for most of such words as were revealed by Allah and uttered by His Apostle can have no equivalent terms in pagan literature. The old Prophets of Israel would have been horrified to see, for example, the name "Ilohim" rendered "Baal," "Mardukh," or any other heathen god. The names "Khuda" and "Tanri," as used by the Persians and Turks respectively before their conversion to Islam, either because of disputed etymology of mythological association, do not express the comprehensive meaning of the holy name of Allah.

The New Testament, on the other hand, contains numerous names and words which were unknown to Jesus Christ and to the Jewish multitudes that listened to his sermons and parables. For this book is not written in the language spoken by Jesus and his disciples. Consequently such names as God Devil, Percolate, heaven, hell and so forth, are not scriptural expressions, but borrowed from pagan mythologies.

The reason why I have selected the name "Iblees" (or Iblis) for the present article is, because it is connected with the first promise made by the Supreme Being concerning the "Seed" of the woman who should bruise the "Serpent's" head (Gen. iii.). I cannot enter here into the questions concerning the authenticity, the date, and the composition of the book of Genesis, nor discuss the theory of typifying man as an image of his Creator and the Serpent as a type of the Evil Spirit, which may be ascribed to a late editor imbued with Zoroastrian views. But I believe in the promise, because I see its fulfilment in Muhammad (upon whom be peace). There are innumerable prophecies and predictions in the sacred writings of the Jews which are literally fulfilled in the Prophet Muhammad, otherwise they would remain senseless absurdities. The word "Iblis" is derived from an old Semitic verb "beles"—that is, from three consonants, *b,l,s,* which when pointed read "beles," which means "to bruise to death," or "to crush underfoot." Therefore, the name "Iblis" signifies "the bruised one."

Of course, it would be useless for any scholar to attempt to discover the exact word used by Jesus for what is rendered in the Greek text of the Gospels as "Diabouls"—or Devil. The Assyrian version called "Pshitta," which is only a translation from the Greek text, has rendered the word "diabolus" "Akhil-Qarsa," which literally means "an eater of strife," and therefore "an accuser" or "adversary." The analogous name for "Iblis" in the Aramaic tongue is "Blisa," just as "Islam, Ahmad, Iqlim, Iklil," correspond to the Aramaic "Shlama, Himda, Quima, Klila" respectively.

It is very remarkable that neither the word "Devil" nor "Iblis" occurs in the Old Testament; and it is very strange too that the authorities of the British and Foreign Bible Society have borrowed from the Qur'an the name Iblis in their translations of the New Testament into Muhammadan languages, forgetting the fact that the Devil was not in the time of Jesus "the bruised one," but the very opposite: he was then the "Bruiser"!

The truth is that no prophet, not even Jesus Christ, ever ventured to use the appellation "Iblis" for the fallen Archangel before the appearance of the last Prophet, Muhammad.

Now let us briefly contemplate the fulfilment of this divine promise. There is a series of divine promises, often repeated, and prophetic allusions concerning a great prophet who, among many other things, would *bruise* the head of the Devil, whom Christ calls the "Liar" and the "Father" of the Jews (St. John viii.). Elsewhere in the Apocalypse, the Devil is described as "the ancient Serpent."

The Holy Apostle of Allah *bruised* the head of the Devil, by the utter destruction of his abominable cult, by the complete uprooting of idolatry from all the lands where his great ancestor Abraham had set his foot; the lands which were promised to this very Muhammad in the person of Ishmael, long before Isaac was born! These lands included all the territories between the Nile and the Great Euphrates (Gen. xv.). In fact, the Covenant between Allah and Abraham was made and sealed by the Circumcision of Ishmael some thirteen years before the birth of Isaac (Gen. xvii.). The only account of the Sacrifice of the "only son" of Abraham, as reported in the book of Genesis (xxii.), and the significant silence of the rest of the Old Testament—and, moreover, the very mention of the tetrogramme Mo RIaH, which is the same in root and meaning as the Qur'anic M*a*RW*a*H (chap. ii.)—leave no room for doubt that the boy taken to Merwah was not Isaac, but Ishmael. The two adjacent hills in Mecca, called Safa (meaning, like "Sion," a stone or rock), and Marwah (the same as Moriah, i.e. "the place where the I*a*HW*a*H was seen"), were two ancient monuments where the Sacrifice of Ishmael was commemorated by the pagan Arabs and is still perpetuated by all Muslims.

No Muslim ever denies that special blessings were also granted to Isaac, and that the land of Canaan was assigned to the people of Israel; but either that land or the royal "Sceptre" and the gift of Prophecy (Gen. xlix. 10) would cease from Judah after the coming of Shiloh—a name which, if not corrupted in its orthography, means exactly the popular epithet of Muhammad before his Apostleship, namely "Emin." But most probably the last letter is not "hi" but "het" and then the correct form would be Shilohah, or S'hiloah, meaning the Ressul Allah! It is quite evident from the prophecy of Jacob (xlix.10) that Shiloh would put a stop to the Power and the Law of the Jewish people, and that he would belong to another nation. However, the truth is safeguarded by the history of the People of Israel, which shows that their greatest kings, David and Solomon, were never able to subdue and possess all the territories extending from the Nile to the Euphrates; that the Jews during their two monarchies were rather idolaters than monotheists; and that they never purged the "Promised Land," including Egypt, Arabia, Syria, Palestine, and Mesopotamia (Gen. xv. 18-21) of idolatry.

All the lands above mentioned were entirely cleansed and purged of idols; so they remain as an inheritance for the Muslim Unitarians, called by the Prophet Daniel (ch. vii.) "the Holy People of the Most High"!

It is wonderful that this vision of Daniel (vii.) is literally fulfilled in Muhammad, who destroyed the fourth Beast, which was the Roman Empire; that the eleventh "Horn" could be none but Constantine the Great; and that the "three centuries and a half" therein predicted correspond to the epoch between that Emperor and the utter destruction of idolatry and the establishment of Islam in the Promised Land by Muhammad and his disciples. Any other interpretation is scarcely tenable.

I am cognizant, of course, of the old Christian archaeology, depicting the skull of Adam and the figure of a serpent under the foot of the cross of Jesus! If the fable of the Crucifixion and all the mythological doctrines attached to it are to be persistently believed as truths, then the Churches and their innumerable sects must indefinitely wait for a second advent of the Christ of their imagination in order to bruise the head of the Serpent! The impartial reader should answer this question for himself: Both Christ and Muhammad found the world in general, and his own country in particular, dominated by the Devil and the practice of idolatry; which of the two, then, rendered more service to the cause of the religion of the true and One Eternal Being, and the extermination of idols from the Promised Land? Did Jesus bruise the head of the Serpent? If you answer in the affirmative, then: Whose servant was Titus, who destroyed Jerusalem? whose servants were the ten Roman Emperors called"ten horns" (Dan.vii.) who persecuted the early Christians? These were all pagans, and consequently the servants of the Devil! It must be logically admitted, therefore, that Muhammad extirpated idolatry or the cult of the Devil once for all, and thus saved not only the Jews, but also the Christian inhabitants of the Promised Land from the persecutions of the pagans, as well as from the Trinitarians.

Is not the Quran, then, absolutely justified in naming the Devi "or the Bruised?"

---

(Revised and edited; originally published in *Islamic Review*, a miscellany.)

# 16

# Bibliographical Essay on Qur'anic Studies

## I. Translations

"There is no substitute for wool." Nothing can replace the Arabic text of the Qur'an yet, even for those who know Arabic, it is very necessary to have a translation to hand. There are numerous English translations available. The following are but a few examples.

Ali A. Yusuf, *The Holy Qur'an* (Text, translation and commentary), first published Lahore, M. Ashraf, 1934, many subsequent editions.

—as is usual with Muslim editions, the Arabic text and the English version are given side by side. The straightforward translation is accompanied by copious notes. There is also a running commentary which attempts to give the essence of the Qur'an in free verse.

Ali S.V. Mir Ahmed, *The Holy Qur'an* (With English translation of the Arabic text and Commentary according to the version of the Holy Ahlul-Bait), Karachi, Muhammad Khaleel Shirazi, n.d. (1964).

—as the subtitle implies, this is a Shi'a Ithna 'ashari publication. It is chiefly valuable for the notes reflecting this standpoint.

Latif Syed Abdul, *Al-Qur'an* (Rendered into English), Hyderabad, India, The Academy of Islamic Studies, 1969.

—rather than a literal translation, this rendering tries to convery the unified ideas connoted by entire sentences.

Bell Richard, *The Qur'an Translated,* Edinburgh, T. & T. Clark, (2 vols.), first published 1937.

—a literal translation which attempts to be as faithful as possible to the original Arabic, getting back behind the traditional Muslim interpretation which is sometimes influenced by later dogmatic developments. There are frequent and enlightening footnotes. The material within the separate suras is re-arranged following Bell's theory that the Qur'anic fragments were assembled in a disordered fashion. This makes the translation rather difficult to use in any way except as a reference book. It should be remembered that the numbering of the verses is that of Fluegel.

Arberry A.J. *The Koran Interpreted*, first published 1955, London, Oxford University Press, 1964 (I volume edition).

—a more literary translation that that of Bell while remaining very faithful to the original. Arberry has been "at pains to study the intricate and richly varied rhythms which—apart from the message itself—constitute the Koran's undeniable claim to rank amongst the greatest literary masterpieces of mankind" (p.x.). He has thus striven to "devise rhythmic patterns and sequence-groupings in correspondence with what the Arabic presents" (*ibid*). For the verse numbers—which follows Fluegel's system—only multiples of five are given, but with practice it is usually east to find references.

Watt. W. Montgomery, *Companion to the Qur'an,* London, George Allen & Unwin, 1967, 355 p.

—this is not a translation but a companion to A.J. Arberry's rendering of the Qur'an. It purports to give alternative renderings when the Arabic original is richer than any single translation, and to indicate the "occasions of revelation" for various passages. The intention is praiseworthy, but the result is rather disappointing.

## II. Introductions

Jomier Jacques, *Bible et Coran,* Paris, Cerf, 1959, 148 p. (English translation, New York, Desclee, 1964).

—rather slight, but could provide a useful starting point for further study. In dealing with the relationship between the Qur'an and the Bible the author has necessarily to discuss not only biblical figures such as Abraham, Moses, Mary, Jesus, but also themes such as God, Judgement, etc. Some of the explicit, or implicit judgements about Islam might be modified if a new edition were being prepared.

Bell Richard, *Introduction to the Qur'an,* Edinburgh University Press, 1953, reprint 1953, x, 190 p.

—given all the technical information necessary in order to undertake an serious study of the Qur'an: the environment in which Muhammad lived and preached, the development of the Qur'an, its actual form and its divisions, structure and style, chronology, contents and relationship to O.T. and N.T. and extra-biblical material.

This work is naturally influenced by the author's theory that "the unit of composition in the Qur'an is not the sura but the short piece" (p. 82) and that these pieces were often recorded on scrads of paper, both front and back, "and that both sides of the paper (were) read and copied consecutively when the Qur'an came to be made up in the from of a codex." (p. 91).

Watt W. Montgomery, *Bell's Introduction to the Qur'an* Edinburgh University Press (*Islamic Surveys 8*), 1970, xii, 258 p.

—a probably more accessible revision of Bell's Introduction presented above. Nothing essential has been omitted, but the material has been arranged in a more orderly fashion, and has been retouched in accordance with Watt's more positive attitude towards Islam. Two chapters have been added: one on "Muslim Scholarship and the Qur'an", the other dealing with "The Qur'an and Occidental Scholarship." The volume also contains a table for the conversion of verse-numbers from Fluegel's system to that of the standard Egyptian text; a table of the suras giving the Arabic names, their English equivalents, and the place of the suras in the different chronological order established by the official Egyptian text and by various orientalists; an extensive index to the Qur'an containing all instances of proper names and a selection of other topics.

Gragg Kenneth, *The Event of the Qur'an,* London, George — Allen & Unwin, 1971, 208 p.

—a less technical, but perhaps more stimulation, introduction than the two previous works. It covers "the charisma, the geography, the poetry, the local idiom of folk and metaphor, the tension and travail that belonged to (the Qur'an), the circumstances of tribe and tongue and territory that made its setting" (p. 182)— well-worked themes yet treated here in a fresh and original manner. Chapter 4 gives interesting explanations of suras 1 *(al-fatiha)*, 112 (*Al-ikhlas*), and 113 and 114 (*Al-mu'dhdhatain*)

Gragg Kenneth, *The Mind of the Qur'an,*—London, George Allen & Unwin, 1973, 209p.

—dealing with the significance of the Qur'an for Muslims first of all (a presentation of the traditional sciences of recitation and interpretation, explaining the technical vocabulary used; the samples of traditional exegesis are given in only approximative translations), but also for non-Muslims (the explanation of a certain number of themes: man's freedom and responsibility, his weakness, creation as a "sacrament" of God's presence, the mystical approach to God.) The final chapter discusses the relevance of the Qur'an today within the traditional Islamic frame of reference, for a world-view Penetrated by secularism, in a Pluralistic world. This book helps to show that the Qur'an can speak to all men.

Gaudeul J.M., *Bible and Qur'an in Encounter* 13(1975), 14 p.

—deals with inspiration, and with the relationship of the Qur'an to their Scriptures.

**III. Technical Instruments**

Fluegel Gustavus, *Concordantiae Corani Arabicae* Leipzig, 1842, x, 219 p.

—gives references only (naturally to his own system of numerotation).

Abc AL-Baqi M.F, *al-mu 'jam al-mufahras li-alfaz al-qur'an al-karim,* Dar al-kutub al-haditha, first Published 1944, 782p.

—far superior to Fluegel because for each word is given not only references but a Phrase from the Qur'an. Extremely useful for the study of Qur'anic themes.

Paret Rudi, *Der Koran, Kommentar und Konkordanz,* Stuttgart, W. Kohlhammer, 1971, 559 p.

—follows the Egyptian numerotation.

Noeldecke Theodor, *Geschichte des Qorans,* first published 1860, 2 edit. revised with Friedrich SCHWALLY, 1909, reprint Hildersheim, Georg Olms, 1961.

part I—the origins of the Qur'an, x, 262 p.

part II—the collecting of Qur'an material, viii, 224 p.

part iii—(with G. Bergstrasse and O. Pretzl, 1937)—the history of the Qur'anic text, xii, 351 p.

JefferyArthur, *Materials for the History of the Text of the Qur'an* Leiden, Brill, 1937, x, 362 p. + 223 p. Arabic text.

—important for the variant reading of the Qur'an.

Jeffery Arthur, *Foreign Vocabularly of the Qur'an*, Baroda, 1938.

HorovitzJosef, *Koransche Untersuchungen,* Berlin, de Gruyter, 1926, iv, 171 p.

—on the narrative sections of the Qur'an (Punishment stories, stories of prophets and men of God) and the Proper names in the Qur'an.

Sabbagh T., *La metaphore dans le Coran,* Paris, Adrien-Maisonneuve, 1943, x, 272 p.

—a study of an aspect of Qur'anic style, with special attention given to the metaphors derived from nature, man's body, his activity and life in society.

Fitzgerald M.L., *Pour une utilisation rationnelle do l' Encyclopedie de l' Islam: le Coran in Etudes Arabes* 36 (1974)) 2-10

—references to articles in the Encyclopaedia on matters connected with the Qur'an.

**IV. Background in the Qur'an**

Bell Richard, *The Origin of the Islam in its Christian Environment,* first published 1926, reprint London, Frank Cass, 1968, vii, 224p.

Henninger J., *L'influence du Christianisme oriental sur I'Islam naissant in L'Oriente Cristiano nella storia della civilta,* Roma, Lincei, 1964, pp, 379-410.

Bravmann M.M., *The Spiritual Background of Early Islam* Leiden, Brill, 1972, vii, 336 p.

—a collection of articles, dating from 1964, which can throw light an different Qur'anic concepts; difficult.

Sidersky D., *Les Origines des Ledgendes musulmanes dans le Coran et dans les vies des Prophetes,* Paris, Geuthner, 1933, viii, 161 p.

—indicated the various parallels with the apocryphal literature of the O.T. and N.T. and with the Haggadah.

Speyer Heinrich, *Die Biblischen Erzaehlungen in Qoran,* Hildersheim, Olms, 1971 (first published 1931), xii, 509p.

—on the same lines as the previous litle, but fuller.

Masson Denies, *Le Coran et la revelation judeo-chretienne,* Paris, Adrien Maisonniuve, 1958 (2 vols.) 828 p.

**V. Qur'anic Themes**

Rahbar Daud, *God of Justice* (A study in the ethical doctrine of the Qur'an) Leiden, Brill, 1960, 446 p.

—an interesting example of a method of approach to Qur'anic studies.

Izutsu Toshihiko, *God and Man in the Koran,* Tokyo, Keio Institute of Cultural and Linguistic Studies, 1964, 244 + 4p.

Izutsu Toshihiko, *Ethico-Religious Concepts in the Qur'an,* Montreal, McGill University Press 1966, xii, 284 p.

—an application of smantic analysis to the Qur'an; useful for studying such concepts as belief (*iman*), unbelief (*kufr*), hypocrisy (*nifaq*), etc.

Moubaracy Y., *Abraham dans le Coran,* Paris, Vrin, 1958, 205p.

Moubaracy Y., *Moise dans le Coran in Cahiers Sioniens,* 1954, pp, 373-391.

Parrinder Geoffrey, *Jesus in the Qur'an,* London, Faber and Faber, 1965, 187 p.

—set out in orderly fashion according to themes, with many references; a useful book.

Hayed Michel, *Le Christ de l'Islam,* Paris, Seuil, 1959, 288 p.

—an anthology of texts in translation.

Merad A., *Le Christ selon le Coran*

—a lecture delivered at the Pontifical Institute of Arabic Studies, giving the point of view of an open-minded Muslim.

in *Revue de l'Occident musulman et de la Mediterranee,* 5 (1968) 79-84.

Raisanen Heikki, *Das Koranische Jesusbitd,* Helsinki, Missiologian ja Ekumeniken Seura Y.A., 1971, 107 p.

—the author, reacting against the over-christianized understanding of the Qur'anic Jesus, emphasizes that the life of Jesus has been reinterpreted in the light of Muhammad's own experience.

O'Shaughnessy Thomas, *The Koranic Concept of the Word of God,* Rome, Pont, Inst. Bibl., 1948, 72 p.

O'Shaughnessy Thomas, *The Development of the Meaning of Spirit in the Koran*, Rome, Pont. Inst. Orient., 1953, 75 p.

Roest Crollius Ary A., *The Word in the Experience of Revelation in the Qur'an and Hindu Scriptures*. Rome, Pont. University Gregoriana, 1974, 273 p.

—contains interesting studies of the concepts of word and book the section concerning Christ had already been published as. *Christ "Word from God". in the Qur'an,* in *Studia Missionalia* 20(1971) 141-162.

Courtois V., *Mary in Islam,* Calcutta, Oriental Institute, 1954, x, 76 p.

—contains translations of representative texts from Islamic tradition, as well as dealing with the Qur'an; largely dependent on the following title ABD EL JALIL J.M., *Marie et l'Islam,* Paris, Beauchesne, 1950, 90 p.

O'Shaughnessy Thomas, *Muhammad's Thoughts on Death,* Leiden Brill, 1969, 89 p.

—a study of the theme of death in the Qur'an.

**VI. Qur'anic Exegesis**

Goldziher Ignaz, *Die Richtungen der Islamischen Koranausle-sung,* Leiden, Brill, 1952 (first published 1920), x. 392 p.

—a fundamental work; after sketching the first attempts at Qur'an exegesis, the author deals with different tendencies; traditional, dogmatic, mystical, sectarian and modernist.

Baljon J.M.S., *Modern Muslim Koran Interpretation* (1880-1960) Leiden, Brill, 1961, x, 135 p.

—a some what unsatisfactory attempt to bring Goldziher's *Richtungen* up to date. Contains interesting material on authors' writing in Urdu, such as Azad, Parwez, etc.

Ahmad Aziz+Von Grunebaum G.E., *Muslim Self-statements in India and Pakistan* 1857-1968, Wiesbaden, Otto Harrassowitz, 1970, x, 240 p.

—contains some material on Qur'an exegesis (Ahmad Khan, Azad, Parwez).

Jansen J. J G., *The Interpretation of the Koran in Modern Egypt* Leiden, Brill, 1974, xii, 114p.

—deals with Muhammad Abduh, "Scientific" exegesis, philological explanations, and practical exposition rather sketchy; English in faulty at times.

Jomier J., *Le commentaire coranique du manar,* Paris, 1954, xvi, 363 p.

—a thorough exposition of M. Abduh's and Rashid Rida's. Commentary of the Qur'an.

Merad Ali, *Ibn Badis; Commentateur du Coran,* Paris, Geuthner, 1971, 267 p.

—a study of the use of the Qur'an in the teaching of Badis (1889-1940), an Algerian of the Reformist school of thought.

Jomier J., *Quelques positions actuelles da l'exegese coranique en Egypte revelees par une polemique recente,* in Melanges de l'Institute Dominicain d'Etudes Orientales (MIDEO), I(1954) 39-72.

—the stir caused by M. Khalafallah's thesis on the narrative style in the Qur'an.

Jomier J., *Le Cheikh Tantawi Jawhari (1862-1940) et son commentaire du Coran,* in MIDEO 5(1958) 115-174.

—an example of "scientific' exegesis.

Jomier J. & Caspar P., *L'exegese scientifique du Coran d'apres ie Cheikh Amin al-Khuli,* MIDEO 4(1957) 269-280.

Casper R., *Vers une nouvelle interpretation du Coran en pays musulman?* in *Studia Missionalia* 20(1971) 115-139.

—discusses various new approaches to the Qur'an.$$$$$

Revised and edited; published originally in Islam and the Modern Age, vol. IX:9.

9655/2
986101